Foundations of Crime Ar

MW00652485

In recent years, the fields of crime analysis and environmental criminology have grown in prominence for their advancements made in understanding crime. This book offers a theoretical and methodological introduction to crime analysis, covering the main techniques used in the analysis of crime and the foundation of crime mapping. Coverage includes discussions of:

- The development of crime analysis and the profession of the crime analyst,
- The theoretical roots of crime analysis in environmental criminology,
- Pertinent statistical methods for crime analysis,
- Spatio-temporal applications of crime analysis,
- Crime mapping and the intersection of crime analysis and police work,
- Future directions for crime analysis.

Packed with case studies and including examples of specific problems faced by crime analysts, this book offers the perfect introduction to the analysis and investigation of crime. It is essential reading for students taking courses on crime analysis, crime mapping, crime prevention, and environmental criminology. A companion website offers further resources for students, including flashcards and video and website links. For instructors, it includes chapter-by-chapter PowerPoint slides.

Jeffery T. Walker is a Professor and Chair of the Department of Criminal Justice at the University of Alabama, Birmingham, USA. He has written 10 books and almost 100 journal articles and book chapters. He has obtained over $12 million in grants from the Department of Justice, National Institute of Drug Abuse, National Science Foundation, and others.

Grant R. Drawve is an Assistant Professor in the Department of Sociology and Criminal Justice at the University of Arkansas, USA. He is a research affiliate of the Center for Social Research (CSR) and Terrorism Research Center (TRC) at UA, Rutgers Center on Public Security (RCPS), and on the executive committee for the National Dialogues on Behavioral Health (NDBH).

"With short, simple chapters that cut to the chase, Walker and Drawve have written a crime analysis book that will be easily accessible to an undergraduate audience."

— **Jerry H. Ratcliffe**, *Professor in the Department of Criminal Justice and Director of the Center for Security and Crime Science, Temple University*

"An insightful and engaging look into the realm of crime analysis that offers readers a practical understanding of the field and its methods, making the crime analysis profession an invaluable resource to public safety agencies and the communities they serve."

— **Joel Caplan**, *Associate Professor at the Rutgers University School of Criminal Justice and Deputy Director of the Rutgers Center on Public Security*

"The emergence of crime analysis has been a driving force in the modern evolution of policing. Indeed, crime analysts, and the work products they produce, are integral to the design and implementation of evidence-based crime prevention practices. In *Foundations of Crime Analysis*, Walker and Drawve present a comprehensive overview of crime analysis techniques. The book is greatly beneficial to both academics and practitioners interested in further developing their understanding of crime analysis."

— **Eric L. Piza**, *Associate Professor in the Department of Law and Police Science, John Jay College of Criminal Justice*

"This book covers a variety of topics relevant to the field and is a great resource for students being introduced to the field, new analysts, and even experienced analysts. As an experienced analyst, I really appreciated the chapters on presenting information and picked up some new tips, tricks, and ideas. I have seen so many changes over the last 20 years, many aspects of my job today that I could not have imagined at the beginning, so I enjoyed the last chapter discussing the future of the field, thinking about where we are all headed, and how it can impact not just law enforcement but other aspects of the criminal justice arena as well."

— **Michelle Belongie**, *Crime Analyst at the Green Bay Police Department and secretary of the WI Law Enforcement Analyst Network*

Foundations of Crime Analysis

Data, Analyses, and Mapping

Jeffery T. Walker and Grant R. Drawve

Routledge
Taylor & Francis Group

LONDON AND NEW YORK

First published 2018
by Routledge
2 Park Square, Milton Park, Abingdon, Oxon OX14 4RN

and by Routledge
711 Third Avenue, New York, NY 10017

Routledge is an imprint of the Taylor & Francis Group, an informa business

British Library Cataloguing-in-Publication Data
A catalogue record for this book is available from the British Library

Library of Congress Cataloging-in-Publication Data
Names: Walker, Jeffery T., author. | Drawve, Grant R., 1986– author.
Title: Foundations of crime analysis : data, analyses and mapping / Jeffery T. Walker and Grant R. Drawve.
Description: Abingdon, Oxon ; New York, NY : Routledge, 2018. | Includes bibliographical references and index.
Identifiers: LCCN 2017036077 | ISBN 9781138860483 (hardback) | ISBN 9781138860490 (pbk.) | ISBN 9781315716442 (ebook)
Subjects: LCSH: Crime analysis. | Criminal statistics. | Criminology.
Classification: LCC HV7936.C88 W35 2018 | DDC 363.25—dc23
LC record available at https://lccn.loc.gov/2017036077

ISBN: 978-1-138-86048-3 (hbk)
ISBN: 978-1-138-86049-0 (pbk)
ISBN: 978-1-315-71644-2 (ebk)

Typeset in Eurostile and Akzidenz Grotesk
by Apex CoVantage, LLC

Visit the companion website: www.routledge.com/cw/walker

Grant: To my nephew and godson, Austin Patrick Egan, wander often.

Jeffery: To Bob Bursik, friend and mentor. Without your guidance, patience, and long discussions about neighborhoods, none of this would be possible for me.

CONTENTS

FIGURES

TABLES

BOXES

ACKNOWLEDGMENTS

We would like to thank the members of the International Association of Crime Analysts (IACA) for responding to our inquiries. We continue to learn from those who do crime analyses daily; and your input made this book what it is.

ABOUT THE AUTHORS

Jeffery T. Walker is a Professor and Chair of the Department of Criminal Justice at the University of Alabama, Birmingham, USA. He has written 10 books and almost 100 journal articles and book chapters. He has obtained over $12 million in grants from the Department of Justice, National Institute of Drug Abuse, National Science Foundation, and others. His areas of interest are social/environmental factors of crime, the study of non-linear dynamics as they relate to neighborhood change, and computer security as it relates to criminal/terrorist groups. He is a past President of the Academy of Criminal Justice Sciences. Editorial experience includes service as Editor of the *Journal of Criminal Justice Education* and *Journal of Critical Criminology*. Previous publications include articles in *Justice Quarterly*, *Journal of Quantitative Criminology*, and *Journal of Criminal Justice Education*, and the books *Leading Cases in Law Enforcement* (9th Edition) and *Statistics in Criminal Justice and Criminology: Analysis and Interpretation* (4th Edition).

Grant R. Drawve is an Assistant Professor in the Department of Sociology and Criminal Justice at the University of Arkansas, USA. Before joining UA, Grant was a post-doctoral research associate at Rutgers–Newark with a dual appointment between the Department of Psychology and School of Criminal Justice. He earned a doctorate in criminal justice from the University of Arkansas at Little Rock, a MA in criminology and criminal justice from Southern Illinois University Carbondale (SIUC), and a BA in administration of justice from SIUC. Grant's research and teaching interests include: crime and place, crime analysis, policing, GIS, neighborhoods and crime, community corrections, and public health. Grant is a research affiliate of the Center for Social Research (CSR) and Terrorism Research Center (TRC) at UA, Rutgers Center on Public Security (RCPS), and on the executive committee for the National Dialogues on Behavioral Health (NDBH).

Chapter 1

Practicalities of crime analysis

CHAPTER OUTLINE

The purpose of this book is to provide a strong foundation for students who are interested in crime analysis while also serving as a reference and overview of topics for practicing crime analysts. Crime analysis and the environmental criminology field have garnered greater attention in recent decades for the advancements made in understanding crime. With the growing popularity of crime analysis as a job opportunity, this book provides a theoretical understanding of crime analysis and main methods used in crime analysis, along with a basic foundation of crime mapping concepts. The goal is to provide you with an understanding of the main areas of crime analysis while providing numerous real-world applications.

Crime analysts are a part of a valuable profession that provides law enforcement agencies with the capability of understanding crime in their jurisdiction. The ability to collect data to assist law enforcement will continue to increase. Large agencies are already making strong commitments to crime analysis. In early 2017, the New York City Police Department (NYPD) had a posting stating they were going to hire around 100 crime analysts to assist their analysis-driven strategies at the precinct level. With large law enforcement agencies seeing the value in crime analysis across their precincts, it is likely the role of crime analysts will continue to expand to smaller agencies looking for guidance on policing matters. This makes sense based on how technology is influencing our lives. Think about how many people have smartphones now and the apps available on the phones, many of which have the ability to track your location, prompt surveys/questionnaires based on where you are located, and have the option for you to provide feedback. Data are the wave of the future, but it is the job of crime analysts to turn "big data" into "smart data" agencies can utilize to improve their communities. This does not necessarily entail knowing complex statistical techniques, but does include understanding the data collection process, potential issues and limitations, and what can be interpreted from the data without exaggerating the findings (see Huff and Geis, 1993; Monmonier and de Blij, 1996). Developing a foundation of data literacy is pivotal as a crime analyst.

Additionally, there is a strong societal movement in transparency among law enforcement agencies, notably influenced by social media coverage of incidents between police and suspects. This played out most proximately in the Michael Brown shooting in Ferguson, Missouri, and the death of Freddie Gray in Baltimore. The argument that arises is the constitutionality of certain policing practices (i.e. stop, question, and frisk). Certain types of policing practices have been argued to infringe on and violate the Fourth (search and seizure) and Fourteenth (equal protection of laws) Amendments. This type of movement necessitates the ability for law enforcement agencies to comprehend and evaluate their current practices to determine if changes are required. This brings the importance of crime analysts to the forefront when trying to understand crime and police strategies in any jurisdiction. Police often are not trained in this capacity, leaving a void in the ability for agencies to identify potential issues or benefits from current practices. This is where crime analysis units and crime analysts enter the equation.

DEFINITION OF CRIME ANALYSIS

Crime analysis is a broad area that can cover many different topics. Because of this, a comprehensive definition of crime analysis is not easy. The definition we will follow in this book is: the study of crime and public disorder problems with the goal of crime prevention, crime reduction, and apprehension of criminals while evaluating tactics and providing translational knowledge to police agencies. When reading that definition, many things come to mind about what contributes to crime analysis. That is what makes crime analysis such a dynamic field. The elements of this definition are discussed briefly in this section, and the chapters in the textbook are ordered to understand the different elements of crime analysis in relation to this definition.

Law enforcement agencies commonly deal with two types of calls-for-service: crime and public disorder. Crime is a bit more obvious and refers to calls such as residential burglaries, theft, homicide, motor vehicle theft, and many other criminal offenses. Public disorder calls typically address problems that reflect societal issues, such as noise complaints, juveniles loitering, prostitution, and others. While public disorder issues can be criminal, they are typically less serious than other crimes. This is an important distinction because crime analysis does not always deal with catching a serial offender, but rather, aiding in making the community safer through public disorder analyses. This distinction was made to allow you to understand that crime analysis does not only pertain to media headline crimes such as homicide, rape, and aggravated assaults, it includes many types of analyses.

Crime analysis relies heavily on data to study crime and disorder problems within a jurisdiction. Technology has greatly influenced crime analysis and the ability to collect, store, and analyze data. The data utilized to study crime and disorder problems are essential in providing quality and translational results. Translational refers to the ability to take findings and put them into policy or strategies, which is an important element in law enforcement agencies. The ability of crime analysis to accomplish this is highly dependent on the type of data that are available. If the data are weak, or analysts must rely on data that does not directly address the issue, the analysis will suffer and possibly misinform police officers and policy makers.

Crime analysis, as with many fields in the social sciences, can be examined with methods of scientific inquiry. While data are essential in the analysis of crime and disorder problems, having theoretical knowledge of information such as how neighborhoods deteriorate, the relationship between social and economic factors (such as housing) and crime, and the geographic patterns of criminal activity helps the understanding of the findings. You might not be testing theory within your analysis, but your results should rely on theoretical principles. This is an important step in taking results and making them translational to police officers. The ability to put findings into terms and theoretical reasoning that makes sense allows for more people to understand the issue.

CAREERS IN CRIME ANALYSIS

Crime analysts can come from a variety of backgrounds. Like any career, there are those who knew what they wanted to do when they grew up and there are other people who never would have imagined becoming a crime analyst. Different backgrounds can aid in the effectiveness of a crime analysis unit because, when starting in crime analysis, it is not possible to be an expert in each aspect. This section discusses career paths into crime analysis and how crime analysts should be a kind of "jack of all trades" when it comes to their capabilities.

It is not uncommon for police officers to switch over to a crime analysis unit because of their working knowledge with a jurisdiction and policing background. This can be appealing for an agency because the officer has experience on how police officers function in the field. With crime prevention being a main goal of crime analysis, police officers are often the personnel trying to reduce and deter crime. The argument could be made that police officers would be more receptive to a crime analyst who is a former officer versus a crime analyst who does not have "policing" knowledge. While "street" smarts might be appreciated among officers, "book" smarts can greatly benefit crime analysis units.

Due to the popularity of crime analysis interest and job placement, criminology/criminal justice departments at many universities have developed crime analysis and crime mapping courses to provide students with beneficial skills on graduation. The International Association of Crime Analysts (IACA; www.iaca.net) published "Crime Analysis Education Recommendations for Colleges & Universities" in 2012. There are a growing number of universities that offer certificates in crime analysis. Certificates can be appealing to law enforcement agencies because it shows that students have taken credit hours specifically in crime analysis. This can help students understand the problem-solving mindset crime analysis requires and gain experience with software programs analysts use on the job.

While it makes sense that college graduates hired as crime analysts probably have a criminal justice or criminology degree, the nature of the crime analyst job can attract people from other educational backgrounds. Technology is becoming a must in most law enforcement agencies; and with the advancements in technology comes the use of computer programs. Additionally, crime analysis is closely associated with crime mapping, a geography component. Overall, the job of a crime analyst requires data gurus, statistics, theoretical application, problem solving, geographical knowledge, and the ability to convey findings to a variety of people from officers to government officials. That is what makes the crime analysis field appealing for people with educational backgrounds in sociology, geography, psychology, political science, and computer science, along with criminology/criminal justice.

Student internships

Preferably, as a part of their college education, students will have the opportunity to intern with law enforcement agencies. This can provide students with valuable experience by allowing them firsthand knowledge of work in the field. Internships also have the potential to lead to full-time positions with the law enforcement agencies. The ability to get your foot in the door and impress the agency could result in a job or, at the very least, offer networking connections. Internships can consist of ride-alongs with officers, attending briefings, and different types of crime analysis projects. Depending on the type of internship, the information handled could be confidential. Because of the confidential nature of the duties, many internships will require background checks, and some internships may require a polygraph examination. This is an important aspect to keep in mind. It is possible that any issues with the criminal justice system (Driving While Impaired (DWI), public intoxication, drug possession, etc.) will disqualify you from getting any position in the police agency, including as a crime analyst.

To summarize, the job of a crime analyst, even an intern, requires the person to have a dynamic and varied set of skills. Not all skills are necessary in the beginning, but anyone looking to become a crime analyst should understand the kind of desired skills, and should start working toward acquiring those skills. As discussed in this section, some of the skills include knowledge of:

Policing terminology and functions
Theoretical basis for people's behaviors
Data collection
Research methods
Statistics
Report writing
Presentation preparation.

There are also very specific skills that are required of crime analysts/interns. These specific skills include knowledge of:

Microsoft Office
Google map
ArcView
SPSS (a statistical program)
LEADS (Law Enforcement Agencies Data System)
i2 Analyst Notebook
ATAC (Automated Tactical Analysis of Crime) (crime analysis software).

Again, these do not necessarily have to be possessed prior to getting the position, but as many of them as possible should be obtained through college courses or other training opportunities. Some of them may be obtained during an internship. The rest will likely be obtained through training if you get a job as a crime analyst.

In an internship or entry-level position as a crime analyst, common duties may include:

Extract data
Criminal profiles
Crime bulletins
Criminal networks/linking charts
Spatial analysis
Crime pattern and trend identification
Aid in patrol activities.

Additionally, there are different types of analytical positions. Often crime analysts are thought of as specifically a law enforcement role. The title might vary but crime analysts can have varied types of employment. There is potential employment in local, state, federal, and private sectors for crime analyst type jobs such as:

Loss Prevention Specialist
Geographic Information System (GIS) Analyst
Financial Analyst
Private Investigator
Intelligence Analyst
Data Analyst
Research Associate
Fraud Analyst.

These are the foundations of crime analysis. They can be learned in an internship or on the job as a crime analyst. You will see these show up in the two job announcements for crime analyst internships in Boxes 1.1 and 1.2.

BOX 1.1 INTERNSHIP POSTING

Agency: UC Irvine Police Department

Summary

Interns will be given several projects or jobs during the quarter so they can experience all the aspects of how the department operates. The responsibilities of the student intern will include assisting the administrative officers with tallying and analysis of crime statistics and filing them; this includes reading police reports to determine how a particular crime/incident should be classified. In particular, federal law (per the Jeanne Clery Act) requires universities to release all crime statistics for each campus and the surrounding community. The UCI Crime Prevention

Officer is currently compiling data as required by that act, and students could assist with this project. Interns may also be asked to create or update documents and forms for administrative use. Students will also assist in conducting research for new programs and formulating new program proposals and implementation. Students may also assist the Crime Prevention Officer with creating brochures, pamphlets, and presentations on crime prevention measures, as well as research new methods of crime prevention for the campus. Additional opportunities include working with dispatchers and assisting them in handling emergency and non-emergency telephone and radio calls and working with the detective division to provide assistance in handling court documents and constructing criminal cases.

Students must be able to write clearly and concisely; they must have good communication and interpersonal skills as well as good time-management skills and the ability to work under pressure and have patience. Interns should be computer literate and able to perform research on the Internet. Competency in using Microsoft Word, Excel and PowerPoint is also required. A one week background check will be performed, so please apply as early as possible. Following the completion of the background check, you will be contacted to schedule a fingerprinting and interview appointment. All applicants must provide fingerprint samples for NCIC [National Crime Information Center], have no felony convictions, and pass a background investigation and criminal record check. Those selected must also be able to deal with confidential criminal documents in a trustworthy manner.

The internship position will provide the student with training on the following: Uniform Crime Report crime classifications and definitions, Jeanne Clery Act, crime analysis skills; Police Band Tactical Radio protocols and procedures, basic understanding of CLETS (California Law Enforcement Telecommunications System) and how it is used, and basic operating understanding of RIMS (Record/Incident Management System).

BOX 1.2 INTERNSHIP POSTING

Agency: Charlotte-Mecklenburg Police Department

Summary

Interns work alongside department personnel in a wide spectrum of assignments throughout the CMPD. Interns will be exposed to effective problem-solving and partnership-building skills as well as gaining a better understanding of day-to-day operations of the police department. The Charlotte-Mecklenburg Police Department offers two internship sessions during the year. CMPD does not provide housing and transportation.

Qualifications

- Interns must be undergraduate or graduate students currently enrolled in a college or university.
- Interns must be taking a minimum 12 semester hours (Fall and Spring Semesters).

- Candidates will be required to successfully complete an oral interview and background investigation, drug test, and polygraph exam as part of the qualification process.
- Meet and maintain the minimum GPA [grade point average] requirement of a 2.0.

Expectations

- Have the capability to work varying hours, depending on the need of their respective assignment.
- Be able to commit at least 20 hours per week for 12 weeks to the program.
- Arrive on time to all assignments, give appropriate notice to their supervisors when absences are anticipated, and attend all necessary training and meetings.
- Behave in a professional manner at all times, treating Charlotte-Mecklenburg citizens, employees of the CMPD, and other interns with respect.
- Perform assigned duties in a timely and efficient manner. If unaware of what duties are to be completed, the intern is expected to obtain clarification from the intern supervisor or the intern coordinator.
- Attend all necessary training and meetings.
- Interns should possess strong research and analytical skills.
- Interns should possess strong oral and written communication skills.
- Interns should possess strong organizational skills.
- Computer skills (Word, Excel, Outlook, and various databases).
- Be able to write or transcribe information using proper grammar and syntax.
- Those selected for an internship must submit to a drug test and polygraph examination.
- Take part in a minimum of five Ride-A-Longs throughout the internship.
- Dress in a manner that is professional and in accordance with CMPD policies.
- Prepare and turn in a 5 page paper and complete an oral presentation on the specific assignments/duties they were tasked with during the course of the internship, lessons learned, and if this experience has led to the further pursuit of a career in law enforcement.

Entry-level analysts

Police agencies vary in their requirements for a position as an entry-level analyst. It is becoming increasingly common for an entry-level analyst position to require a Bachelor's degree with preference given to those in the field of criminal justice, political science, geography, sociology, or related field. While some positions may require a certificate before hiring, most positions do not or will require you to obtain certification once hired. As discussed previously, many universities offer certificates in crime analysis, and there are also organizations that offer certification courses/exams. Additionally, a good way of becoming an entry-level analyst is completing an internship with an agency before graduating because that provides you with a working knowledge of entry-level tasks and gives you a chance to prove yourself to the agency. While some entry-level positions only require an undergraduate degree, some positions will require a level of analytical experience. Typically, graduate coursework can be substituted because of the level of research methods, statistical, and theoretical courses taken. When just starting as an analyst, the type of crime analysis conducted can be limited until more knowledge and analytical know-how is obtained. With greater experience and a potential move to a mid-level or senior analyst, the depth and quality of analysis required will increase.

Boxes 1.3 and 1.4 show typical examples of postings for crime analysts. You will notice that many of the job qualifications and duties discussed in this section are contained in the job announcements. Anyone who is seeking a position as a crime analyst should be prepared for these kinds of qualifications and requirements.

BOX 1.3 EXAMPLE JOB POSTING

Agency: Chattanooga Police Department
Position: Crime Analyst

Summary

Incumbent in this classification conducts a variety of crime and statistical analysis in support of crime analysis activities; collects and analyzes data describing crime patterns, crime trends, traffic analysis and potential suspects; assists with administering crime analysis database and RMS system; assists in monitoring and researching known felons within the city; assists with creating local, state and federal statistics for City-wide and in-house reporting requirements; ensures work quality and adherence to established policies and procedures.

Examples of Duties:

- Collect, collate and analyze a variety of economic, geographic or social information in support of crime analysis activities; utilize sources from various calls-for-service, census, demographic and other related data; display informational analysis to police administrators and City officials.
- Perform a variety of statistical analysis; provide information to assist in identifying crime problems; develop and test crime prediction and resource allocation statistical models; assist in advising sworn staff of areas of high crime probability; assist in developing and preparing charts, graphs, maps, reports and related materials in order to track and present findings related to criminal activity.
- Monitor local, regional and national crime trends.
- Establish and maintain effective communication and working relationships with city employees, representatives of other agencies, the media and the general public.
- Create confidential law enforcement bulletins regarding crime trends, repeat offenders and officer safety.
- Develop and produce crime maps using geographic information systems (GIS) applications and conduct spatial analysis of crime data.
- Analyze known offender's MOs and establish timelines to perform suspect/crime correlation to provide suspect leads and targets for surveillance or directed patrol.
- Make written and oral presentations using maps, charts and graphs to inform police officers, detectives, investigators and commanders on emerging or existing crime series, patterns, and trends, as well as suspect and victim profiles.
- Predict or forecast criminal trends based on computer analyses of current and past criminal activity.

- Answer inquiries from the public, businesses, community groups and websites regarding crime activity, trends and patterns.
- Collect, analyze and interpret data and statistics using quantitative and qualitative methodology. Employ principles and applications of mathematics and statistics, which may require knowledge of research methodology and techniques.

Minimum Qualifications:

- Bachelor's degree from an accredited school in criminal justice, public administration, mathematics/statistics or related field. Three years of building databases, collecting, organizing and summarizing data to provide usable analyzed information. Must be able to interpret and make inferences from statistical information.
- Any combination of education and experience that would provide the required knowledge and abilities is qualifying.

BOX 1.4 EXAMPLE JOB POSTING

Agency: Raleigh Police Department in North Carolina
Position: Crime Analyst
Salary: $35,165.25–$56,492.12 annually

Position Duties

This involves non-sworn analytical work in the assimilation and comparison of trends in reported crimes in the City as a Crime Analyst assigned to the Detective Division. Work requires the collection, analysis, and dissemination of sensitive information. Work requires development and maintenance of multiple databases and their application in a computer environment. Work includes the retrieval and analysis of crime data, the preparation of informational reports for various user groups, and providing technical assistance for special projects.

Essential Job Functions:

- Tracks citywide criminal trends and patterns.
- Produces hot sheets and reports associated with crime patterns.
- Prepares weekly crime numbers reports and specialized maps.
- Monitors criminal activity, performs analysis, and prepares reports utilizing crime data.
- Maintains a thorough knowledge of the police reporting system; data entry, storage, and retrieval techniques; uniform crime reporting procedures; and computer skills.
- Demonstrates a high level of independent thinking, completes most tasks with limited supervision, and organizes and participates in many projects at the same time.
- Provides maps and statistical information for the Detective Division and other divisions as needed.

- Responds punctually to request for assistance from departmental members, city employees, the media, and the public.
- Maintains effective interpersonal relationships with members of the department, the city departments, and the public.
- Prepares written correspondence and statistical reports that are accurate, clear, concise, and completed on time.
- Processes and files warrants, maintains quality control for wanted persons per DCI regulations, and performs validation of all NCIC wanted persons entered on behalf of the Department.
- Works rotating shifts.
- Safely operates city-owned vehicles, as needed, for various administrative tasks.
- Performs additional work as required.

Education:

- Associate (2-year) college degree or equivalent, preferably in criminal justice, GIS, or a related field. May substitute additional relevant experience for the required education.

Experience:

- At least 1 year of relevant experience is required. Applicants may substitute additional relevant education for the required experience.

Preferred Experience Includes:

- Analysis of trends
- Logic and analytical process for solving problems
- Link, temporal, and predictive analysis techniques
- Databases and spreadsheets
- GIS technology.

Computer Skills:

- Advanced knowledge of Microsoft Office applications (Excel, Word, Access, and PowerPoint)
- Advanced knowledge of GIS software (ESRI ArcView or similar programs)
- Use of Structured Query Language (SQL) for select statements in our records management system
- Basic networking knowledge.

Also, Boxes 1.5 and 1.6 are interviews with practicing crime analysts Levi Giraud and Damien Williams where they tell about their jobs and views on being a crime analyst. This should help you understand more about the daily life and duties of a crime analyst.

BOX 1.5 CRIME ANALYST INTERVIEW WITH LEVI GIRAUD, FARGO POLICE DEPARTMENT

Serving population size: 112,000

Years as analyst: 2

I earned a Master's in Criminal Justice with a Certificate in Crime Analysis from Seattle University in 2012. After finishing my degree, I began applying for positions as a crime analyst for departments across the U.S. and ultimately found a place with the Fargo Police. I have been working as their first crime analyst since March of 2013.

Education:

- Master's Degree in Criminal Justice with a Certificate in Crime Analysis from Seattle University
- Bachelor's Degree in Criminal Justice from Eastern Washington University

Starting salary range: $49,500

How did you get into crime analysis?

I was actually working on my Master's without a clear direction of what I was going to do. I knew I wanted to work in the field of criminal justice, I just was not sure in what capacity. I had begun to lean toward going on to law school. Then I took a crime mapping class, and then an advanced crime mapping class. I was hooked. Crime analysis just made so much sense to me as a criminal justice/public safety policy that I knew I had to become a part of it.

Main duties:

- Daily review of crime reports to search for trends, patterns, or series
- Compilation of data for monthly Compstat meetings
- Production of intelligence reports, BOLOs [Be on the Look Out], and alerts as needed
- Assessing needs and making recommendations for purchasing new equipment or software
- Developing tools for automating crime analysis functions using Access, Excel, Crystal Reports, ATAC Workstation, and others.

Highlights of job:

The most rewarding part of the job is helping to catch criminals. I also enjoy the people I work with. I am in an office with all of the detectives and they are a great group of people and I could not imagine having a better time in an office with a bunch of accountants or lawyers.

Favorite task/analysis/approach:

I really love learning to do new things on the job. The first thing I realized I would have to learn was SQL. When I first got here it was extremely time consuming to get the RMS system to give me any answers I was looking for. That is when I began to experiment with Access and teach myself SQL. I have not looked back, it is an amazing tool.

Words of wisdom/thoughts for up-and-comers:

Any program that promises to teach you how to be a crime analyst should include courses on SQL, Access, Excel, and Crystal Reports. SPSS is fine, but unless you work for a major metro agency you will not have SPSS, it is too expensive. Demand they offer courses in the more basic programs because those are what you will be working with. If the criminal justice department itself does not offer the classes, make them let you take them as electives from another department. You will be much better prepared as an analyst if you have a foundation in these subjects. One less class on Strain Theory or Anomie will not hurt you, I promise.

Also, I have a blog on what it is like to be a brand new analyst in an agency that has never had an analyst before. Hopefully, the lessons I have learned can help newer analysts find their footing faster, or at least let them know that they are not alone (www.crimeanalysthot spot.com/).

BOX 1.6 CRIME ANALYST QUESTIONNAIRE: DAMIEN WILLIAMS, ROCK HILL, SC POLICE DEPARTMENT

Serving Population Size: 70,000

Years as Analyst: 12

Crime Analysis Experience: Internship and Analyst at 3 city police departments

Education: Bachelor's degree and Master's degree in Sociology/Criminology

Starting Salary Range: $40,000

How Did You Get into Crime Analysis: Internship; love of crime and geography

Main Duties:

- Crime analysis patterns/trends, maps, data analysis, annual reports, etc.
- Assist all other city departments in crime data and crime map requests
- Assist citizens and media with crime analysis and crime information
- Manage social media accounts and websites
- Edit police department app
- Manage the data that goes on citizen/public crime map
- Add users to records management system
- Edit reports for correct UCR classification

- Speak at neighborhood meetings
- Speak at local universities
- Attend career fairs.

Highlights of Job: Analytical work with crime data, calls-for-service, and any other data source

Favorite Task/Analysis/Approach: Using GIS to analyze crime in multiple ways; using link analysis to spot trends in data and groups of people.

Words of Wisdom/Thoughts for Up-and-Comers: INTERNSHIP, INTERNSHIP, INTERNSHIP!

Mid-level to senior analysts

As in any type of career, with experience comes more responsibility and knowledge. The more experience gained while on the job (often determined by years of experience) allows analysts to advance in rank and specialty areas. Depending on the size of the agency, there will be a need to have different levels of analysts. Not everyone will have the same amount of experience, allowing for mid-level and senior analysts to accept more responsibility while also helping entry-level analysts learn the profession. Additionally, as analysts gain more knowledge and analytical knowledge, they can become a specialist in a certain type of analysis. Some common specialty areas are motor vehicle theft, GIS, violent crime, and sex crimes.

Box 1.7 is a job posting for a senior-level analyst. You can see the difference in qualifications and skills between this and the job posting for an entry-level position. You do not have to worry about having these skills right away as an analyst. Obtaining them over time is what qualifies you to move up or move to a higher-level position.

BOX 1.7 SENIOR ANALYST JOB POSTING

Agency: Escondido Police Department, San Diego North, California

Summary Description

Supervises, assigns, reviews, and coordinates the day-to-day activities of the Crime Analysis Unit, including collecting, compiling, and analyzing data from a variety of sources to identify and evaluate crime series, trends, and patterns; oversees and develops reports on crime series, trends, and patterns; oversees and participates in preparing crime summaries, statistical reports, spreadsheets, charts, maps, diagrams and graphs; ensures work quality and adherence to established policies and procedures; and performs technical and complex tasks relative to assigned area of responsibility.

Ability to:

- Coordinate and direct the day-to-day activities of the Crime Analysis Unit.
- Supervise, organize, and review the work of assigned staff.
- Select, train, and evaluate staff.
- Recommend and implement goals, objectives, policies and procedures for providing crime analysis services.
- Understand the organization and operation of the city and of outside agencies as necessary to assume assigned responsibilities.
- Understand, interpret, and apply general and specific administrative and departmental policies and procedures as well as applicable federal, state, and local policies, laws, and regulations.
- Perform statistical research and analysis.
- Compile and interpret statistics.
- Analyze various crime data and develop analytical reports.
- Track and present findings related to criminal activity, patterns and trends.
- Prepare predictions of criminal activity based on previous reported activity and an analysis of typical behavior patterns.
- Prepare extensive reports, maps, charts, graphs and other visual aids.
- Recommend and implement goals and objectives for providing crime analysis and research.
- Respond to requests and inquiries from the public.
- Operate office equipment and supporting crime analysis programs and databases.
- Prepare clear and concise reports.
- Participate in the preparation and administration of assigned budgets.
- Plan and organize work to meet changing priorities and deadlines.
- Effectively represent the city to outside individuals and agencies to accomplish the goals and objectives of the unit.
- Work cooperatively with other departments, city officials, and outside agencies.
- Respond tactfully, clearly, concisely, and appropriately to inquiries from the public, city staff, or other agencies on sensitive issues in area of responsibility.
- Demonstrate an awareness and appreciation of the cultural diversity of the community.
- Communicate clearly and concisely, both orally and in writing.
- Establish and maintain effective working relationships with those contacted in the course of work.

WHAT TO EXPECT WITH THE REST OF THE BOOK

This book is divided into three main parts: background (chapters 1–5), statistics (chapters 6–10), and applications (chapters 11–15) related to crime analysis. The first part is designed to provide context into what crime analysis is, including common concepts, theories, and strategies. Understanding the progression of crime analysis becoming a common term within police agencies will also highlight potential hurdles you might encounter while on the job. Some law enforcement officers are fine with status quo and do not believe change is necessary, even more so when being informed by civilian personnel and not a fellow officer. This is why it is important to be able to translate analytical findings into relatable theoretical and discussion points officers in the field often encounter.

The second part of this book focuses on a statistical foundation that will ease the transition into crime analysis techniques. The focus of the second part is to introduce different types of commonly utilized data and to provide an introduction to statistical techniques that can be conducted in Excel. Understanding limitations of data sources is as important as conducting statistical analyses themselves. Not only does this provide knowledge into understanding and interpreting data, but it will also ease the transition if additional crime analysis courses are taken. Additionally, learning these statistical techniques assists in making you more marketable when applying for jobs.

The final part of the book relates to common applications of crime analysis techniques in practice and research. These chapters offer a starting point for you to build from, with the thought process of you taking a geographic information system (GIS; crime mapping) course. These chapters also highlight the convergence of how theoretical concepts and assumptions inform analyses and, in turn, the findings are then discussed in relation to what is supported theoretically.

What about maps?

A must-have within crime analysis is visualizations. Charts and graphs can show fluctuations of numbers, but the ability to put crime on a map is often desired. The focus of this book is to provide background on the problem-solving mindset, concepts, terminology, data, and statistical techniques that can be used jointly with crime mapping. There will be places where maps will be addressed in the book, and we will offer some general advice on constructing maps. For those interested in GIS applications, additional classes and texts are available, such as:

Crime Analysis with Crime Mapping by Rachel Boba Santos
Fundamentals of Crime Mapping by Bryan Hill and Rebecca Paynich
GIS Mapping for Public Safety by Joel M. Caplan and William D. Moreto.

Worth discussing now is one of the most common terms known within crime mapping: "hot spots." There are numerous variations of the term hot spot but, in general, hot spots refer to small geographical areas that have a high volume of crime occurring there. That is why law enforcement agencies rely on hot spot maps; they show where crime clusters in their jurisdiction. Showing clusters of crime in space can be completed a number of ways (see Eck, Chainey, Cameron, Leitner, and Wilson, 2005); but, as seen in the two right-hand panes of Figure 1.1, simply putting dots on a map becomes cluttered. Yes, you can see general dark areas that resemble where more crime is located, but there are multiple ways to better display crime clusters. One of the ways to better display density is through kernel density maps. Examples of density maps are shown in the two left-hand panes of Figure 1.1. This introduction gives you an idea of the kinds of crime mapping that are possible, and what we will be addressing in this book.

Crime analysis in action

Throughout the book, there are features that will give you a glimpse into the world of crime analysis. This starts in the practice assignment in Chapter 2 by giving you a task that would be something a crime analyst would have to accomplish. This gets you started looking at crime data and making sense out of it in a way that can be used to help police officers do their job. In the chapters that follow, you will see these kinds of "practitioner links" that show the normal activities of crime analysts and how they view their job. These are provided to give you both the academic and training side of crime analysis, and how this plays out in a career as a crime analyst.

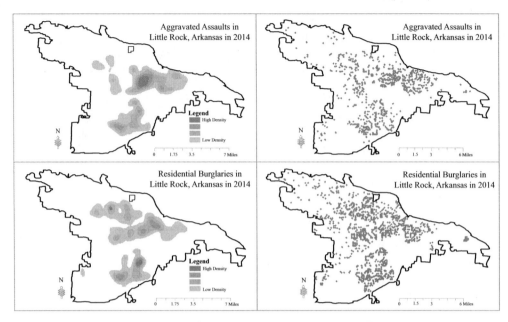

Figure 1.1 Pin and Kernel Density Maps of Aggravated Assaults and Residential Burglaries

CONCLUSION

Much of this chapter was focused on introducing you to the crime analysis field. Specifically, what crime analysis is and potential paths of how to learn what you want to do after graduation. The insights offered by real-world crime analysts provide valuable insights into what to expect and the importance of different elements. We cannot understate the importance of student internships. Even if you are taking this class as an elective and not interested in being a crime analyst, internships are extremely helpful in shaping a career path.

BIBLIOGRAPHY

Eck, J.E., S. Chainey, J.G. Cameron, M. Leitner, and R.E. Wilson. 2005. *Mapping Crime: Understanding Hotspots.* Washington, DC: National Institute of Justice.

Farrell, G. and K. Pease. 2001. *Repeat Victimization.* New York, NY: Criminal Justice Press.

Huff, D. and I. Geis. 1993. *How to Lie with Statistics.* New York, NY: W.W. Norton.

International Association of Crime Analysts. 2012. Crime Analysis Education Recommendations for Colleges and Universities. (White Paper 2012–02). Overland Park, KS.

Matthies, C. and T. Chiu. 2014. *Putting a Value on Crime Analysts: Considerations for Law Enforcement Executives.* New York, NY: Vera Institute of Justice.

Monmonier, M. and H.J. de Blij. 1996. *How to Lie with Maps.* Chicago, IL: University of Chicago Press.

Pease, K. 1998. *Repeat Victimisation: Taking Stock.* Crime Detection and Prevention Series, Paper 90. London: Home Office.

Townsley, M., R. Homel, and J. Chaseling. 2003. Infectious burglaries. A test of the near repeat hypothesis. *British Journal of Criminology,* 43(3): 615–633.

QUESTIONS AND EXERCISES

1   What is crime analysis and what is it used for? Who does it benefit?
2   Why is data literacy important? What are the consequences of interpreting data wrong as an analyst?
3   How can crime analysis be used to benefit society and what events/incidents show support for crime analysts within police agencies?
4   What does crime analysis help police agencies do?
5   From the interviews and job postings in this chapter, what skills seem to be of most importance to have? Why are these skills important?
6   What are "hot spots" and what role do they play in crime analysis?
7   This chapter pointed out that now there are many degrees outside of criminal justice and sociology that can be beneficial in crime analysis. What are the benefits of having experience in a police agency?
8   Search for free crime analysis tools, including mapping. What do the tools/features allow you to do related to crime analysis? Are there software programs or analytical skills you should learn before applying for a position? Are there courses offered at your university/college that would make you a more attractive job candidate?
9   What are potential internship opportunities related to crime analysis in your area? Are there federal opportunities for students?

What is crime analysis?

This chapter provides a historical overview of crime analysis and the thought process behind analytical approaches. The history of crime analysis is discussed to provide a foundation of how the analytical movement became what it is today. A focus of the chapter is to provide you with examples of tasks and problems analysts respond to on the job. This will provide you with an understanding of what is expected and sought after within the crime analysis profession. It will also provide a foundation for what you will learn in the chapters to come.

HISTORY OF CRIME ANALYSIS

The study of crime is not a new profession, but has become more prominent as time has progressed. Crime analysis has its roots in the 1800s with the London Metropolitan Police; not surprising with England's influence on policing practices in other regions. During a similar time period, you can trace crime mapping back to the works of Guerry and Quetelet, who utilized demographic data from the French census to provide reasoning to the distribution of crime in France. In particular, Quetelet found factors like climate, poverty, alcohol, age, and gender to be influential on crime. While Guerry and Quetelet were conducting research on social factors and how they influence crime in the 1800s, it was the London Metropolitan Police that employed pattern identification.

When the London Metropolitan Police (LMP) was formed, there were just over 1,000 different types of people on the force, such as constables, sergeants, inspectors, and superintendents. A focus of the LMP style of policing was crime prevention, which differed from crime detection. This can be seen in the writings of the founder of the LMP, Sir Robert Peel, and his "Principles of Law Enforcement." His principles begin and end with crime prevention. The first principle stated, "The basic mission for which police exist is to prevent crime and disorder." After enumerating the relationship between the police and the public, Peel returned to crime prevention in his final principle, which stated, "The test of police efficiency is the absence of crime and disorder, not the visible evidence of police action in dealing with them."

In 1842, the LMP formed a detective department, and by 1846 it had two plain-clothed detectives per division. The LMP was recording crime information and keeping track of discipline issues among officers by 1847. The formation of a detective department is evidence the LMP thought there was a need for crimes to be given more attention with the hopes of being solved. With the recording of crime information, the LMP was able to analyze the collected data. Unknown at the time, this was the groundwork with developing crime analysis.

At this point, you have probably taken an introduction to criminal justice or criminology course that highlighted the United States law enforcement growth being influenced by European models. One of the most well-known police reformers in the United States was August Vollmer, who is also known as the Father of Modern Policing. Vollmer was the Chief of Police for Berkeley, California, from 1905–1932, during a time when many police agencies were influenced heavily by local politicians and suffered from corruption. For Vollmer to be considered the Father of Modern Policing, numerous changes had to be made in policing based on the current standard when he became Chief of Police.

With a focus on prevention and evolving policing methodologies, Vollmer transformed policing with many advancements still utilized by law enforcement today (Vollmer, 1936). Motorized patrols (motorcycle and patrol car), radio communications, fingerprinting, and the development of a juvenile unit/division were all contributions to policing by Vollmer. Vollmer is also known for the implementation of pin mapping, which is just what it sounds like, putting pins on an actual map to represent where crimes occurred. This is essential for understanding spatial patterning in data during this time period. He also led the development of a records management system (RMS). While basic at the time, it assisted in the ability to make scientific inquiries with the data. Many of these advancements assisted in the creation of police patrol districts. Based on the list of contributions by Vollmer, it should not be surprising many of them helped the development of crime analysis.

A protégé of Vollmer's, Orlando W. Wilson, continued advancing policing and became an influential police reformer. Wilson was the Chief of Police for numerous jurisdictions and was also a professor in the School of Criminology at the University of California at Berkeley. One of Wilson's most notable books, *Police Administration* (1950), was utilized for educational purposes into the 1970s because of the detail on police department management and organization. In the second edition of *Police Administration* (1963: 103), we see the term "crime analysis" discussed:

> Crime Analysis. The crime-analysis section studies daily reports of serious crimes in order to determine the location, time, special characteristics, similarities to other criminal attacks, and various significant facts that might help to identify either a criminal or the existence of a pattern of criminal activity. Such information is helpful in planning the operations of a division or district.

While this point in time is often associated with development of the term "crime analysis," the description provided by Wilson leads to the assumption crime analysis was already in use within police agencies. This description also highlights the value of developing operations by division of district, suggesting different resources could be needed depending on the subunit (i.e. district or division). Recall in Chapter 1, this necessity is still relevant today with NYPD looking to hire district crime analysts. This allows for tailored analysis per district/division.

In the early 1970s, the Law Enforcement Assistance Administration (LEAA) began to provide money to law enforcement agencies, encouraging Wilson's discussion of crime analysis to be a part of departments. This is an important aspect that police agencies still face today: the cost associated with developing a crime analysis unit. For some, the solution to crime problems is often a greater number of police officers and cracking down on certain types of offenses; however, arresting their way out of a problem does not assist in understanding the problem. The LEAA funded numerous manuals/handbooks on crime analysis in the 1970s to share ideas and approaches to the topic area.

Additionally, in the latter part of the 1970s, LEAA developed the Integrated Criminal Apprehension Program (ICAP), making crime analysis one of the four focal points of LEAA. ICAP helped develop crime analysis units in numerous agencies, and some remain today based on the early efforts of these programs.

In the 1990s, there was a renewed interest of crime analysis in police agencies in what was described as the "Golden Age of Crime Analysis." There are many factors that contributed to the revitalization of crime analysis. During this time, technology was becoming much more popular and available; and advancements were enhancing the types of analyses possible by analysts. There was also an emergence of problem-oriented policing, brought to the forefront by Herman Goldstein. Goldstein brought attention to the need to focus on crime as a problem rather than individual incidents, and this is still seen today with the POP Guides.

POP Guides provide tailored approaches to problems encountered in all types of jurisdictions. POP stands for Problem-Oriented Policing, and is a common acronym used in law enforcement. There are POP Guides that address many different types of problems; and this is what makes the Center for Problem-Oriented Policing such a valuable resource. Currently, popcenter.org provides a starting point for analysts and agencies to search and examine what has been done in the past in other jurisdictions. Topics include street prostitution, loud car stereos, shoplifting, drunk driving, student party riots, and many others. There are also resources related to responses to crime, identifying what works best, and tools agencies can utilize to examine their problem. This was an essential step in furthering crime analysis because it required the identification of a problem that needed to be analyzed so it could be understood.

Also during the Golden Age of Crime Analysis, the International Association of Crime Analysts (IACA) was founded. This organization is a leader in providing educational opportunities; developing standards; and sharing knowledge among researchers, practitioners, and analysts. IACA is a great resource of what has worked for agencies and how to troubleshoot problems. IACA has an annual conference that allows members to present on research topics, test for certifications, learn new techniques, and network (among many other benefits).

Toward the mid-1990s, the "CompStat" (Comparable Statistics) system was developed and used in the New York Police Department. The CompStat system is a strategy that involves crime analysis, and puts emphasis on the inclusion of crime mapping and data analysis. NYPD saw a reduction in serious violent crime in the first half of the 1990s. Based on the influence the NYPD has on setting precedent, and for reduction in violent crimes, police agencies around the United States were using CompStat meetings to help officers understand crime problems by aiding their findings with visualizations from maps. CompStat is still a relevant strategy that agencies use to examine crime and public disorder problems.

Throughout the twenty-first century, there has been continual growth in the crime analysis field. The expansion of technology has led to numerous programs and potential certifications for a variety of software programs. These certifications can assist in obtaining an entry-level job or trying to move to more advanced positions. Through IACA, members can become Certified Law Enforcement Analysts (CLEA). These certifications have led to the development of Crime Analysis certificates at universities throughout the world. These programs help students obtain knowledge and expertise in crime analysis.

The September 11, 2001, terrorist attacks spurred greater interest in the prevention and forecasting ability of analytical work, including crime and intelligence analysis. The prominence of terrorism across multiple social media sources and news outlets will continue to drive a movement to better understanding terrorism events. Although rare, the effect terrorism events have on the greater audience necessitates a preventative focus.

By no surprise, technology greatly assisted the progression of crime analysis; however, without early innovators such as Vollmer and Wilson, policing would look very different. The discussion of crime analysis in this section is an abbreviated historical timeline, but referenced important people and organizations along the way. More detail into the theoretical side and analysis side of crime analysis will provide a greater understanding of how crime analysis progressed.

PRACTICE ASSIGNMENT

Now that you are familiar with the historical side of crime analysis, let's try an exercise. Crime analysts are often tasked with a variety of duties, many of which lack any real detail. As a crime analyst, you have to think through a problem and try to analyze it to the best of your ability. Often, time restraints and data availability will hinder what is possible when given a task. Try your hand at conducting a crime analysis by following the task below as an example.

Task

You are asked to examine the top prevalent crimes (aggravated assaults and residential burglaries) for the calendar year of 2014 in Little Rock, Arkansas, and provide insight on the crimes' temporal

Table 2.1 Aggravated Assaults and Residential Burglaries in Little Rock in 2014

Crime Type	Number of Incidents
Aggravated Assaults	
Nonfamily – Gun	639
Nonfamily – Other Weapon	190
Family – Strongarm	181
Nonfamily – Strongarm	131
Nonfamily – Knife	119
Family – Other Weapon	90
Family – Knife	82
Family – Gun	45
Residential Burglary	
Forced Entry	2,126
No Forced Entry	3

elements to aid officers in their patrol/crime prevention efforts. *Temporal* relates to the time characteristics associated to crime or other outcomes of interest.

- Where do you start? This may seem relatively straightforward; but within crime analysis, connecting the dots is a vital role. The ability to go through data and detect problems, patterns, and trends is important; but what is essential is the skill to translate those findings into understandable presentations.

Step 1: Since you know the two types of crimes you are examining, you should pay attention to how the data are coded and the numbers behind the data. Throughout 2014, there were a total of 1,477 aggravated assaults and 2,129 residential burglaries reported to Little Rock Police Department. Table 2.1 provides a breakdown of the different type of offenses with descriptions about the incidents.

As shown in Table 2.1, a majority of the aggravated assaults included the use of a weapon, specifically a gun. What is interesting is the difference between family and nonfamily weapon use. For nonfamily incidents, guns were more likely to be used; whereas in family incidents, "other" weapons were the most common, with guns being the least frequently used weapon.

- Why do you think there are differences in weapon use between family incidents and nonfamily incidents?
- Do you think that family incidents are reported as frequently? This is an important question to keep in mind when examining the description of the incidents. Black (1976) discusses the "relational distance" between the victim and offender in the context of reporting to police. The closer the victim and offender are in terms of relationships, the less likely the criminal justice system is involved. By not reporting to the police, the incidents are handled within families, keeping them

out of the eye of law enforcement. Now imagine that the victim and offender are not related, stranger or acquaintance incidents. Because there is a greater "relational distance," law enforcement is more likely to be contacted in hopes of holding the offender(s) accountable for their actions. While this type of analysis is not evident by just looking at the numbers, crime analysts have to put thought into what is behind the numbers.

For residential burglaries, a large number of the incidents were conducted with the use of force. This means that the offenders had to gain access to the residences that did not include an unlocked door or open window. The current data do not include descriptions concerning method of entry, but many law enforcement agencies record that element. For example, offenders could have gained access through a back door, front door, side window, garage, and so on.

- Following this frame of thought, what makes one residence more attractive to offenders than others?
- Are there certain environmental cues that signal a suitable target (see Cohen and Felson, 1979) or flag a house as a target and increase the likelihood of victimization (see Farrell and Pease, 1993; Pease, 1998)?
- Are there similar methods of entry and/or are there near repeats? Near repeats mean, once there is an initial residential burglary, the likelihood of an additional burglary in close proximity and time is likely to occur (see examples Grubb and Nobles, 2016; Townsley, Homel, and Chaseling, 2003).

Step 2: Now that the numbers have been examined, where can you go from here? Crime is known to have temporal patterns. You could examine crime in terms of hour, day, and month to help inform administrators and officers to variations.

- What do you think the temporal patterns will look like for aggravated assaults and residential burglaries? Hour of the day; Day of the week; Month of the year? Why would you expect change?

Figure 2.1 shows the frequencies of aggravated assaults and residential burglaries by the hour of the day (0 = 12:00 am, 13 = 1:00 pm). Examining aggravated assaults first, around 7:00 am is the low point, with 14 incidents. Around 7:00 am, many people are waking up and getting ready to start their day, meaning that many people would still be sleeping or not have left the place where they slept the night before. As the time of day progresses, there is a general increase in the number of aggravated assaults. This would be expected with the increase in people traveling outside of their homes for work, school, errands, and other activities, resulting in a higher number of potential victim and offender intersections. Aggravated assaults were most frequent during late evening hours, 8:00–9:00 pm. This could be viewed as a time when people are off from work and not at home. People may be out at bars or other activities that bring them in contact with others. This could increase the potential for aggravated assaults.

Now compare the aggravated assault line to the residential burglary line. See a distinct difference? Based on the crime type, why would you expect differences between the occurrence of the crimes? While aggravated assaults had their lowest occurrence around 7:00 am, this was the highest frequency time for burglaries. Residences can become attractive targets as residents leave for their daily activities, limiting the guardianship of the home. Further examining the residential burglary line, there is a general decrease as the day progresses with a few spikes. There is a spike around normal lunch hours when offenders who do work normal hours commit burglaries, and there is a spike in early afternoon that could be when adolescents are released from school for the day. There are a number of reasons for what can happen, and it is the job of a crime analyst to sift through the reasoning and delve deeper into understanding the task. Crime analysts are tasked with connecting these dots.

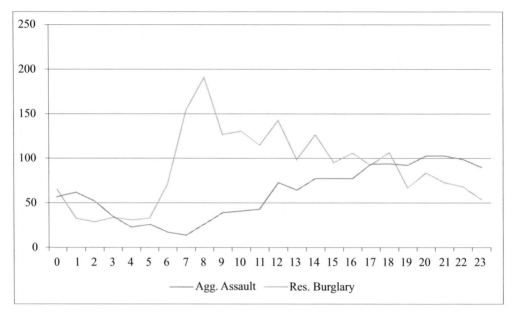

Figure 2.1 Aggravated Assaults and Residential Burglaries by Hour for 2014

Identifying patterns and trends is just one piece of the pie, but being able to explain these patterns and trends provides officers with valuable insights when developing strategies.

In Figure 2.2, the two crimes are separated by the day of the week. As you can see, residential burglaries are more common during the week while aggravated assaults are more prevalent during the weekend. A greater number of people work during the week, leaving their homes as suitable targets while at work versus the weekend. There is less guardianship (potential occupancy and neighbors as on-lookers) during traditional working hours, creating greater potential anonymity for burglars to go undetected, even during the day. Aggravated assaults are violent crimes that occurs between people. During the weekend, there is greater potential to have victim and offender intersections as they conduct weekend activities. The argument could also be made that more people are out patronizing bars and restaurants, increasing intoxication, which could alter judgment on criminal opportunities, resulting in the number of aggravated assaults.

Crime could also vary by the month of the year, as shown in Figure 2.3. Residential burglaries are more likely to occur between September and December when compared to the other months. Little Rock is known to have hot and humid summers that could limit activities; while fall and spring months allow for greater activities to take place (i.e. kickball, baseball, softball, soccer, concerts, etc.). With more people away from their homes, there are more targets for offenders. While more activities take place in the fall and spring in Little Rock, the summer still sees an increase in people outside of their homes, in part, because school is not in session.

Going through this task, can you think of other relevant points to look into?

- Do you think the temporal patterns would vary by police district or neighborhood?
- What about temporal patterns by day and hour (temporal heat map/pivot table)?
- What would you have done differently or added to the task?

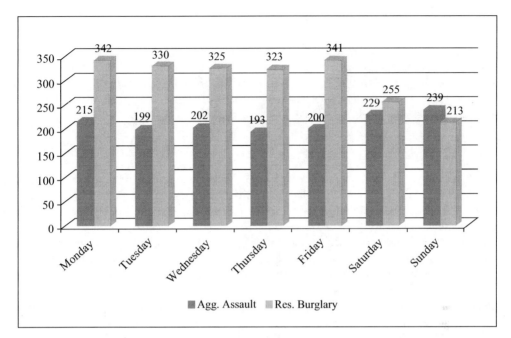

Figure 2.2 Aggravated Assaults and Residential Burglaries by Day of the Week for 2014

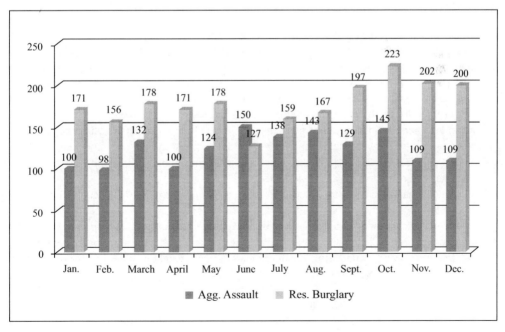

Figure 2.3 Aggravated Assaults and Residential Burglaries by Month for 2014

Later, in the second part of the textbook, crosstabs will be discussed along with other statistical applications. The temporal patterns described previously could be further examined. For example, the hour of the day when crime occurs could differ depending on the day of the week and/or the month. During the weekend, crime could be more prevalent during later hours since not as many people work on Saturday or Sunday. This process of thinking and problem solving is essential for a crime analyst to more thoroughly aid police administration and officers. The descriptive analysis discussed above can be written up in research briefs that can be used by administrators and officers.

CRIME ANALYSIS IN ACTION

Because crime analysis is a growing field and many crime analysts have skillsets they are open to share, we thought it would be beneficial to include applications of crime analysis that were used by police agencies. Following are two research briefs that were completed by a crime analyst from St. Louis Metropolitan Police Department, Christy Oldham. Accompanying the research brief is a description of the task given to Christy and steps she took throughout the project. Christy's insight is a great example of crime analysis projects, the thought process, and analytical process when aiding law enforcement. In the first example, Figure 2.4, pay close attention to Christy's inquisitive nature throughout the project. She has a problem-oriented mindset to gain a better understanding of the assignment. The second example, Figure 2.5, discusses a common task assigned to crime analysts: aid law enforcement in identifying high crime areas where crime reduction and prevention strategies can be targeted. Both examples provide you with an understanding of how crime analysts are utilized within law enforcement agencies and why they are crucial for law enforcement agencies.

Research Brief #1: District 3 – Cherokee Street Analysis

In April 2014, I received a phone call from an officer who had recently been assigned back on the streets, and who wanted to familiarize himself with a few areas within his newly appointed district. One of the areas he was most interested in was Cherokee Street. Cherokee Street is a popular street in south St. Louis that is home to many locally-owned businesses, art galleries, restaurants, and festivals. Knowing Cherokee Street to be a busy place, the officer wanted to know what kind of criminal activity had occurred since the beginning of the year, how that activity was structured along the street, and the days and times in which that activity was most likely to occur. He then planned to take this information and meet with the business owners and community leaders of Cherokee Street, and not only discuss what is happening, but also how they can proactively approach and manage such activity together.

Using the analytic software ATAC, I pulled data from the neighborhoods surrounding Cherokee Street for all crime types (Part I and Part II crimes) and calls-for-service. I saved that as my main database and then filtered that subset down to just incidents with addresses listed on Cherokee Street. I chose to look at both crime incidents and calls-for-service because I did not feel there was an adequate amount of activity along Cherokee Street to develop a proper analysis when looking at just crime incidents. Also, when working with the public and the public's perception of what goes on within a particular area, the old adage of "where there is smoke, there is fire" is essential. I found that calls-for-service made up almost 80% of the activity along Cherokee Street; so, had I excluded them from this study, much of what went on would have been overlooked.

After pulling and cleaning the data, I geocoded the incidents within ArcGIS. Next, I created a hot spot map using the kernel density tool because many of the incidents would not be visible on

District 3—Cherokee Street Analysis
January 1, 2014—April 21, 2014

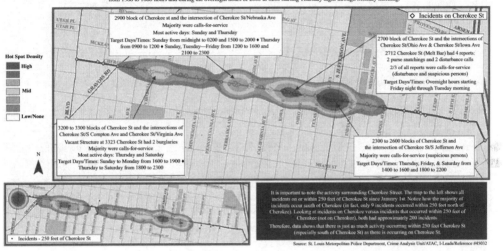

Figure 2.4 St. Louis Metropolitan Police Department: Cherokee Street

a point map due to overlapping. A hot spot map would represent those incidents stacked underneath others and would give a better visual representation of where the most active areas are along Cherokee Street. In addition to this, I decided to keep the points on the map along with the hot spot densities so that those individuals reading the map would understand that activity still existed outside of the hot spot areas, but just not at as high of an intensity. To determine what kind of incidents the hot spot was constructed of and if activity was targeted within certain days and times, I selected each hot spot individually using the select tool, and then analyzed those incidents highlighted within the attribute table.

The results of the analysis left me curious to see how the activity surrounding Cherokee Street compared. I went back to the original database I pulled and geocoded all incidents within the surrounding neighborhoods. I used both the buffer tool and the clip tool within ArcGIS to create a 250-foot buffer around Cherokee Street and then cut the incidents that occurred within that buffer. Using that subset of data, I created another hot spot density map. Upon reviewing the hot spot map, I was not surprised that the hot spots along Cherokee Street had minimized in some central locations and intensified toward the west. The west end of Cherokee Street intersects with S. Grand Boulevard. S. Grand Boulevard is a major thoroughfare in St. Louis with lots of traffic and many commercial properties, including a large chain grocery store located just south of where the two streets intersect. I was surprised to learn there was just as much activity within 250 feet of south of Cherokee Street as there was on Cherokee Street itself. A further analysis could look into the relationship between Cherokee Street and its surrounding area more thoroughly.

I spoke with the officer a little while after I sent him the analysis and he said that the business owners were elated with the map and the information presented to them. This analysis informed them on what areas they should focus on improving, what activities they should look out for, and what times the activities are most present. The officer, business owners, and community members plan to continue to collaborate together to keep Cherokee Street a place where people want to go.

Christy provided a very detailed response to her project task. There might be terminology and takeaway points not fully understood and deserve greater attention. Do not worry, below we provide details. Below are a few of the common terms you saw in this example and will see throughout the rest of the book.

- *Community-Oriented Policing* (COP): COP is a strategy that actively engages community members to assist in policing efforts. The officer putting in the request wanted to take the information back to local business owners and community leaders to get feedback and work proactively. Additionally, the officer reaching out to Christy is an important step in itself because some police underestimate the importance of crime analysts assisting their policing efforts. This strategy will be discussed in greater detail in Chapter 5.
- *ATAC*: Automated Tactical Analysis of Crime software. ATAC is a useful crime analyst program used to identify patterns, trends, and other crime analysis needs. ATAC was developed by BAIR Analytics; then BAIR Analytics was acquired by LexisNexis (www.lexisnexis.com/risk/government/crime-analytics-mapping.aspx).
- *Parts I and II*: Parts I and II refer to Uniform Crime Reporting (UCR) data. UCR crime data are reported to the Federal Bureau of Investigation (FBI). Part I are more serious crimes (e.g. homicide, rape, arson, among others).
- *Buffer*: Christy applied a 250-foot buffer around Cherokee St. Imagine any street, then drawing a 250-foot catchment area around that street (i.e. buffer). Buffers are often used to understand how much crime is occurring around certain features (e.g. roads, bars, schools, bus stops). Christy then selected only the data points (crimes) occurring within the buffer, resulting in a subset of data.
- *Data Subset*: Christy created a data subset based on the crimes within the buffer around Cherokee Street. These crimes could potentially have different patterns and trends about their occurrence. Selecting these incidents out from the larger area allows for a geographic specific analysis.
- *ArcGIS*: ArcGIS is a mapping program utilized by numerous fields, not only criminal justice. If you are interested in learning mapping techniques and your agency does not have a geographic information system (GIS) type course, most likely other agencies will offer GIS/mapping courses. Often, these courses are taught using ArcGIS. This would be a great program to become familiar with if you have the opportunity.
- *Geocoding*: When crimes are reported to the police, addresses are often supplied to dispatch or on reports. Geocoding is the process of taking addresses and mapping them through a software program. In a sense, an automated process as if you were to have a large map in an office and put a pin on a map representing each crime. This is done electronically and much quicker.
- *Kernel Map vs. Point Map*: Christy used both point and kernel maps in her analyses. When multiple points are at the same address, or in close proximity, it distorts the appearance of the map. Also, if multiple crimes occur at the same address, one point could represent numerous crimes. This is where kernel maps are beneficial. Kernel maps, also known as Kernel Density Estimation Maps (KDE), is a common technique for identifying hot spots. Hot spots are clusters of crime, or any event displayed spatially in small geographical areas.

Research Brief #2: Gravois Park – Benton Park West – Tower Grove East: Blitz

In the summer of 2014, the St. Louis Metropolitan Police Department decided to do a blitz within the following south city neighborhoods: Gravois Park, Benton Park West, and Tower Grove East. This blitz not only focused on crime reduction, but also set out to improve the overall atmosphere of the neighborhoods by collaborating with other city services and outreach programs. Aside from reducing crime in general, some key components of the blitz included identifying and arresting as many actively wanted persons as possible, conducting consent searches at specifically chosen residences, cleaning up streets and alleyways, trimming overgrown trees and bushes, towing illegally parked cars, and replacing or upgrading street lighting. My role in this blitz was to provide a map detailing where the hot spots existed within these three neighborhoods, which then informed the officers and other municipal agencies the areas to focus their efforts on.

Using the analytic software ATAC, I pulled all Part I crime incidents (excluding larceny – shoplifting and domestic-related incidents) from August 1st, 2011 to July 27th, 2014. I then geocoded the data within ArcGIS and created a hot spot density map using the Kernel Density tool. Once the hot spot map was completed, I wanted to determine which blocks within the blitz area had the most activity. The Major had listed a number of blocks he felt should be targeted, and I wanted to see if his predictions and the data reflected each other. To do this, I used the spatial join tool to join points (crime incidents) to polylines (streets), and then symbolized the streets with

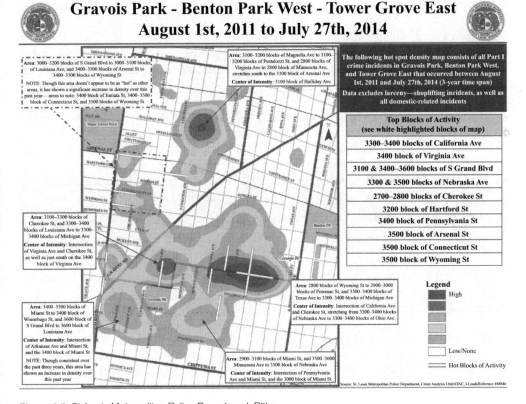

Figure 2.5 St. Louis Metropolitan Police Department: Blitz

the highest incident counts using a thick, solid white line. This way, the hot blocks would be visible on the map, but not overshadow the hot areas indicated in the density.

The Major's prediction and the data-based hot blocks were the same. As predicted, the hot blocks fell within or were adjacent to the hot spot areas. There were, however, a couple of hot blocks that were not expected. These were the blocks located in the central west portion of the area, just southeast of Tower Grove Park. To determine how these blocks were hot but not located within a hot spot area, I decided to look at how the hot spot areas evolved over time. Using a definition query within ArcGIS to create new point layers by year, I ran the Kernel Density tool on each layer, creating three new hot spot maps. When I compared the three maps, I found that the majority of hot spots shown on the overall map were also present during each individual year. Though they ranged in intensity, their presence indicated a continuing problem within that particular area. More interesting though, I found that the area just southwest of Tower Grove Park did not become active until the third year. It did not appear to be as hot on the overall hot spot map because the first two years of little to no activity almost neutralized the last year, which experienced a significant increase in activity. This was important to note and inform the officers of because the activity was recent; and, although the area did not appear to be problematic, it was an area of growing concern.

The feedback I received from this assignment was very positive. I was told that the maps were helpful and informative. All agencies involved were able to focus their time and energy on the hot spot areas, which resulted in a better use of the city's finite resources. The maps also allowed the Nuisance and Problem Properties Sergeants to center in on smaller areas and send their officers door-to-door with information on Crime Stoppers and the city's nuisance process in hopes of educating the residents living within these areas of concern.

Many of the same concepts used in this brief were seen in the prior one. As you work your way through this book, you will notice overlapping concepts and the common terminology used within the field. Below are brief descriptions of concepts and terminology you might be familiar with at this point.

- *Clean-up efforts around hot spots*: In this example, a blitz of efforts at hot spots sought to, not only focus on crime, but the larger context of neighborhoods. Hot spot analyses were used to identify hot spots of crime; but, rather than solely directing police to the problem areas, multiple stakeholders partnered to tackle problems in those hot spots.
- *Comparing the data to the officer's prediction:* This cannot be discussed enough. Crime analysts deal with many skeptics because analysts deal with data while officers are on the street. The interesting point though is the analysts' data are often collected by officers. Crime analysts are utilizing analytical techniques to make sense of the data being collected. While in Christy's brief, the Major's prediction and the data supported one another, this is not always the case. Then it becomes the analyst's duty to link the two together and show the reality versus perception.

CRIME ANALYST QUESTIONNAIRE

In Boxes 2.1 and 2.2, there are additional crime analyst questionnaires. These are examples of what to expect from different positions and analytical work throughout the United States. Pay close attention to the duties and tasks to identify if these types of everyday responsibilities are what interest you career wise. Additional crime analyst questionnaires are located in Appendix A. We highly recommend going through these to see the words of wisdom, duties, pay, and experience.

BOX 2.1 CRIME ANALYST QUESTIONNAIRE: CHRISTOPHER PRITCHETT, SENIOR DETECTIVE, LAGRANGE, GA POLICE DEPARTMENT

Serving Population Size: 35,000

Years as Analyst: 4

Crime Analysis Experience: see below

Other Related Work Experience: fraud and computer investigations

Education: BS-security management, starting graduate school at Columbus State University – Law Enforcement Command College, completed crime and intel analysis certification through Alpha Group

Starting Salary Range: detective starting salary is about $45,000

How Did You Get into Crime Analysis: I was approached by the section commander and asked if I would be interested in taking this position. LPD had never had an analyst before, so I was tasked with getting trained, creating policy, and creating everything else from scratch. Previously, I was a case detective specializing in fraud and computer crimes. I was working with the Internet Crimes Against Children Task Force.

Main Duties: Creating staff meeting presentations (CompStat), keeping information up to date for the department intel site (policeintel.com), maintaining pin maps, identifying serial offenders, downloading surveillance videos from homes and businesses, maintaining the department social media sites, plotting anything on a map, fixing anything electronic that is broken or does not work properly, maintain the department televisions, and research anything and everything.

Favorite Task/Analysis/Approach: My favorite thing to do is identifying a serial offender and predicting his next target. I think it is the pinnacle task that shows what crime analysts can do for everyone in the agency.

Words of Wisdom/Thoughts for Up-and-Comers: For newcomers, you are smarter than the average bear. Do not let others in your agency dictate the work you do. Do what you know is right. And realize that impossible does not exist, but improbable does; do not get overworked.

BOX 2.2 CRIME ANALYST QUESTIONNAIRE: JEFFREY WELLS, SENIOR CRIMINAL INTELLIGENCE ANALYST, ARMY THREAT INTEGRATION CENTER

Serving Population Size: 500,000

Years as Analyst: 8

Crime Analysis Experience: 25

Other Related Work Experience: Military Police; Federal Special Agent

Education: Master's Degree

Starting Salary Range: Military so appears low

How Did You Get into Crime Analysis: After 9/11 the need was seen, so some of us were "chosen" to be analysts

Main Duties:

- Collection, analysis, production, and dissemination of fused criminal intelligence and military intelligence products for community consumption.
- Provide Terrorist threat warning and situational awareness reports to Senior Army Leadership, Army Staff, Army Commands, Army Service Component Commands, Direct Reporting Units, and Army National Guard.
- Analyzes, assimilates, and evaluates all available criminal intelligence and military intelligence information collected.
- Extracts and organizes statistical data.
- Prepares reports and oral briefings.
- Works independently, establishes work procedures, exercises judgment in applying advanced criminal intelligence and military intelligence techniques, and evaluates validity and pertinence of data and reporting.
- Establishes procedures for issues that do not appear to be able to be resolved by applying generally accepted criminal intelligence and military intelligence methods and applies an understanding of patterns and knowledge of current and past terrorist events, making recommendations on controversial matters.
- Expertly uses law enforcement and intelligence databases, applications, and counter-terrorism specific secure portals to perform work and uses in-depth knowledge of Secret Internet Protocol Router Network (SIPRNET) and Joint Worldwide Intelligence Communications System (JWICS) in daily tasks.
- Assists in serving as liaison to develop working relationships with counterparts in other law enforcement and intelligence agencies to exchange pertinent information and provide free flow of information on matters of mutual interest.

Highlights of Job: Liaison with other agencies

Words of Wisdom/Thoughts for Up-and-Comers: I have learned, at the highest levels of the Federal Government that, "criminal intelligence analyst," is different by agency. The same job title can do completely different things, even in the same room/agency.

CONCLUSION

Crime analysis is a growing field as police agencies and government agencies realize the benefits. With growing technology, the capabilities of crime analysts continue to increase. Understanding where crime analysis came from and the direction it is heading offers insights into potential agencies that will be looking to hire in the future. The Crime Analysis in Action section provides a brief introduction to what analysts do on a daily basis based on requests from command staff. A valuable way of getting into crime analysis is understanding thoughts and perspectives from current analysts. There are three links that analysts might find valuable (both new as well as experienced analysts):

- www.iaca.net

  The International Association of Crime Analysts website provides numerous resources, both education and professional. Becoming a member of IACA is a valuable choice with the amount of knowledge you can gain from other members. IACA has an annual conference that includes presentations and classes for attendees.
- www.crimeanalysthotspot.com

  This website was constructed by Levi Giraud, whose profile was in Chapter 1. The website entails topics of, "I wish I had known that earlier!", interviews with relevant analysts/researchers, and many helpful links.
- www.crimemapping.info

  This website is part of The Police Foundation, that also re-launched their newsletter, *Crime Mapping & Analysis News* in 2014. This newsletter provides innovations and advancements in crime mapping, allowing readers to be up to date with new analytical techniques.

Through these resources and others, you have an opportunity to become involved in a dynamic and interesting field. With this introduction complete, we now turn to some of the background theories and knowledge that are a part of being a crime analyst.

BIBLIOGRAPHY

Beirne, P. 1987. Adolphe Quetelet and the origins of positivist criminology. *American Journal of Sociology*, 92(5):1140–1169.

Black, D.J. 1976. *The Behavior of Law*. New York, NY: Academic Press.

Cohen, E.C. and M. Felson. 1979. Social change and crime rate trends: A routine activity approach. *American Sociological Review*, 44(4): 588–608.

Farrell, G. and K. Pease. 1993. *Once bitten, twice bitten: Repeat victimisation and its implications for crime prevention*. Crime Prevention Unit Series Paper no. 46. London: Home Office Police Department.

Grubb, J.A. and M.R. Nobles. 2016. A spatiotemporal analysis of arson. *Journal of Research in Crime and Delinquency*, 53(1): 66–92.

Morris, A. 1975. The American Society of Criminology: A history, 1941–1974. *Criminology*, 13(2): 123–167.

Pease, K. 1998. *Repeat Victimisation: Taking Stock*. London: Home Office.

Reibstein, L. 1997. "NYPD black and blue." *Newsweek*, June 2, 66–68.

Townsley, M., R. Homel, and J. Chaseling. 2003. Infectious burglaries: A test of the near repeat hypothesis. *British Journal of Criminology*, 43(3): 615–633.

Vollmer, A. 1936. *The Police and Modern Society*. Berkeley: University of California Press.

Wilson, O.W. 1963. *Police Administration*, 2nd ed. New York, NY: McGraw-Hill.

QUESTIONS AND EXERCISES

1 What police reforms did August Vollmer make? How did early reforms shape crime analysis?
2 How has technology affected/changed crime analysis over the last 100 years?
3 What are POP Guides and how are they beneficial to the police?

4   When faced with a problem or question, what steps would a crime analyst take?
5   In Research Brief #1, why was a hot spot map used?
6   What are the crimes that make up UCR Part I and II categories?
7   Review the Center for Problem-Oriented Policing website (popcenter.org). What POP Guides should be added to the list? Briefly summarize the problem.

Chapter 3

Places and individuals

Environmental criminology

Much of what we do in law enforcement, criminological theory, and all of the criminal justice system, deals with people. After all, it is people who commit crimes. But focusing only on individuals leaves out a lot of what is important in understanding crime – places. Individual behavior must take place in a context – in a place. Some places are riskier than other places, and more likely to produce violent and/or criminal behavior. For example, you cannot get into a bar fight in a church. It is not that all bars produce fighting customers; but there is a higher chance of getting in an interpersonal conflict in a place with a lot of people and alcohol than in other places. Other places are perfectly normal and safe most of the time, but can also occasionally produce criminal behavior. For example, your home is one of the safest places you can be, but there are more people killed in homes than any other single place.

This chapter deals with the foundations of one criminological perspective, environmental criminology, that focuses on place, along with the other elements of the "what, who, and where" that is central to crime analysis. The environment we will be discussing in this chapter is the social, particularly urban, environment where people reside. You will be introduced to the foundations of environmental criminology in the form of social disorganization theory. We will then discuss some of the early theoretical perspectives in this area, such as routine activities theory and crime prevention through environmental design (CPTED). We will then move through the development and expansion of environmental criminology, beginning with the work of Paul and Patricia Brantingham and moving to the most recent theories in this perspective.

EARLY FORMS OF THEORY THAT WOULD AID CRIME ANALYSIS

As discussed in Chapter 2, some of the earliest forms of crime analysis began in the 1800s in England and France. The government in England began collecting data on crime in 1805, followed by the French government in 1825. Not long after, researchers began using this data to examine crime in its social context and to make comparisons between geographic units (counties, cities, and soon parts of cities). In some of the very first examinations of the geographic distribution of crime, Guerry (1833) and Quetelet (1842) examined crime at the department (county) level in France. Guerry found that property crimes were mostly found in the northern part of France and violent crimes were more likely located in southern France. Guerry is also credited with being the first person to shade maps (at the department/county level) related to crime – arguably making him the first crime analyst. Also, both Guerry and Quetelet found crime was very stable over time as it related to age, sex, economics, and location.

One of the earliest studies examining the characteristics of crime within a single urban area was conducted by Mayhew (1862/1968), who found that there were certain areas of London that consistently had high crime. Mayhew found these areas were typically on the outer edge of London. These areas were typically near areas of wealth but characterized as being high in poverty and crowded conditions. These studies began the process of examining crime and its social context; providing the "who" and "where" of crime.

SOCIAL DISORGANIZATION THEORY

The Chicago School of Sociology brought the study of crime and its geographic relationship to social factors to the United States beginning in the late 1800s. One of the first studies linking crime to social characteristics in the U.S. was a study examining the distribution of the homes of juvenile delinquents in Chicago by Breckenridge and Abbott in 1912. They found the homes of juvenile delinquents were disproportionately clustered in certain parts of the city.

The geographic study and representation of crime took another step forward when Ernest Burgess (1924) proposed that many of the social problems of cities followed a concentric zone pattern (see Figure 3.1 and the discussion below). Burgess proposed that cities had a core and that all cities grew in rings around that core. Because the areas closer to the core were older (and often more run-down), these areas were more likely to have problems such as low birth weights, low income, and crime.

In one of the most significant studies of crime and the urban environment, Clifford R. Shaw and Henry D. McKay (1942) studied the association and, more specifically, the physical relationship between the characteristics of neighborhoods in Chicago and juvenile delinquency. In this research, Shaw and McKay examined three characteristics of neighborhoods in Chicago.

In examining the physical characteristics of neighborhoods, Shaw and McKay looked at population change, the proximity of neighborhoods to areas of industry (commercial areas), and vacant and condemned houses – all characteristics that would be studied by modern-day crime analysts. They found that areas with high levels of juvenile delinquency were associated with high levels of physical deterioration and older homes, had residents who often had not lived in the area long (and many were new immigrants to the U.S.), and were close to the center of the city and to areas of industry.

The primary economic characteristics studied by Shaw and McKay were the number of homes owned and the median rental price. Although these may not seem to be something that analysts

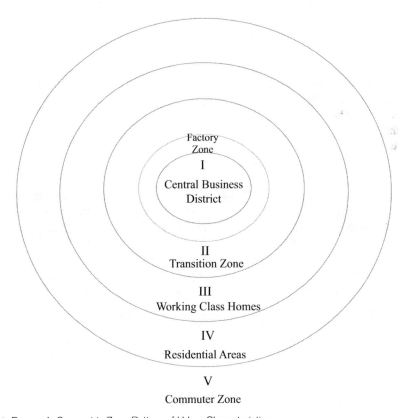

Figure 3.1 Burgess's Concentric Zone Pattern of Urban Characteristics

would study to predict crime, they are actually quite important if viewed in the correct way. Home-ownership can reflect a population capable of affording a home. Further, homeowners are more likely to have developed a better sense of community since homeowners typically reside at a location longer than those who rent. These neighborhoods could form a higher degree of collective efficacy (Sampson, Raudenbush, and Earls, 1997) and social organization (for the other end of the spectrum, organization to disorganization, see Sampson and Groves, 1989). Shaw and McKay also studied the number of families receiving social assistance (families on relief in their study). While this is something that might be studied by current crime analysts, it should be undertaken with caution. Social assistance is really just another measure of the wealth in the area – and a closely related measure could be median income. Further, there are different types of social assistance, some of which are inversely related to crime and delinquency. For example, an area that is high in the number of retired people may show high social assistance (social security and Medicare) but be very low in crime. It is important, then to know the area and the total characteristics and not just work from one measure.

Finally, Shaw and McKay examined the population characteristics of neighborhoods. They found an association between crime and the percentage of foreign-born and Black heads of households. They cautioned, however, that there was little to draw a direct relationship between a person's race or nativity and juvenile delinquency. They supported their findings by examining all the characteristics over almost 50 years. What they found was that, when immigrants from a certain country were in the areas characterized by other problems, their delinquency rate was high; but when they moved to areas characterized by more prosperity and stability, their rates of delinquency declined. Thus, Shaw and McKay attributed the association with juvenile delinquency to the economic and physical characteristics of the areas, not to race or ethnicity.

Overall, Shaw and McKay concluded that the environment was such in certain parts of the city that it resulted in the social disorganization of the residents. In essence, residents lost (or never had) their informal social control. Examining the geographic distribution of the characteristics and delinquency, Shaw and McKay found their results supported Burgess's patterns of concentric zones surrounding the central part of the city.

SPATIAL PATTERNS OF CITY GROWTH AND SOCIAL DISORGANIZATION

A primary contribution of the Chicago School to sociology, criminology, urban studies, and crime analysis was Burgess's work on the pattern of social characteristics in urban areas. Burgess found that the central business district of a city is usually centered where the city was founded. He argued that cities begin at this location and then grow in concentric zones at about one mile increments from the center as new developments are constructed (see Figure 3.1). Burgess also argued that the characteristics of the zones changed dramatically from one zone to the next. Specifically, he proposed that there was a zone of manufacturing that surrounded the central business district of the city. Outside this "factory zone" was an area of very low-income housing and was predominantly occupied by the low-wage earning population. In the third concentric ring, the predominate residential characteristic was working class homes. Finally, in the fourth and fifth zones from the center of the city were middle and upper-class homes. Burgess labeled this pattern the "Burgess Zonal Hypothesis."

Following Burgess, there were others who proposed cities develop in different spatial configurations, not always following a concentric zone model. The two most popular of these are Hoyt's successive sectors model and Harris and Ullman's multiple nuclei model.

Hoyt (1939) contended that cities grew in sections that followed specific direction of growth, as shown in Figure 3.2. In his model of urban growth, areas of new growth or new popularity in a city would grow in smaller "slices" of the concentric zone rather than taking up an entire ring as in Burgess's model. Part of the potential difference between concentric zones and successive sectors can be attributed to the change in transportation of cities. In Burgess's model, city streets were laid out primarily in grid fashion, with streets essentially the same size throughout the city. By the time of Hoyt's work, cities started using larger, high-speed automobile routes and better public transportation that would allow people to move further away from the city center. This sector development often showed a pattern that followed these transportation avenues. This was made even more prevalent with the development of expressways and interstate highways that provided rapid automobile access to areas even farther from the city center.

Another pattern of the spatial layout of urban areas was the multiple nuclei, shown in Figure 3.3 (Harris and Ullman, 1945). This model proposed that urban areas are organized around several areas of attraction, such as a port, factory center, or shopping area, that draw people to that area to live. In Figure 3.3, the different numbers are the nuclei of the outlined areas. This theory is not mutually exclusive of other theories because it proposed that a city could expand in either concentric or successive sector patterns around the nuclei. These multiple nuclei will be a part of examining crime areas later in the chapter when we discuss crime generators and attractors.

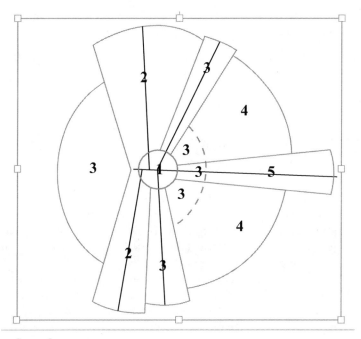

Legend

1. Central Business District
2. Commercial and Manufacturing
3. Low Income Housing
4. Medium Income Housing
5. High Income Housing

Transportation Avenues

Figure 3.2 Hoyt's Successive Sectors Model

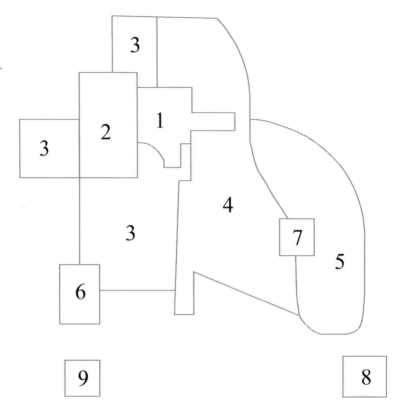

Figure 3.3 Harris and Ullman's Multiple Nuclei Model

RESEARCH ON DETERIORATING CITIES

Increasing crime rates and the deterioration of American cities in the 1980s and 1990s resulted in a renewed interest by police and criminologists in examining the relationship between crime and social characteristics – particularly the geographic relationship. The focus of this interest was somewhat different from the earlier work in social disorganization, however. Now, the focus was on how to control crime at the neighborhood level. A focal point of this effort was how police could move beyond random patrolling to reducing crime and improving the quality of life.

One of the earliest and defining statements on this new focus on crime and justice was an article written by Wilson and Kelling (1982). This article proposed that crime may begin with something simple like a broken window. Wilson and Kelling argued that if the window was replaced quickly, there would be no further deterioration. If the window was not fixed, however, it could lead to other types of crimes such as graffiti and loitering; and eventually to higher levels of other crime. This "Broken Windows" theory somewhat changed police and crime analysis efforts to focus more on "order and disorder" crimes. The earliest and strongest statement of this focus was the New York Police Department's focus on stop and frisk and aggressively policing minor crimes. This also required a change in the way police gathered data on crime and how they were analyzed – which led to the development of CompStat.

In a study that provided some interesting results that would help shape future examinations of crime, Schuerman and Kobrin (1986) examined data from the juvenile court in Los Angeles for the years 1950, 1960, and 1970, and compared it with measures of land use, population composition, socioeconomic status, and subculture. This study broke new ground in two ways. First, Schuerman and Kobrin proposed that neighborhoods move through three stages of delinquency over time: emerging, areas with very low delinquency rates; transitional areas with moderate levels of delinquency; and enduring crime areas, which maintain high levels of delinquency for many years. While others had implied such "progression," Schuerman and Kobrin made it explicit. They also used a novel technique – cross-lagged regression – to examine the temporal ordering of characteristics. They found that changes in the social and economic characteristics related to crime typically precede a rise in delinquency in emerging and early transitional stages; but, as neighborhoods move to the enduring stage, increases in delinquency precede deterioration. This shows that, at certain times, changes in delinquency are dependent on changes in neighborhood characteristics; while at other times, delinquency may be driving deterioration.

Roncek (1981) also examined neighborhood characteristics and crime, but with a change in the geographic level. While his findings were important in that they supported most other social disorganization research, instead of using neighborhoods or Census tracts for his unit of analysis, Roncek worked at the city-block level. He could move to a more refined area of examination because of advances in the quality of data and because of advances in statistical sophistication (particularly advances in GIS technology). Roncek's research is important for our understanding of crime and social characteristics because he found that while the concentration of residents, the concentration of apartment housing, and the percentage of Black residents at the city-block level had strong effects, they did not "dominate the regressions in the same way as in studies using data for census tracts or larger units of analysis" (Roncek, 1981: 88).

Efforts to examine urban crime in the 1970s and 1980s made substantial progress on data, statistical analysis, and GIS technology. About this same time, environmental criminology added strong theoretical understanding to the geographic behavior of criminals as it related to neighborhood characteristics, opportunities for crime, and patterns of human behavior.

ENVIRONMENTAL CRIMINOLOGY

Around 1970, Jeffery (1969) and Newman (1972) separately began a line of inquiry called Crime Prevention through Environmental Design (CPTED). They each proposed that the physical environment often influenced crime. For example, they argued that houses with bushes close to windows provide a safe place from which a burglar could break into the house. By changing the design of the physical environment (such as increasing lighting), they proposed crime could be reduced.

Brantingham and Brantingham (1991) took the research of Jeffery and extended it to include more elements of the social environment and changed the focus to examine places and the patterns of events that occur in those places. This was also a strong step in furthering crime analysis. Although maps had been a part of neighborhood research for years, most of the maps were simply static representations of a characteristic (the number of vacant and condemned homes). Environmental criminology began to examine the movement of people in time and space – examining the patterns of victims and offenders.

One of the core theories of environmental criminology is routine activities (Cohen and Felson, 1979). Routine activities theory examines the movement and activities of offenders and victims and the places where their movement may bring them together. It acknowledges that victims go about their daily lives (work, school, etc.) with little thought of being a victim. Also, offenders go about their daily lives in similar ways, often not focused on committing crime. Sometimes they may plan for crime, but often it is more the opportunities that are presented. A crime occurs when the "routine activities" of victims and the "routine activities" of offenders bring them together in a time and place where there are no "capable guardians" who would prevent the crime from occurring.

Capable guardians in routine activities theory can take many forms, and may be categorized into two groups: formal and informal guardians. The most obvious form of guardian (which is a formal guardian) is the police. Informal guardians can be friends, family, and coworkers who may also provide some protection from crime, such as watching your purse while you go to the bathroom. Guardians can also go beyond people, and be part of the physical environment as in CPTED. For example, the presence of a security system for a home could be a guardian against residential burglary.

Clarke and Eck (2004) built on routine activities theory, particularly the capable guardians, to develop the "crime triangle." The crime triangle is considered a "problem analysis triangle" because it uses an understanding of crime theories to address police problems.

As shown in Figure 3.4, there are two triangles that construct the crime triangle. The inner triangle resembles elements of routine activities theory that must converge in time and space for crime to occur. In the outer triangle, handlers, guardians, and managers (what Cohen and Felson would have called capable guardians) reflect different types of "controllers" that can prevent a crime from occurring.

Guardians in this model follow routine activities theory. They are people who have some formal or informal control over a potential offender or a place where crime might occur. Handlers are people who are close to the offender in relational, personal, or supervisor capacities. Common types of handlers include parents, coaches, teachers, friends, and probation/parole officers who can apply control over the offender's actions.

The final part of the outer crime triangle are managers, who can affect places. These may be managers of apartment complexes, liquor stores, bars, hotels, etc., who can influence control over a place by enforcing rules and being cognizant of the behavior of patrons. By doing so, managers can influence the crime at places. The most typical example of a manager is a bouncer at a bar.

Another part of environmental criminology that is important to crime analysis is journey to crime. Journey to crime is just as it sounds – the journey a criminal takes to commit a crime. Journey to

Figure 3.4 Eck's Crime Triangle, Extension of Routine Activities Theory
Source: Clarke and Eck (2004).

crime research has shown that criminals travel relatively short distances to commit their crimes. Note, however, that there often can be reasons for criminals committing crimes farther away from their homes (such as committing crimes near their work or school, which may be farther away from home). The reasons for the short distances vary, but common explanations are that there is more information available at locations near the residence because of familiarity with the surroundings (awareness space), and criminals have a greater opportunity to have more random crime opportunities near their homes where they spend more of their time (activity space). Journey to crime and distance decay are discussed further in Chapter 11.

Brantingham and Brantingham (1993a) proposed in their crime pattern theory that people develop travel patterns based on routine activities. For example, most people travel the same path from home to work, or even home to buy groceries. The geography of this movement Brantingham and Brantingham called activity space. Activity spaces are locations where people spend most of their time; so, they are able to develop an awareness of opportunities for crime in their environment. They argued that the movement of people within their activity space results in development of a cognitive map of the area. Because of this, "the likely location for a crime is near this normal activity and awareness space" (Brantingham and Brantingham, 1993a: 84).

Within activity space are nodes, paths, and edges. Nodes are locations such as homes, work, school, shopping malls/centers, and recreation sites. Among these nodes are places where people are most likely to commit crimes (Brantingham and Brantingham, 1993b). Paths refer to the routes taken when traveling from one node to another. Here, the activity spaces (nodes) of individuals shape the routes (paths) taken between nodes. The more often paths are traveled, the greater awareness of space people have of the surrounding area, which creates an environment where a criminal opportunity can be identified. Edges are places where there are noticeable changes in the geography. These can be definite breaks, such as a river or lake; more fluid but still defining breaks, such as a major street; or more social breaks, such as in Chicago, where one block may be predominately Polish (including street signs and shop names in Polish) and the next block in German.

When the activity spaces of many people (both offenders and non-offenders/victims) converge at one place, they can create clusters of crime. Brantingham and Brantingham (1981) called these places crime generators and crime attractors (CGAs). They proposed that some places attract or generate crime because of the people who access the businesses during their routine activities. These CGAs could exist because victims could be attracted to the place for the type of activity and offenders could be attracted to the place because of people who go there. For example, large crowds (sporting events, concerts, etc.) are good places for pickpockets. CGAs can also exist because of crime opportunities. Many people go to bars for entertainment. Sometimes, circumstances happen such that people get in fights or have other opportunities for crime they did not initially plan when they went to the bar.

EXTENDING ENVIRONMENTAL CRIMINOLOGY AND CRIME ANALYSIS

Environmental criminology built on the understanding of the social, economic, and geographic influences on crime by extending our understanding of crime to include offenders, non-offenders/victims, and locations. Environmental criminology studies provided insight into the patterns of crime in space and time. They provided a foundation for crime analysis by showing how to examine where crimes are most likely to be located; when they are likely to occur; and the characteristics of the crime, criminals, location, and victims. More recent studies have refined this knowledge and provided a more refined understanding and better analytic techniques.

One of the most extensive, recent projects at the micro level is that of Weisburd, Morris, and Groff (2009). They found that juvenile crime was concentrated in certain areas of Seattle, Washington. They proposed this is in part because juveniles have restricted routine activities, allowing juveniles to concentrate at certain places. The authors found many juvenile crimes occurred at school or youth centers (17 to 31 percent). Other locations with high percentages of juvenile arrests occurred at shops, malls, and restaurants. Think about the discussion of routine activities theory and how this fits with the routine activities for this age range. These places where juvenile crimes occurred fit exactly with what would be proposed by environmental criminology and routine activities theory. The authors also found the locations of juvenile arrests occurred in only 0.29 percent of the street segments, but accounted for about a third of juvenile arrests.

Taylor, Ratcliffe, and Perenzin (2015) utilized an ecological framework to focus on predicting long-term crime problems. They gathered crime data from 2009 in Philadelphia and demographic data from the American Community Survey (ACS) to predict 2010 crime counts in Philadelphia. There were three different approaches to predicting 2010 crime counts: 2009 crime counts, 2010 demographic data, and both crime counts and demographic data. The crime plus demographic approach was a better approach for aggravated assault, robbery, burglary, and motor vehicle theft, but not for murder and rape. Showing the increasing relevance of crime theory for crime analysis, Taylor et al. (2015: 18) specifically provided context for crime analysts,

> Crime analysts would benefit from the use of demographic predictor variables for strategic estimates of future crime concentration. The generation of improved maps depicting future long-term crime potential within jurisdictions will assist with the strategic planning operations of police departments and other agencies concerned with community harm. If such tools are developed and routinely used to guide law enforcement strategic planning, agencies should be alert to how tools with demographic variables might impair police–community dynamics even while they boost the accuracy of crime predictions.

The last sentence in that quote is important for predicting crime and how to maintain healthy police–community relations. When using demographic data to predict crime, there is potential for misuse of the data; in other words, profiling based on demographics. This becomes very problematic for police agencies. Demographic variables are important for crime analysis and crime prevention/control, but there must be an understanding of the theory behind the data or they can be misunderstood and misused – resulting in bad relations between the police and the community.

Song, Andresen, Brantingham, and Spicer (2017) extended Brantinghams' work on journey to crime by focusing on crime on the edges. Edges refer to boundaries between different areas – spatial transition points. These can be actual, physical boundaries such as interstates and major roads, railroad tracks, and bodies of water, or they can represent more subtle gradation, such as changes between neighborhoods. The authors examined crime in metro Vancouver, Canada. Crime data were collected for five years and land-use data were collected to assist in defining edges. The land-use data had classifications such as high rise apartments, commercial establishments, single-family residential areas, agricultural, and others. The hypothesis was that when other types of land uses bordered single-family residential areas, crime would be greater nearest those edges. The authors found support for an edge effect on crime. When single-family residential land uses bordered another type of land use, crime was higher at those edges. Also important was that the amount of crime at the edges decreased the further away from the edges, usually within 40 meters. This furthers the understanding of the effect place has on the surrounding area.

CONCLUSION

The efforts of Guerry, Quetelet, and other early criminologists provided a foundation for studying crime in a geospatial manner. The work of Shaw and McKay and others at the University of Chicago set the tone for the study of crime in urban areas, and gave us the beginnings of the tools of crime analysis. As this line of research continued over the years, it broadened in scope to a number of areas. A primary line of research in this area grew from the insights of both Jeffery and Newman that cities, neighborhoods, and residences could be constructed or altered in a way that could reduce the chances of crime. This "crime prevention through environmental design" has grown into environmental criminology. And environmental criminology has developed a foundation that brings a theoretical perspective to crime analysis in how it provides the "what and why" and especially the "where" of criminal behavior. This is the foundation of crime analysis. It gives crime analysts the understanding of why the data they see are behaving the way they do.

REFERENCES

Brantingham, P.J. and P.L. Brantingham. 1981. Notes on the geometry of crime. In P.J. Brantingham and P.L. Brantingham (Eds.), *Environmental Criminology* (pp. 27–54). Thousand Oaks, CA: Sage.

Brantingham, P.J. and P.L. Brantingham. 1991. *Environmental Criminology*. Prospect Heights, IL: Waveland Press.

Brantingham, P.L. and P.J. Brantingham. 1993a. Environment, routine and situation: Toward a pattern theory of crime. In R.V. Clarke and M. Felson (Eds.), *Advances in Criminological Literature* (pp. 259–294). New Brunswick, NJ: Transaction Books.

Brantingham, P.L. and Brantingham, P.J. 1993b. Nodes, paths, and edges: Considerations of the complexity of crime and the physical environment. *Journal of Environmental Psychology*, 13: 3–28.

Breckinridge, S.P. and E. Abbott. 1912. *The Delinquent Child and the Home*. New York: Russell Sage Foundation.

Burgess, E.W. 1924. The growth of the city: An introduction to a research project. *Publications of the American Sociological Society*, 18: 85–97.

Clarke, R.V. and J.E. Eck. 2004. *Crime Analysis for Problem Solvers: In 60 Small Steps*. Retrieved April 2015 from: www.popcenter.org

Cohen, L.E. and M. Felson. 1979. Social change and crime rate trends: A routine activity approach. *American Sociological Review*, 44: 588–608.

Guerry, A.M. 1833. *Essai sur la Statistique Morale de la France*. Paris: Crochard.

Harris, C.D. and E.L. Ullman. 1945. The nature of cities. *Annals*, 242 (November): 7–11.

Hoyt, H. 1939. *The Structure and Growth of Residential Neighborhoods in American Cities*. Washington, DC: Federal Housing Administration.

Jeffery, C.R. 1969. Crime prevention and control through environmental engineering. *Criminologica*, 7: 35–58.

Mayhew, H. 1862/1968. *London Labour and the London Poor*, Volume IV, *Those that Will Not Work, Comprising Prostitutes, Thieves, Swindlers, and Beggars*. New York: Dover Publishers.

Newman, O. 1972. *Defensible Space*. New York: Macmillan.

Quetelet, L.A.J. 1842. *A Treatise on Man and the Development of His Faculties*. Edinburgh: W. and R. Chambers.

Roncek, D.W. 1981. Dangerous places: Crime and residential environment. *Social Forces*, 60: 74–96.

Sampson, R.J. and B. Groves. 1989. Community structure and crime. *American Journal of Sociology*, 94: 774–802.

Sampson, R.J., S.W. Raudenbush, and F. Earls. 1997. Neighborhoods and violent crime: A multilevel study of collective efficacy. *Science*, 277(5328): 918–924.

Schuerman, L. and S. Kobrin. 1986. Community careers in crime. In A.J. Reiss Jr. and M. Tonry (Eds.), *Communities and Crime*. Chicago, IL: University of Chicago Press.

Shaw, C.R. and H.D. McKay. 1942. *Juvenile Delinquency and Urban Areas: A Study of Rates of Delinquency in Relation to Differential Characteristics of Local Communities in American Cities*. Chicago, IL: University of Chicago Press.

Song, J., M.A. Andresen, P.L. Brantingham, and V. Spicer. 2017. Crime on the edges: Patterns of crime and land use change. *Cartography and Geographic Information Science*, 44(1): 51–61.

Taylor, R.B., J.H. Ratcliffe, and A. Perenzin. 2015. Can we predict long-term community crime problems? The estimation of ecological continuity to model risk heterogeneity. *Journal of Research in Crime and Delinquency*, 52(3): 635–657.

Weisburd, D., N.A. Morris, and E.R. Groff. 2009. Hot spots of juvenile crime: A longitudinal study of arrest incidents at street segments in Seattle, Washington. *Journal of Quantitative Criminology*, 25: 443–467.

Wilson, J.Q. and G.L. Kelling. 1982. Broken windows. *Atlantic Monthly*, March: 29–38.

QUESTIONS AND EXERCISES

1   What was the significance of the Chicago School of Sociology?

2   What was Burgess's Concentric Zone Model; what were its implications?

3   What characteristics did Shaw and McKay study about crime and neighborhoods or zones?

4   What is Broken Windows theory and how did it change the way police analyzed crime?

5   When applying routine activities theory to juveniles, what is shown? What is different about juvenile routine activities?

6   How do handlers, guardians, and managers affect crime generators?

7   How does environment affect crime? What kind of environment is more conducive to criminal activity?

8   Writing assignment/outside of the classroom in the field:

Think of an area or community that is more prone to crime. What is the environment like and what are some changes that could be made to help prevent crime in that area through its design? Visit the area and take note of the environment. What are some elements of environmental design? How could zoning be beneficial when planning? Prepare and plan new design elements for the area or community that would potentially prevent crime through environmental design.

Strategic and tactical crime analysis

The purpose of this chapter is to discuss two relevant types of crime analysis: strategic and tactical. The main difference between the two types of analysis discussed is that strategic analysis pertains to the long-term, bigger picture, while tactical deals with the short-term, immediate analysis of crime to aid officers. This chapter will discuss the main aspects of the two analytical approaches and provide a general knowledge of crime analysis concepts. The analysis types will be further discussed in the last part of the textbook that relates to the application of crime analysis.

STRATEGIC CRIME ANALYSIS

Strategic crime analysis refers to the examination of crime and disorder problems to identify long-term trends in the data that indicate chronic issues. The key aspect of strategic crime analysis is the long-term aspect. By examining longer time periods, evaluation of tactics and policies can be identified to aid in policing strategies. Strategic crime analysis entails the use of quantitative and qualitative methodologies that will be discussed in a later chapter.

One main component of strategic crime analysis is the identification of long-term crime problems. This requires extensive use of data, ranging from calls-for-service to arrests made. Strategic crime analysis will work with thousands of records based on the time period being analyzed. Strategic analyses may range from as little as six months of data to ten years or more of data.

A way of examining crime over a long period of time is through the Uniform Crime Reports (UCR) (discussed in greater detail in Chapter 6). The UCR started recording data in 1929. The Federal Bureau of Investigation (FBI) was then given the responsibility of collecting, publishing, and archiving the crime data, and now collects data from about 18,000 law enforcement agencies. Of particular concern is the reporting of Part I crimes, which are murder and non-negligent manslaughter, rape, robbery, aggravated assault, burglary, larceny–theft, motor vehicle theft, and arson. Table 4.1 presents Part I violent and property crime rates for Little Rock, Arkansas, for 2008–2012. If you look over the five-year span, the rates fluctuate but generally increase. An important element of Table 4.1 is that the rates take into account the population of Little Rock, rather than only reporting total numbers of crime, which can be deceiving.

Table 4.2 is an example of why it is important to take population into consideration when examining crime. Philadelphia, Pennsylvania, is a major metropolitan city with a population around 1.5 million; and Little Rock, Arkansas, is a smaller city with a population close to 200,000. Looking at violent and

Table 4.1 Little Rock UCR Rates per 100,000 Persons

Year	Population	Violent Crime Rate	Property Crime Rate
2008	187,978	1,251.7	7,981.3
2009	190,205	1,472.1	8,352.0
2010	193,524	1,521.8	7,664.7
2011	194,988	1,489.8	7,951.3
2012	196,055	1,315.4	8,061.0

Source: www.ucrdatatool.gov

Table 4.2 UCR Crime Counts Comparison

Year	Philadelphia, Pennsylvania					Little Rock, Arkansas				
	Population	Violent Crime Total	Violent Crime Rate	Property Crime Total	Property Crime Rate	Population	Violent Crime Total	Violent Crime Rate	Property Crime Total	Property Crime Rate
2008	1,441,117	20,771	1,441.31	62,580	4,342.46	187,978	2,353	1,251.74	15,003	7,981.25
2009	1,547,605	19,163	1,238.24	55,888	3,611.26	190,205	2,800	1,472.10	15,886	8,352.04
2010	1,526,006	18,535	1,214.61	57,788	3,786.88	193,524	2,945	1,521.78	14,833	7,664.68
2011	1,530,873	18,268	1,193.31	59,617	3,894.31	194,988	2,905	1,489.84	15,504	7,951.26
2012	1,538,957	17,853	1,160.07	56,997	3,703.61	196,055	2,579	1,315.45	15,804	8,061.00

property crime totals by themselves, you would think that Philadelphia has a greater crime problem than Little Rock. Once the population is accounted for, Little Rock had a greater violent crime rate for all but 2008. For example, the violent crime rate in 2012 for Little Rock was 1,315 per 100,000 people and for Philadelphia it was 1,160. Additionally, the property crime rate in Little Rock was almost double the property rate per 100,000 compared to Philadelphia.

Another main aspect of strategic crime analysis is the evaluation of policing practices. Many of the tactics used are discussed in the third part of the book so a brief discussion is provided here. There are two main types of policing: reactive and proactive. Reactive policing relies on crime to occur, then police react to the problem. This type of policing can be described as chasing calls/crime because crime must occur first before any action is taken. The other type of policing is proactive, that seeks to prevent crime. Proactive policing takes steps to increase police effectiveness and usually involves community leaders to aid in crime prevention efforts. Both types of policing still have crime reduction strategies that agencies use to reduce crime.

In the next chapter, problem identification strategies will be discussed that analysts use to help agencies understand their crime problems. From there, prevention strategies can be implemented. The evaluation of these strategies is a focus of strategic crime analysis. A main element that analysts face when evaluating prevention strategies implemented by police agencies is if crime was displaced rather than reduced.

Displacement

A common concept that police agencies use when trying to prevent crime is displacement. Gabor (1978: 101) defined displacement as, "the reappearance of criminality along some dimension(s) following the implementation of an ostensibly effective prevention program." This typically means that, because of some crime prevention efforts, either crime will just move down the street to occur, or it will come back to the area after the "newness" of the effort has worn off. Displacement can be seen in both good and bad lights, depending on what is being measured. As a negative, displacement is a situation where policing activities may not actually prevent crime but they simply move it away from where the police are active. For example, police may make several arrests in a drug market area. Beyond stopping the drug dealers who may be incarcerated, the effect of the police actions may be to move the drug market a few blocks away to resume operations. The issue becomes how much crime is actually being reduced; and, therefore, what is the actual effect of the police actions. The alternative is what is called diffusion of benefits (discussed below). This is where police activity in a certain area influences that area but also reduces crime in nearby areas.

The foundation of displacement is that an area is selected as the study area (it could be examining crimes in general or could be determining the effectiveness of a crime prevention strategy). This area is then compared to another area (typically surrounding the study area, like a bull's-eye, but could also be an adjacent area selected based on the likelihood of displacement). How the study area and displacement area are identified is a critical factor that is subject to much debate. The most basic method of indicating the study and displacement areas is radial buffers (a circle around a point). Other methods include examining areas right outside the study area (see Roncek and Maier, 1991, for a discussion of adjacent block measurement), or using more sophisticated measures related to creating polygons of the areas (see Bowers and Johnson, 2003, for a discussion of weighted displacement quotients). The selection of the type of indication of the study area can be very important for any analysis. For instance, Murray and Roncek (2008) found that using the adjacent block method produces a statistically significant *positive* relationship with assaults, while using a 500-foot radial buffer produced statistically significant *negative* results. This underscores the need by crime analysts to use careful and well-thought-out methodology in analyses.

Bowers and Johnson (2003) argued there are six different types of displacement that may occur as a result of police actions:

1   Temporal – offenders change the time of offending.
2   Tactical – offenders change their tactics to commit the same crime.
3   Target – offenders select a different target (change from single-family home to apartment).
4   Spatial – offenders move to new locations.
5   Type of crime – for example, offenders change from robbery to theft.
6   Perpetrator – incarcerated offenders are replaced with new ones.

It is difficult to account for all of these different types of potential displacement; but crime analysts should at least be aware of them in any analyses they undertake.

Temporal

Temporal displacement refers to a change in time in criminal activity. The temporal shift in crime can be the result of crime prevention efforts, or it can be a part of the natural cycle. For example, some crimes are more likely to occur at night. But in the summer, it gets darker much later, which may change the time of the crime in the summer months. For temporal displacement through crime prevention efforts, think from an offender standpoint, an increased effort to prevent a crime from a police agency will increase the risk associated with that crime. Committing that crime when the risk is high can lead to a greater likelihood of being caught/arrested. Prevention efforts may only be put in effect during a particular patrol shift, however, leaving out times of the day less risky to commit crime. Offenders may notice this and change their temporal offending patterns as a result. This would fall under the category of temporal displacement.

It may be very tempting to look at the potential of displacement using time series analyses. For example, the amount of crime in an intervention area and the potential displacement area(s) could be examined for each month for a year before the intervention and a year after the intervention. Bowers and Johnson (2003) pointed out potential problems with this strategy. They argued that an area can have wide and essentially random variation month to month. They used the example of an area in their study that varied between 1 and 73 burglaries over two years. This can cause problems for time series analyses. Using quarterly counts are more stable, but then there would only be four data points before and four data points after the intervention, which is a problem for time series analyses. They also argued that there may be time lags in offending; where crime may initially go down in either or both the intervention area and the displacement area, but then may begin to creep back up over time.

Tactical

Tactical displacement happens when offenders change their strategy or technique to commit a crime. Think about residential burglaries, burglars could gain access through the front door or window. With the implementation of neighborhood watch groups, neighbors could be on the lookout for suspicious people going up to homes. Burglars could change their tactics to gain access to residences through a back door. The burglars still achieved their goal of burglarizing a residence but changed their tactics of how they gained access.

Target

Target displacement refers to the change in selection of subjects, objects, or targets. This type of displacement can occur from target-hardening efforts. Target-hardening is what it sounds like, a potential target of crime has prevention efforts applied to it to make it less attractive to offenders. For example, many types of cell phone and automobiles have locator apps/programs, allowing them to be located if stolen. Because of this, offenders may target certain types of cell phones that do not have that capability or an automobile that does not have a locator.

Spatial (geographical; territorial)

Spatial displacement, also known as geographical or territorial, is the most commonly thought about type of crime displacement. Simply, when prevention efforts are targeted at a certain location, crime moves to where there are not prevention efforts. For example, say residential burglary is high in a neighborhood, Hillcrest, and police increase patrols and ask residents to lock their homes in response to this problem. With the increased police efforts, offenders find the homes in Hillcrest less attractive targets based on increased perceived risk. Offenders may then move to a new neighborhood. This is known as spatial displacement.

A common assumption of spatial displacement is that if crime is displaced, it will move to the near vicinity (i.e. the next couple streets). Imagine that police efforts were increased in an outlined circle where aggravated assaults are high. Displacement is often measured by a buffer, which is a "catchment area" around the outlined circle area. Picture a donut, the circle in the middle is where police are implementing prevention efforts and the donut itself is the buffer area where crime is suspected to be displaced to during the prevention efforts.

In addressing displacement, crime analysts need to also be aware that how the spatial aspect of displacement is defined is critical to the obtained results. A buffer zone that is too close to the intervention area may not fully capture the potential displacement of crimes; while a buffer zone that is too big may overestimate the displacement. It is also quite possible that the shape of the displacement is irregular rather than round. For example, a major street that passes through an intervention area may allow displacement that is much farther away than in other directions. Alternatively, something that may block access, such as a sports stadium or park, may limit any diffusion in that direction. In effect, the awareness space of offenders who might be displaced may vary, even within a potential area of displacement. In this way, displacement also links with journey to crime and distance decay, as talked about elsewhere in this chapter and in other chapters. Another consideration in any analyses involving displacement is that any displacement area should be closely examined before the intervention. This way, any changes in crime can be more theoretically linked to the intervention. This information must also be linked to changes in the intervention area. For example, if crime decreases in the intervention area, the displacement area, and more generally in the larger area surrounding the intervention area, then it is possible there is a general decline in crime not related to the intervention.

Weisburd, Wyckoff, Ready, Eck, Hinkle, and Gajewski examined spatial displacement in an article titled, "Does Crime Just Move Around the Corner? A Controlled Study of Spatial Displacement and Diffusion of Crime Control Benefits" (2006). The title alone brings attention to the thought of crime moving around the corner, or in close proximity, once police target hot spots of crime. They found that crimes, such as drugs and prostitution, did not move around the corner, but, there was a diffusion of the policing efforts to nearby areas.

Think about this question: is it fair to assume that crime will move to the area immediately surrounding the place where crime prevention efforts occur? What if criminal opportunities are not as prevalent in the surrounding area; would offenders still choose those areas? Based on arguments in environmental criminology, offenders have activity spaces throughout an environment (home, work, school, stores, etc.). Do you think offenders would move to an activity space that has similar criminal opportunities but with less risk of getting caught? As an analyst, it is important to put yourself in the offenders' shoes to think what you might do in their situation.

Type of crime

Crime type displacement is a change in the type or form of criminal behavior of the offenders. This brings up the argument of whether offenders specialize in a certain type of crime or are generalists who commit different types of crime. A police agency could implement interventions to target business robberies. A past robber could change to commercial burglary, moving from a violent crime to property crime. While the criminal is still obtaining goods (i.e. stolen property), the change in crime type could be the result of the prevention efforts. Table 4.3 provides an example of different forms of displacement for auto theft; but also potential diffusion of benefits based on policing efforts.

Perpetrator

Finally, there may be displacement of perpetrators. People get arrested all the time for crimes. Sometimes, this may serve to reduce crime in the area. Other times, the perpetrator may just be replaced by another offender (perhaps even an apprentice). Take, for example, drug sales. The arrest of a drug dealer may stop the flow of drugs (at least in the short run). Or, another drug dealer, or a member of that original dealer's group, may simply step in and continue the business.

Diffusion of benefits

Displacement and diffusion are often confused in their meaning. Because of the idea that crime will reappear, displacement is often thought of as a taboo concept for police agencies. Displacement, however, is not necessarily a bad thing when there is a diffusion of benefits. Diffusion refers to the sometimes extra benefits achieved by crime prevention efforts. In essence, the tactics used to prevent crime have a greater effect than what was expected, resulting in a diffusion of benefits (www. popcenter.org/learning/60steps/). For example, if police increase patrols to reduce drug sales in a particular area, it may also reduce other types of crime in the area; or it may reduce crime in a larger area than just where the patrols are operating.

Where the relationship between displacement and diffusion gets complicated is whether, if displacement occurs (where crime is moved in time or space), does the diffusion of benefits (of the reduction in crime in time or space) outweigh the amount of crime displacement. Specifically, does the total amount of crime prevented outnumber the amount of crime displaced? Were the crime prevention efforts

Table 4.3 Types of Displacement and Diffusion of Benefits for Auto Thefts

Type	Description	Displacement	Diffusion
Temporal	Time of day change	Switching from early morning to late afternoon	Reducing auto theft throughout the course of a day
Tactical	Change in MO	Switching to busting out windows to gain access	Reducing auto thefts of unlocked autos
Target	Change in object	Change to truck auto thefts	Reduction in sedan auto thefts
Spatial	Location change	Movement to another parking lot or neighborhood	Reduction in auto thefts in parking lot and surrounding streets
Functional (Crime Type)	Crime swap	Change from auto theft to auto break-ins	Reducing both auto thefts and auto break-ins

overall successful? These are questions that analysts must examine when police agencies implement crime prevention efforts.

In a perfect world, there would be no displacement of crime but rather diffusion of benefits based on policing efforts. Imagine a donut with no center. The center, missing part, is where police target the crime prevention efforts, but since the surrounding areas are in close proximity to where police are implementing their strategies, the greater area of the donut, also sees a reduction in crime. This would be valuable because police were not allocating resources in the donut or haloed area, so there was "more bang for the buck."

Guerette and Bowers (2009) conducted a systematic review of 102 crime prevention projects with 574 observations to determine potential displacement and diffusion of benefits effects. They found there was a diffusion of benefits in 27 percent of the 574 observations. While the researchers did find there was a higher observed percentage of displacement than diffusion, there still is potential for diffusion of benefits. The benefit of a systematic review is that it is how researchers and practitioners can learn from projects resulting in displacement and diffusion to tailor crime prevention efforts around what has been successful.

Strategic crime analysis is essential for police agencies to determine if what they are doing has any influence on reducing crime and disorder. Common data and statistical tools used for strategic crime analysis will be discussed in the second part of this book, while applications will be discussed in the final part. In the next chapter, problem identification techniques will be discussed to provide you with an understanding of how police agencies rely on analysts to help the understanding of crime problems, both long term and short term. But not all crime analysis happens at the strategic level. Some occurs at the tactical level.

TACTICAL CRIME ANALYSIS

Short-term analysis that examines the how, when, and where elements of criminal activity is known as tactical crime analysis. What differentiates tactical and strategic crime analysis is the time frame of crimes being analyzed. Shorter time periods of crime data being analyzed assist officers in apprehending criminals and distinguishing crime patterns. Tactical crime analysis is an important aspect of crime analysis that aids in short-term resource deployment and helping in investigations.

Pattern detection: how, when, and where

The ability to detect patterns in the commission of crimes is essential for police operations. One of the key components of pattern detection is identifying the "how" aspect of crime. In many television shows, you hear the acronym MO. MO stands for modus operandi, which is how a crime is committed and what technique(s) the offender used to commit the crime.

The ability to detect similar MOs for crimes can indicate if it is the same criminal committing multiple crimes. When two or more crimes are highly similar, it is helpful to try and link the criminal events if possible. A common crime that is regularly examined in terms of MO are burglaries. Say in the past week there has been a spike in residential burglaries. A question should be asked: are these residential burglaries linked together? One of the first things to examine is the method of entry used by the offender. As shown in Table 4.4, when examining MOs, there is a commonality in the type of entry point used. The residential burglaries occurred through doors on the back of the house. This can provide cover for the burglars while gaining access to the residence. Additionally, if you pay attention

Table 4.4 Example of Residential Burglaries

Date Reported	Address	Time (estimate)	Entry Point	Burgled Items
12/20/2014	1XX S. 6th St.	20:00	Rear door – force	TV and video game consoles
12/20/2014	2XX S. 6th St.	19:00	Rear door – no force	Surround sound system
12/21/2014	1XX S. 8th St.	22:00	Rear door – force	TV and DVD player
12/22/2014	1XX S. 7th St.	20:00	Rear door – force	TV and smart watch

to the items that were taken from the homes, there are similarities – consumer electronics. With the advancements in online sites that allow you to sell second-hand goods and also pawn shops, consumer electronics are easy items to resell for profit with little questions asked.

Table 4.4 also shows when and where the residential burglaries took place. The residential burglaries were clustered to a few street segments and in later times of the day. The times show the residential burglaries took place between 7:00 pm and 10:00 pm. The time of day could reveal that the burglar preferred the cover of darkness while gaining entrance to the property from the rear. If you pay attention to the dates of the burglaries, you notice that they are close to a holiday. During holidays, people are more likely to travel and be away from their homes, making residences more attractive to target by criminals. All of these commonalities and similarities between crime incidents to determine if they are linked are part of tactical crime analysis. That is, tactical crime analysis is designed to look for patterns within crime and disorder events to help with immediate police actions, from preventing future crime to apprehending criminals.

Pattern detection: when

A point that was touched on above that deserves to be expanded is the "when" element of crime. The temporal analysis of crime can reveal a great amount of information related to criminal activity. Temporal refers to the time element of crime. Taking a step back, our human routine activities reflect general temporal patterns. When we go to school/work, eat breakfast/lunch/dinner, go out for drinks, and numerous other activities have general temporal patterns. These temporal patterns extend into criminal activity.

Imagine you are new to a law enforcement agency and you want to understand the temporal patterning of gun crimes the past few months. You decided to examine 2011 March–May gun crimes based on month, day of week, and time. There were a total of 310 gun crimes that occurred between March and May 2011. As shown in Figure 4.1 there is a general increasing trend in the number of gun crimes.

Think about the months being examined; can you think of a reason why there would be an increase? One possible explanation is an increase in routine activities of people during these months. The temperature would be increasing, moving from winter to spring, allowing for more activities to take place outdoors. For example, there could be an increase in people walking to and from stores and a general desire to be outside, creating more criminal opportunities that offenders identify. A crime analyst could expect to see increases in gun crimes and crime in general depending on the month. The "seasonality" of crime needs to be remembered when looking at month to month crime data.

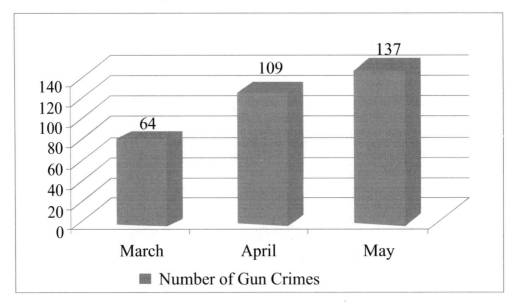

Figure 4.1 Number of Gun Crimes by Month in Little Rock, 2011

Next, in Figure 4.2, the gun crimes are further examined in relation to the day they were committed. Logically, it makes sense that gun crimes are more prevalent on weekends, when more people may be engaged in recreation activities or in potentially criminal behavior and not working as much (normal Monday–Friday job). While the increase in crime throughout the week is not dramatic, there are more gun crimes that happened on Saturday and Sunday than any other days of the week.

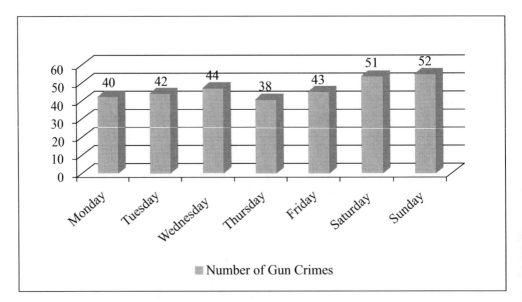

Figure 4.2 Number of Gun Crimes by Day between March and May, 2011

The last temporal time frame discussed in this example is presented in Figure 4.3. Gun crimes were more prevalent depending on the time of day. During evening and late night/early morning hours, there were more gun crimes than during the day. This could be because people are at work or school during the day, limiting the criminal opportunities. Also, at some point during the day, people will go to sleep and people tend to have similar sleeping hours.

In Figure 4.3, there are three spikes, at 9:00 am, 11:00 am, 3:00 pm, and a general increase in gun crimes during late night hours (9:00 pm–1:00 am). Can you think of any possible reasons for increases in gun crimes during these time periods? The spike at 3:00 pm could be because schools are letting students out around then. Knowing these kinds of time patterns can help a police agency in when to deploy more officers. But they also need to know where to deploy them in the high crime times.

Pattern detection: where

We have discussed the how and when, but the where aspect of tactical crime analysis helps bring the analysis all together. When many people think of crime analysis, maps are used to drive home the findings. There is visual output that can help sell the findings versus just numbers. We often think spatially and look for patterns, and this is no different with crime analysis. Is there a uniform pattern, clustering, or do the data seem random? Look at Figure 4.4 to see different types of spatial patterns.

The distribution of crime in space is visually easier to understand than discussing where it is located. Look at Figure 4.4A. Here, crime appears to be random without a true pattern. This makes the detection of patterns in the short term and aiding officers difficult. In Figure 4.4B, crime is more uniform across the area. While random and uniform spatial distributions of crime are possible, it is more likely that you will find clustering of crimes, such as shown in Figure 4.4C. That is not to say that there

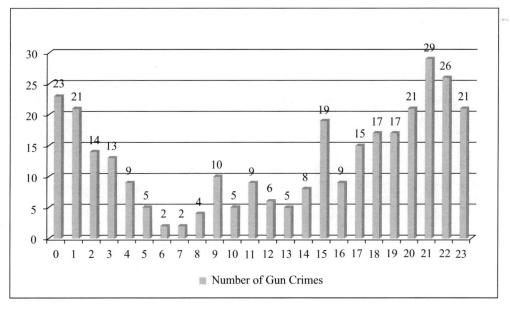

Figure 4.3 Number of Gun Crimes by Military Hour between March and May, 2011

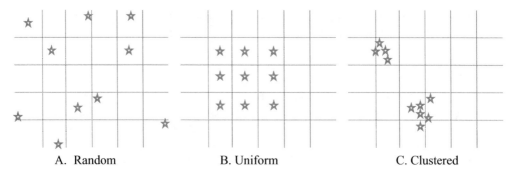

A. Random   B. Uniform   C. Clustered

Figure 4.4 Spatial Distributions of Crime

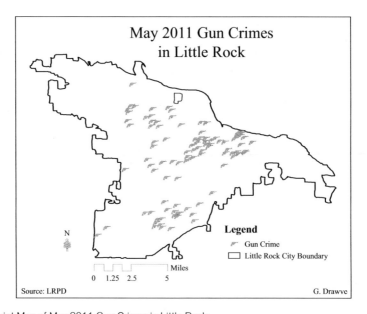

Figure 4.5 Point Map of May 2011 Gun Crimes in Little Rock

will not be random crimes throughout a jurisdiction, but crimes may cluster in small groups throughout an area, forming hot spots of crime. Another way of displaying the clustering of crimes is shown in Figure 4.5. Here, gun crimes are mapped, showing the clustering of crimes in the city.

The maps here are limited on the layers included to simply show the gun crimes. Layers is a mapping term referring to data files. For example, police districts or divisions could be added to the map as an additional layer, or streets/arterial roads could be included. Before advancements in technology, and for those of you who remember overhead projectors, each transparency could be viewed as one layer; and, as additional transparencies are laid on top of one another, greater context is provided. There is the potential to include too much data or too many layers, however, and overwhelm the reader, losing the context and initial point of map visuals.

As Ratcliffe (2010: 7) stated, "The growth of interest in crime mapping from police agencies has thus spurred practitioners to seek out both theoretical explanations for the patterns they see and remedies to the crime problems that plague the communities they police." As an analyst, part of the job is to make these connections. That is why it is important to have a strong theoretical foundation to be able to make sense of patterns.

Keep in mind that pattern detection requires the joint use of how, when, and where to detect patterns. This section was subdivided, but you can see how easily tied together each aspect is to identifying patterns. For example, where crime is occurring depends on the time of day; and how offenders choose targets depends on where and when offenders want to commit crime. It is not a surprise that crime mapping is often the first thought in crime analysis because the "where" aspect can visually be represented.

OTHER TYPES OF CRIME ANALYSIS

Administrative crime analysis is conducted to provide police administration, government/city officials, and neighborhood groups answers to law-enforcement related questions. Administrative analysis is different from other crime analysis in that it is meant more to talk about the "state of the city" or other geographic area, and is not really meant to address the actual crimes. Since the tasks will vary, administrative analysts are required to have knowledge of multiple data sources and analytical capabilities. For example, an analyst may have to construct a report that shows the demographics across a jurisdiction with their respective rates of crime by neighborhood. This sounds straightforward, but data would be needed from the Census or American Community Survey (ACS) at the tract or block-group level to identify demographic differences within a city. The analyst would not only have to be familiar with how to extract the data and join it with crime data, but also how to construct crime rates based on the amount of crime per neighborhood and overall population. This example task would utilize a number of different software programs and downloaded data sources to produce one report.

In relation to theory, a common pairing that is researched is social disorganization (discussed in Chapter 3) and crime rates. An administrative analysis could be to show the level of disadvantage in relation to the rate of crime with the purpose of identifying if the two are related (for example, as the level of disadvantage increases, the level of crime also increases). Other administrative tasks could be generating presentations, support for grant solicitations, data preparation for national databases, and general crime statistics reports.

Another type of analysis is known as intelligence analysis. Intelligence analysis pertains to the criminal network and organizations. This could be larger criminal organizations, such as the mafia, for federal agencies; but is often more about gangs at the local level. A main purpose of intelligence analysis is to identify the hierarchy of a criminal organization. From here, analysts can begin to "connect the dots." This includes identifying organizational members, how the members are criminally connected, the exchange of money and goods, properties/shell companies, and current locations/activities. Think of this process as identifying each criminal's role and how they are connected within the larger criminal organization.

The last type of crime analysis is police operations analysis. This includes resource allocation within the agency; from personnel to money and equipment. This requires a different type of analysis that could, for example, identify the optimal number of officers needed for each patrol district and shift. This extends to how many officers are needed within the agency to function properly. Operations analysis also overlaps with strategic analysis based on the needs for the agency. Within strategic analysis, much of the evaluation that may be conducted can be justified by operations analysis. Imagine a cost–benefit mindset, such as trying to determine whether increasing the amount of police resources

Table 4.5 Overview of Different Crime Analysis Types

Type of Analysis	Description
Strategic	Long-term approach to identify patterns and trends, evaluate policing efforts and tactics, and organizational/personnel allocation
Tactical	Analytical approach in the short term to assist in operations, identifying series of connected crime incidents, identifying potential suspects of crimes
Administrative	Provide information to administrators and the greater audience through presentations, reports, and briefs
Intelligence	Identify criminal networks and organizations through inter- and intra-agency collaboration
Operations	Pertains to policing operations such as deployment of resources and shift assignments to improve agency operations

(time, patrol, officers) to try and reduce crime is worth the investment. Operation and strategic analyses can be used together to optimize policing strategies and get the best bang for the buck.

CONCLUSION

Crime analysts are typically called on to conduct a variety of analyses within a police agency. The types of analyses are summarized in Table 4.5. Strategic and tactical crime analyses are important elements of a crime analyst's job. The two types are not all-encompassing of the types of analysis conducted by analysts but are two prevalent types. Strategic crime analysis examines the long-term crime problems and often evaluates policing strategies to determine if the strategies have been successful. Tactical crime analysis focuses more on the short-term problem issue to identify patterns in criminal activity and to aid officers and detectives. A pivotal responsibility of crime analysis, no matter what type, is the ability to identify problems. This chapter discussed two types of crime analysis that agencies often rely on. The next chapter will discuss problem identification techniques and strategies used that help guide the analyst.

REFERENCES

Bowers, K.J. and S.D. Johnson. 2003. Measuring the geographical displacement and diffusion of benefit effects of crime prevention activity. *Journal of Quantitative Criminology*, 19: 275–302.

Gabor, T. 1978. Crime displacement: The literature and strategies for its investigation. *Crime and Justice*, 6: 100–107.

Guerette, R.T. and K.J. Bowers. 2009. Assessing the extent of crime displacement and diffusion of benefits: A review of situational crime prevention evaluations. *Criminology*, 47(4): 1331–1368.

Murray, R.K. and D.W. Roncek. 2008. Measuring diffusion of assaults around bars through radius and adjacency techniques. *Criminal Justice Review*, 33(2): 199–220.

Ratcliffe, J. 2010. Crime mapping: Spatial and temporal challenges. In A.R. Piquero and D. Weisburd (Eds.), *Handbook of Quantitative Criminology* (pp. 5–24). New York, NY: Springer.

Roncek, D.W. and P.A. Maier. 1991. Bars, blocks and crimes revisited: Linking the theory of routine activities to the empiricism of "hot spots." *Criminology*, 29: 725–753.

Weisburd, D., L.A. Wyckoff, J. Ready, J.E. Eck, J.A. Hinkle, and F. Gajewski. 2006. Does crime just move around the corner? A controlled study of spatial displacement and diffusion of crime control benefits. *Criminology*, 44(3): 549–592.

QUESTIONS AND EXERCISES

1   There are five types of crime analysis discussed in this chapter. What are the two that were discussed more in depth? What are their strengths and how are they evaluated?
2   What is displacement and its role in crime analysis? What are the different types of displacement?
3   What is a MO and how can it assist an investigation? What should be looked for during an investigation through MOs?
4   In tactical crime analysis, why is it important to look for patterns?
5   What are the different spatial distributions of crime and what do they mean?
6   Writing assignment/outside of the classroom in the field:

What crime analysis type does your local police agency use? Do they rely on one more so than the others or multiple? What are some problems in your community and how are they addressed? Do they have an officer with a crime analysis certificate/training or do they outsource help into the community to seek an analyst? What are some benefits to the community of having an individual trained in crime analysis? If your local police agency does not have anyone certified/trained on staff, what are some of the setbacks this could cause in the community? Have they experienced any problems because of this?

7   Apply routine activities theory to what was discussed in this chapter. How can routine activities affect how we interpret patterns and data? Why is this important?
8   Review from previous chapters: CompStat; routine activities theory; social disorganization.

Problem identification

This chapter will discuss the process of problem identification commonly used within police agencies. This strategy relies on what is known as a SARA model (Scanning, Analysis, Response, and Assessment) to identify problems within communities. Following this, typical policing strategies will be introduced. Many of these types of policing and their use in law enforcement agencies will be discussed throughout later chapters based on their relationship to crime analysis.

The focus of problem-oriented policing is understanding the problem itself. This is a time-consuming process that deserves attention. With a focus on understanding the problem, responses can be directed in a manner more suitable for the problem. Not every problem can be solved with a quick glance to determine how to alter or negate the problem.

SARA MODEL FOR PROBLEM IDENTIFICATION

The SARA model is a way for police agencies to maintain a problem-oriented approach. SARA is an acronym that stands for *Scanning*, *Analysis*, *Response*, and *Assessment* (Eck and Spelman, 1987).

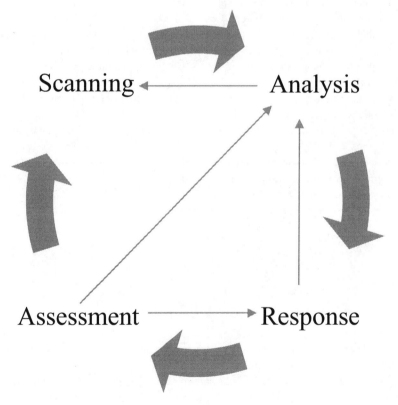

Figure 5.1 SARA Model
Source: Adapted from Eck and Spelman (1987).

SARA is a four-stage process for problem identification and problem solving. This is a common approach used by police agencies to aid in crime reduction and prevention. The SARA process is visualized in Figure 5.1.

Scanning is the first step of the process. It pertains to the ability to identify problems in the community. Problems do not have to be illegal, such as crimes; they could also be issues that concern the community. Because of the general nature of problem identification, problems can be identified or brought to the forefront by many stakeholders, beyond the police. Community members, business owners, schools, hospitals, neighborhood watch groups, and police officers can all identify problems within the community. While many different people can indicate a problem, the role of a crime analyst is crucial in the identification of potential problems. That is, crime analysts deal with data and information on a daily basis as part of their job, so they have the ability to see issues before they become problems. Overall, police agencies should partner with outside stakeholders to identify and understand problems within the community. Each stakeholder provides a different viewpoint and insight into the problem, emphasizing a collaborative nature to problem solving.

A main role of the police is to handle community problems, in part, because the public expects this is part of their role. As discussed in Chapter 4, crime has characteristics about it that can be identified and monitored. As incidents grow in number and share commonalities, crime concentrations can develop. For example, close to two-thirds of parolees released from 30 states in 2005 were rearrested within three years of being released (Durose, Cooper, and Snyder, 2014). What drives home this point even more is that 16.1 percent of the prisoners released were responsible for 48.4 percent of the nearly 1.2 million arrests that occurred within a 5-year follow-up from their release. Repeat offenders can create large problems within communities as shown by the amount of crime committed just by known offenders who were caught again.

One of the most important skills of a crime analyst is the ability to map crime. Evident in many of the job descriptions included in Chapter 1 and profiles of crime analysts, crime mapping is a vital role for police agencies. When examining a problem area, identifying "hot spots" is a common way of indicating where crime is clustered in a small geographical area. Hot spots identify areas where incidents are occurring in close proximity to each other. Hot spots are typically utilized for targeted policing since an area is identified where crime occurs. Christy Oldham, a crime analyst from St. Louis Metropolitan Police Agency provided a narrative of how hot spot policing is used within their agency to aid in scanning and problem identification. This is shown in Box 5.1.

BOX 5.1 CRIME ANALYSIS IN ACTION

Hot spot policing is one of the most well-known types of policing. It is based on using past crime locations to target certain areas. Christy Oldham provides an example of how hot spot policing is utilized within St. Louis Metropolitan Police Department. She provides a description of the project and gives insight into the methodology for using hot spot policing. A hot spot map that Christy used is shown in Figure 5.2. In the kernel density technique used in Figure 5.2. the center is the highest intensity. In other words, the center is the hottest area of the hot spot with an intensity decay the further you are from the center.

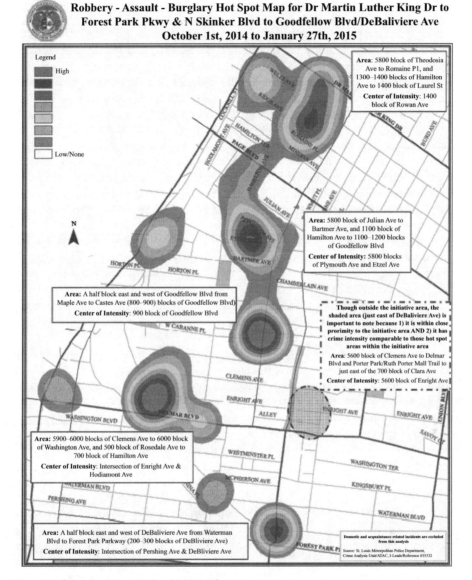

Robbery - Assault - Burglary Hot Spot Map for Dr Martin Luther King Dr to Forest Park Pkwy & N Skinker Blvd to Goodfellow Blvd/DeBaliviere Ave October 1st, 2014 to January 27th, 2015

Legend

High

Low/None

Area: 5800 block of Theodosia Ave to Romaine Pl, and 1300–1400 blocks of Hamilton Ave to 1400 block of Laurel St
Center of Intensity: 1400 block of Rowan Ave

Area: 5800 block of Julian Ave to Bartmer Ave, and 1100 block of Hamilton Ave to 1100–1200 blocks of Goodfellow Blvd
Center of Intensity: 5800 blocks of Plymouth Ave and Etzel Ave

Area: A half block east and west of Goodfellow Blvd from Maple Ave to Castes Ave (800–900) blocks of Goodfellow Blvd)
Center of Intensity: 900 block of Goodfellow Blvd

Though outside the initiative area, the shaded area (just east of DeBaliviere Ave) is important to note because 1) it is within close proximity to the initiative area AND 2) it has crime intensity comparable to those hot spot areas within the initiative area
Area: 5600 block of Clemens Ave to Delmar Blvd and Porter Park/Ruth Porter Mall Trail to just east of the 700 block of Clara Ave
Center of Intensity: 5600 block of Enright Ave

Area: 5900–6000 blocks of Clemens Ave to 6000 block of Washington Ave, and 500 block of Rosedale Ave to 700 block of Hamilton Ave
Center of Intensity: Intersection of Enright Ave & Hodiamont Ave

Area: A half block east and west of DeBaliviere Ave from Waterman Blvd to Forest Park Parkway (200–300 blocks of DeBaliviere Ave)
Center of Intensity: Intersection of Pershing Ave & DeBliviere Ave

Domestic and acquaintance-related incidents are excluded from this analysis
Source: St. Louis Metropolitan Police Department, Crime Analysis Unit/ATAC, I-Leads/Reference #55532

Figure 5.2 Crime Analysis in Action: MLK Hot Spot

Hot Spot Policing Initiative – Dr Martin Luther King Dr to Forest Park Pkwy

The St. Louis Metropolitan Police Agency implemented a number of "hot spot" policing initiatives in 2015. Based on the success of initiatives conducted during the first half of 2014, the purpose of the initiatives was to combat crime by focusing efforts on the areas within the city that were being hit hardest by criminal activity. The city of St. Louis experienced a decrease in overall crime in 2014 (hitting an 8-year record low). This decrease is said to be a result of the "hot spot" policing initiatives conducted in the first half of the year. Though a decrease was recorded overall, an increase in violent crime (crimes against persons) occurred, including a 32.5% increase in homicides. This increase in violent crime was concentrated in certain areas across the city and had become all too familiar to the officers and residents within those areas. By increasing police presence and employing "hot spot" policing initiatives within these "hot" areas, the police agency hoped to not only build relationships with residents but to also work toward continuing the decrease in crime the city had seen over the past decade.

My role within these hot spot policing initiatives was to provide a map listing the "hot" areas within a larger general area to which the officers would focus their efforts. Unlike other hot spot maps I had created in the past, this larger general area given to me by the command staff was not defined by district or neighborhood boundaries. Though not difficult to execute, I had to perform a few extra steps to get only the data I needed.

Using the analytic software ATAC, I pulled all robbery, aggravated assault, and burglary incidents within the previous four-month period for the neighborhoods the initiative area was encased in. From there, I selected out all domestic-related and acquaintance-related incidents and saved that as my main database. Working from my main database, I opened the map feature in ATAC and loaded the city streets map layer. Then, using the "select points" button, I selected all the incidents within the initiative area, as well an area just outside to confirm that the entire initiative area was included within the selected data. Since points are highlighted when they are selected from the map, I ran a query for highlighted records only, which gave me a smaller subset of data. I then went through that smaller subset manually and unhighlight those incidents that fell outside of the initiative area. After the smaller subset was reduced down to just those incidents within the initiative area, I saved that as my final database and geocoded the incidents using ArcGIS. I then created a hot spot map using the kernel density tool and labeled those areas on the bulletin, giving the officers the specific streets and blocks of concern, as well as the center of intensity.

The hot spot policing initiatives employed by the St. Louis Metropolitan Police Agency have been very successful. Across the three initiatives conducted so far this year (January–March 2015), over 160 arrests have been made, more than 15 guns have been seized, and large amounts of drugs and cash have been confiscated. One stop in particular within the hot-spot initiative that resulted in 3 suspects being taken into custody, led to the recovery of 4 firearms (including an AK-47 assault rifle and an AR-15 pistol), a large quantity of suspected marijuana and suspected heroin, and a large amount of cash. This is just one of the many successful stops conducted within the hot spot policing initiative that shows that hot-spot policing works.

The second step of SARA is *analysis*. Similar to problem identification, analysis is best when more than just police agencies are involved. The analysis stage involves understanding as much as possible about the identified problem. This is why having outside stakeholders involved in the SARA process can greatly help learning about the problem from multiple angles. If you refer back to the crime triangle in Chapter 3, many of the elements are identified during the analysis stage in the SARA model. For example, say the problem is theft from retail stores. After conducting some analysis, it is determined that most offenders are juveniles and the incidents tend to occur right after school hours. It would be important to bring school officials, retailers, youth organizations, and the police agency together to discuss the problem and how to address it effectively. Each stakeholder will have varying insights into the problem that can be beneficial when trying to prevent/reduce crime. For example, the retailers may want to increase the controllers from the crime triangle to keep better watch on juveniles in the stores.

Additionally, when there are outside agencies partnering with law enforcement agencies, it is an opportunity to identify potential data sources relevant to the problem. Outside agencies can be local community groups, nonprofit organizations, youth centers, schools, and many others. Data could be gathered from multiple agencies, allowing for a better picture of the problem. Also, this could provide potential outcome data used to assess the response. This will assist in identifying what resources are available to address the problem and develop a potential response.

With analysis tailored to a specific problem, a *response* can be developed that will aim to reduce and prevent the problem in the future. Through the community collaboration in the analysis stage, how to handle and respond to the problem will come about and guide the response. For example, schools could offer more after-school programs that aim to provide a place for students to interact, but under supervision.

The response can be police focused, having another stakeholder be more involved, or a joint partnership from multiple parties to help curb the problem. Identifying the intervention and stake-holders allows for a distributed leadership model. In a distributed leadership model, each party is responsible for their task in the response plan. This process allows for a multi-prong approach to the problem when multiple organizations are involved; hopefully, resulting in an effective response to the problem.

After implementing a response, it is crucial to make an *assessment* of the response. This is the final stage of the SARA model, and one that influences each of the prior stages in the model. The assessment evaluates the effectiveness of the response. It is often best to have assessments ongoing with weekly, biweekly, or monthly meetings to discuss the efforts and determine if there are any potential issues that need to be addressed. This can continue to assist in the problem-solving efforts. The implementation will never be perfect, so having ongoing assessments will help overcome issues. During the assessment phase, questions are asked pertaining to:

- Did the response achieve the goals desired? The desired goals are established during the prior stages. This includes defining what success is or the desired outcome. This could be less truancy, crime reduction, increased community support, or a number of other outcome measures.
- Was the response implemented correctly? If there are multiple stakeholders, were some responses implemented better than others?
- What were unexpected hurdles? How can these be overcome in the present effort and taken into consideration in the future?
- Are there other strategies that could be implemented, either at the present time or in the future? Other stakeholders could be identified throughout the implementation/response and included in the effort.
- Were there any unexpected negative effects?

The assessment will help guide further iterations of the SARA model based on obstacles encountered, what worked, and what could be changed. The SARA model is an ongoing cycle process that continues to evolve/change. This ongoing process of upgrading to create the most efficient and effective SARA models is part of the growing nature of problem-oriented policing. The SARA model, if implemented correctly, can provide police agencies with a solid framework of how to problem solve and implement responses while assessing their effectiveness. The amount of resources made available through the POP Center (www.popcenter.org) can assist agencies as they undertake SARA-based efforts.

POLICING STRATEGIES

There are many police strategies that can be greatly enhanced with strong crime analysis. Some of the more traditional strategies are discussed here. More recent and innovative techniques are discussed in later chapters.

Traditional model of policing

The traditional model of policing is a generic approach to responding to crime through generalized strategies (see Weisburd and Eck, 2004). There is typically a focus on enforcing laws through arrests and alleviating short-term problems. This approach is what the public often expects of law enforcement agencies. Other examples of traditional policing responses to crime include (Weisburd and Eck, 2004: 44):

- Increasing the size of police agencies
- Random patrol across all parts of the community
- Rapid response to calls-for-service
- Generally applied follow-up investigations
- Generally applied intensive enforcement and arrest policies.

These generic approaches are often not efficient for police agencies. For example, we have discussed at multiple points in the book that crime is not random and clusters in space. Allocating patrols randomly throughout the community will result in police being in areas where crime has not occurred and is not likely to occur. Additionally, it is crime-centric in that the agency waits for crime to occur then responds to the problem (i.e. retroactive). Weisburd and Eck (2004) discussed how this model of policing relied on criminal justice system agencies for partnerships and not the greater community. This could result in a divide between the community and police, fostering tension over a longer period of time.

Table 5.1 provides an overview of the traditional policing model compared to the community policing model (Sparrow, 1988). These are very different approaches to crime and public safety issues. Follow the questions on the left column of the table and note the differences between the two approaches. The next section will expand on community-oriented policing.

Community-oriented policing

Community-oriented policing is a broadly implemented strategy by law enforcement agencies in recent time (Weisburd and Eck, 2004) that relies heavily on law enforcement agencies fostering relationships with the community. Community-oriented policing rests on the notion that to respond to, prevent, and lower crime and disorder issues, the public must be engaged. By creating community partnerships with multiple stakeholder involvement, a larger group can problem-solve and more fully address the problems at hand.

Table 5.1 Comparison of Traditional Policing to Community Policing Models

Questions	Traditional	Community
Who are the police?	A government agency principally responsible for law enforcement.	Police are the public and the public are the police: Police officers are paid to give full-time attention to the duties of every citizen.
What is the relationship of the police force to the other public service departments?	Priorities often conflict.	The police are one department among many responsible for improving the quality of life.
What is the role of police?	Focusing on solving crimes.	A broader problem-solving approach.
How is police efficiency measured?	By detection and arrest rate.	By the absence of crime and disorder.
What are the highest priorities?	Crimes that are high value (e.g. bank robberies) and those involving violence.	Whatever problems disturb the community most.
What, specifically, do police deal with?	Incidents.	Citizens' problems and concerns.
What determines the effectiveness of police?	Response times.	Public cooperation.
What view do police take of service calls?	Deal with them only if there is no real police work to do.	Vital function and great opportunity.
What is police professionalism?	Swift effective response to serious crime.	Keeping close to the community.
What kind of intelligence is most important?	Crime intelligence (study of particular crimes or series of crimes).	Criminal intelligence (information about the activities of individuals or groups).
What is the essential nature of police accountability?	Highly centralized; governed by rules, regulations, and policy directives; accountable to the law.	Emphasis on local accountability to community needs.
What is the role of headquarters?	To provide the necessary rules and policy directives.	To preach organizational values.
What is the role of the press liaison department?	To keep the "heat" off operational officers so they can get on with the job.	To coordinate an essential channel of communication with the community.
How do the police regard prosecutions?	As an important goal.	As one tool among many.

Source: Sparrow (1988).

Throughout the years, there have been many different trendy programs attempting to increase community involvement, and some of these are still present. For example, neighborhood watch programs are still common. Depending on the neighborhood, there could be signs along the street indicating that neighborhood has a Neighborhood Watch Initiative. This is where neighborhood residents provide an additional level of security for the neighborhood. Another example is "Crime-Stoppers." The program has a tip hotline for citizens to call and provide crime tips. In some cases, there are rewards offered for valuable tips. A benefit of CrimeStoppers is the ability to provide an anonymous tip if the tipster does not feel comfortable enough providing his or her personal information. There are many other programs offered, many of which are likely featured on your local policing website.

In more recent times, there has been a discussion of "us" versus "them" between community members and law enforcement. This can come from over-policing of certain areas and profiling of certain residents. This makes community policing difficult when there have been years of mistrust in police from the public. It is important to remember this will not change overnight or in the span of a few months. Agencies wanting to be more community-oriented with a history of mistrust with residents should expect change at a slower rate based on the history.

With the changing of times, and more so with changing technology, law enforcement agencies have multiple outlets of engaging the public. Social media accounts can assist law enforcement reaching residents in their jurisdiction. From local events to crimes in progress, social media provides a real-time outlet for agencies to relay information to their constituents. Police can advertise community meetings or a coffee/donut with a cop event, which allows community members to meet with officers in a different type of environment. Police often deal with people on their worst days (responding to a crime call), so these events provide opportunities for police and community members to meet under normal conditions. Additionally, the Internet allows citizens to file reports or complaints online. Some agencies provide notifications and submission points so persons filing a report can know where the complaint/report stands. This increases the level of transparency.

Much of the expansion of community-oriented policing can be linked to the development of the Office of Community Oriented Policing Services (COPS; https://cops.usdoj.gov/) in the Department of Justice (DOJ). COPS has distributed money to numerous programs and agencies since 1994, nested in the idea of community-oriented policing strategies. Table 5.2 provides an overview of COPS money throughout the years and examples of where money was awarded. The COPS website has resources for law enforcement agencies, recent news, and potential funding opportunities. COPS also has monthly e-newsletters users can sign up to receive.

Problem-oriented policing

Problem-Oriented Policing (POP) is just what it sounds like, a focus on identified problems that require policing efforts. What makes this approach different from other methodologies is the steps it takes to recognize the underlying causes of crime and disorder problems. Traditionally, crime incidents occur and police respond to them, often without the time or resources to understand the causes behind the problem. This is known as reactive or incident-based policing; and is a part of the traditional model of policing. POP focuses on the underlying reasons behind the emergence of crime or disorder problems, seeking to prevent crime rather than reacting to it. By re-focusing police agencies (or parts of police agencies such as community policing patrols) to concentrate on crime problems, prevention strategies can be developed based on analysis of the problem.

Herman Goldstein is considered the founder of the problem-oriented approach (Goldstein, 1979). Goldstein argued that too much attention was put on the organizational structure of a police agency rather than crime problems. By identifying the underlying cause to problems, tailored policing strategies can be implemented to overcome the problems. POP takes a proactive, preventative approach that relies on police officers' decision-making process. Officers have more independence in their decision-making process when using a POP strategy. The decisions and actions of the officer need to be analyzed, however, to determine their effectiveness.

Table 5.2 COPS Office Yearly Appropriated Money and Yearly Descriptions

Year	Money Appropriated to COPS	Examples of Funding, Awards, and Spending
1994	$148.4 million	Office of Community Oriented Policing Services established
1995	$1.3 billion	Grants for Youth Firearms Violence Initiative
1996	$1.4 billion	Anti-Gang Initiative; Community Policing to Combat Domestic Violent; 311 program; funded more than 52,000 officers hired
1997	$1.42 billion	Problem-Solving Partnerships Initiative; Advancing Community Policing; Police Integrity Training Initiative
1998	$1.63 billion	Safe Schools Initiative; Small Communities Grant Program; Technology Program; School-Based Partnerships Program
1999	$1.46 billion	Launches COPS in Schools (CIS); Tribal Resources Grant Program (TRGP); COPS funds used to hire reaches 100,000 officers
2000	$913 million	In-Car Camera Initiative used $12 million to purchase 2,900 in-car cameras
2001	$1.042 billion	Launches two new publications: COPS Innovations and POP Guides
2002	$1.1 billion	Secure Our Schools Program
2003	$977 million	Homeland Security Overtime Program (HSOP)
2004	$748 million	$82 million awarded to 23 communities to develop Interoperable Communication Networks
2005	$598 million	Government Accountability Office (GAO) found COPS funding resulted in significant declines in crime rates
2006	$472 million	COPS hosts National Community Policing Conference
2007	$541 million	Distributed millionth technical assistance publication to the law enforcement field
2008	$587 million	Funded Child Sexual Predator Program (CSPP)
2009	$1.55 billion	Awards $1 billion in Recovery Act funds to hire, rehire, or retain about 5,000 law enforcement officers
2010	$791 million	Coordinated Tribal Assistance Solicitation (CTAS) is developed
2011	$495 million	COPS Hiring Program applicants are asked to identify a public safety problem then provide reasoning of how to respond to the problem through supported community policing strategies
2012	$198.5 million	Under the 2012 COPS Hiring Program, required to hire military veterans who served after 9/11 and who were honorably discharged
2013	$222.5 million	Awards nearly $500,000 to Virginia Tech Family Outreach Foundation to develop a new school safety model; Disseminated more than 2 million training and technical assistance publications
2014	$214 million	Solicitations for Anti-Methamphetamine Program and Collaborative Reform Initiative for Technical Assistance
2015	$208 million	Led the President's Task Force on 21st Century Policing by hosting Listening Sessions throughout the United States
2016	$212 million	Presidential proclamation creating the first National Community Policing Week (Oct. 2–8, 2016)

Source: https://cops.usdoj.gov/about

Beyond the police agency, the relationships officers develop in the community aid in the understanding of a problem. Working with the community through these relationships, more information can be collected on the underlying causes of the problem and ideas of how the community would like to see it overcome. This process also allows preventative measures to be developed and implemented. A commonality among the POP strategies is the amount of attention given to understanding the problem, which requires a substantial amount of data to be collected. The use of the SARA model is closely related to problem-oriented policing.

The identification of problems (and particularly using data to understand problems) is where crime analysts play a vital role. POP relies on the implementation, evaluation, and reporting of strategies aimed at solving a crime problem and using the results in prevention efforts. Crime analysts are able to connect the dots and identify how the problems develop (discussed in Chapter 4). Once strategies are developed to overcome the problem, the strategies have to be evaluated to determine their effectiveness. For example, neighborhoods could have a problem with drug dealers using their homes as places to sell drugs. Police could meet with neighborhood watch group members and community leaders to discuss how the issue grew to be a problem, and develop strategies to curb drug selling in their neighborhoods. What becomes important is whether the efforts taken were successful at reducing drug sales in the neighborhood. Crime analysts are capable of evaluating the strategies to assist in police agencies understanding what efforts are successful.

The implementation of problem-based strategies allows police agencies to identify what strategies are effective for certain crime and disorder problems. This is essential in sharing knowledge with other law enforcement agencies, but also allows agencies to advance their policing strategies. Knowing how others have approached similar problems can provide a foundation to build a tailored approach to a local problem. The POP Center website (www.popcenter.org) contains numerous POP Guides that are available to users for free. The guides provide insight into how police can reduce issues caused by crime and disorder problems. The guides are reviewed by a patrol officer, a police executive, and a researcher before the guide is published. This is a great resource to consider when dealing with problems in a community. Topics for which guides are available on the PopCenter website include:

- alcohol and drug problems
- animal problems
- burglary and theft
- business-related problems
- disorder and nuisance problems
- elderly problems
- endangerment
- frauds
- gang problems
- misuse of police resources
- robbery
- school and college problems
- sex-related problems
- traffic problems
- vehicle-related problems
- violence problems
- youth/juvenile problems.

In many of these general topics, there are specific guides to problems. For example, under business-related problems, there are guides on bank robbery, identity theft, shoplifting, check and credit card fraud, and others.

Hot spot policing

Hot spots are clusters of crime in small geographical areas. One of the most frequently cited and well-known hot spot studies was conducted in Minneapolis by Sherman, Gartin, and Buerger (1989). They found that 3 percent of places accounted for 50 percent of all police calls; and when focusing on all robberies, 2.2 percent of places; and for all rapes, 1.2 percent of places accounted for over half of the calls. Knowing crime clusters and forms hot spots allows police to direct their resources at the hot spots. Police resources are typically limited, so allocating resources where needed the most becomes important. Usually police presence is increased in the hot spot, or target areas, to reduce crime.

Other types of policing strategies used within hot spots include foot patrols, arrests, directed patrol, and many others. The overall purpose is to increase police presence and/or change tactics used within the high crime areas. With software programs capable of identifying clusters of crimes, or simply putting pins on a map, law enforcement agencies will continue to utilize hot spot policing strategies.

CONCLUSION

The first step in dealing with any issue, be it a crime or other community issue, is problem identification. Crime analysts are often at the center of problem identification since they have (or can get) the data necessary to identify the problem. Sometimes, crime analysts learn of problems through their normal projects or routine monitoring of crime. They may find hot spots of crime or other anomalies that warrant further investigation in the SARA model. Even if the identification of the problem comes from an officer or the community, it is generally required that crime analysis is used to verify the problem or to further understand it. That puts it back in the job of crime analyst. The role of crime analysis remains important throughout the SARA model, certainly in the analysis stage, helping determine the response and providing the assessment of the effectiveness of the response. As such, crime analysts should be familiar with policing strategies and the SARA model.

REFERENCES

Durose, M.R., A.D. Cooper, and H.N. Snyder. 2014. *Recidivism of prisoners released in 30 states in 2005: Patterns from 2005–2010.* Washington, DC: Bureau of Justice Statistics.

Eck, J.E. and W. Spelman. 1987. *Problem Solving: Problem-Oriented Policing in Newport News.* Washington, DC: Police Executive Research Forum.

Goldstein, H. 1979. Improving policing: A problem-oriented approach. *Crime & Delinquency,* 25(2): 236–258.

Sherman, L.W., P.R. Gartin, and M.E. Buerger. (1989). Hot spots of predatory crime routine activities and the criminology of place. *Criminology,* 27: 27–56.

Sparrow, M.K. 1988. Implementing community policing. *Perspective on Policing,* 9: 1–12. Washington, DC: U.S. Department of Justice. (https://www.ncjrs.gov/pdffiles1/nij/114217.pdf)

Weisburd, D. and J.E. Eck. 2004. What can police do to reduce crime, disorder, and fear? *Annals of the American Academy of Political and Social Science,* 593: 42–65.

QUESTIONS AND EXERCISES

1   Search for law enforcement agencies utilizing POP. What are they utilizing the framework for in relation to policing efforts?
2   Search for a recently published journal article focusing on crime hot spots and policing. In the article, what are strengths and weaknesses of the approach? If the article does not discuss these points, and even if they do, what do you think are positives and negatives with hot spot policing?
3   Search the Center for Problem-Oriented Policing website (popcenter.org) and examine the POP Guides. Find a topic worth creating a POP Guide for and outline the main elements of the POP Guide. Utilize the examples online to tailor your approach to your location.

Data

The foundation of crime analysis is data. Crime analysts must have data to be able to do their job. Without data, it is just guesswork. Data are becoming easier to access as advancements in technology continue. Depending on where you live, cities are starting to form data portal websites that contain an array of data pertaining to that city. For example, Chicago (data.cityofchicago.org), Denver (data. denvergov.org), and Baltimore (data.baltimorecity.gov) each have a data portal allowing users ease of access to their data. When President Obama took office, he voiced the need for open and transparent government. A product of this effort was the development of a website (data.gov) which centralizes regional, state, county, city, and international country data. While not having the data needed is a definite problem, there is also the possibility that there is so much data, and it is being added to and changed so fast, it is impossible to keep up. As far back as 1994, Block argued that

> Contrary to conventional wisdom, we are not plagued by a dearth of information in criminal justice. The problem is just the opposite. There are often so many pieces of information that it is impossible for the human mind to assimilate them, to sort them out, and to use them for tactical or crime analysis decisions before the window of opportunity has passed.

Many of these data resources contain more than just crime data but that is crucial for crime analysis. Remember, as an analyst, part of your job is to connect the dots related to crime. The greater access you have to data, the more social characteristics you can account for in your analyses. The key to conducting strong crime analyses is trying to truly understand the problem you are trying to address (it is not just crime in a park; what are the social factors that are at play?). Knowing what you are looking for can provide insight into what other types of data you could merge into your analyses.

Can you think of possible agencies or where you could potentially find access to data for the following questions?

1   What is the relationship between neighborhood unemployment rates and crime rates?
2   What is the average distance from parolees' homes to social service agencies?
3   What is the relationship between liquor store locations and crime?

In the first question, you would need to find data on unemployment rates for neighborhoods and make a measure of crime rates. Unemployment data are found in the Census or American Community Survey (ACS) at levels that can be defined as a neighborhood (block group or tract). Crime rates would be determined by having a population estimate for each neighborhood, also found in the Census or ACS. Typically, crime rates are discussed in terms of 1,000 or 100,000 persons. Since this question is asking about neighborhoods, it would be more appropriate to discuss crime rates per 1,000. The crime data would be obtained from the police agency and geocoded and spatially matched to a neighborhood, providing you the ability to sum the number of crimes per neighborhood. We will further discuss these data sources and types of data later in this chapter.

The second question calls your attention to an aspect often overlooked in analysis. You might wonder, as a crime analyst, "Why do I care how close probationers are to the services?" Hipp and colleagues (2010) studied parolees in California and the neighborhoods the parolees returned to on release. They found that a one standard deviation increase in the amount of social service providers within 2 miles of the parolees decreased the likelihood of recidivating by about 41 percent. From this standpoint, greater access to social services could influence the volume of crime police respond to because offenders are getting the help they need. Police officers are usually aware of known offenders through prior experiences, making parolees an important consideration since they are returning to communities. Where parolees reside would often be obtained from a corrections agency. Keep in mind the addresses provided are often the reported addresses of where the parolees reside, meaning it is the best estimate of where we can say parolees reside. The corrections agency usually has access to social service agencies throughout the state but, if not, the state or city you work for probably has a record of their locations.

The final question pertains to liquor store locations and crime in and around those establishments. Liquor store locations can be obtained from a variety of different sources, depending on how your city and state records businesses. At the city level, businesses need a license to operate, and they have to file taxes; so an agency within the city government should have access to an up-to-date list of liquor store locations. If not, or you want to compare, states have Alcohol and Beverage Control agencies. This state agency would monitor these businesses since they are selling alcohol.

Beyond the examples discussed here, data collection can be a tedious task. What can make your experience easier is networking with other agencies and individuals. Even if you do not need access to data that a specific agency could offer right away, by networking within multiple agencies you have a point of contact if you do need data in the future. This can save time and effort when searching for data.

To fully understand the spatio-temporal patterns of crime, you need to understand the greater context of the environment. As data continue to become easier to obtain and include in analyses, crime analysts will have to discuss why the various data can help the police agency better understand crime in their jurisdiction. Throwing additional data into analyses is pointless unless you can justify why they are included and how to interpret the results. The best way to fully understand your problem and to justify gathering data beyond crime is to understand the theory of the urban environment as it relates to human behavior and crime.

In this chapter, we discuss the types of data available to analysts. These include crime data of different types – local data, Uniform Crime Reporting (UCR) data, National Incident-Based Reporting System (NIBRS) data, and National Crime Victimization Survey (NCVS) data – as well as data on community characteristics (Census and ACS data). We also address the strengths and limitations of each of these kinds of data.

POLICE AGENCY DATA

Many police agencies have data systems they use to analyze and report their crime. As technology continues to advance and become more affordable, data systems are no longer a luxury of large police agencies. One of the more commonly known police data systems is referred to as CAD, or computer-aided dispatch. This is the foundation of the 911 system of responding to emergencies. This type of system is not only used by police agencies but also fire, ambulance, and courier services. Here, we will focus only on CAD as it is used for police.

CAD is a specialized communication platform capable of assigning and tracking police responses to emergencies and calls-for-service. This requires geographic technology and warehousing details about calls. It is possible that officers initiate their own "service" so this is also recorded in the CAD system. The CAD system records, along with details input by the dispatcher, items such as officer dispatched, call type, time of day, date, dispatcher name, when the officer arrived, and the disposition of the call. Often CAD data are updated by officers with narratives describing the call.

Based on the amount of data input into CAD, storing the data becomes troublesome. Not only is storing data an issue but, depending on the type of CAD system, pulling the data out of the system for crime analysis can be a complex and time-consuming task. While it should be easy to do something like link data from several police agencies that are near one another, many record management systems charge enormous amounts of money to do so, even if all of the agencies use the same system. In recent years, it has become easier to export queries out of CAD to spreadsheets or other usable forms, but that is dependent on the CAD system used. Some police agencies might only have the ability to print reports, so then it would be on you to transfer the hardcopy to an electronic version for analysis.

Access to police agency primary data is ideal for crime analysts, but this does not mean that the data are perfect. An issue with using crime-related data from police agencies is the data only represent crimes reported to and known by the police agency. This misses out on the "dark figure of crime" discussed below.

Crime analysts often deal with spatial components of their police agency's data. In a geographical sense, there can be neighborhoods underreporting and overreporting crime. Neighborhoods that have less trust in the police might not report every crime, especially for more petty crimes. Violent and more public crimes can increase the likelihood of police being contacted, but certain neighborhoods still underreport crime. At the other side of the spectrum, some neighborhoods contact police for every incident from minor to major types of offenses. While police agency crime data are often utilized, crime analysts must acknowledge that these data only reflect crimes known by the agency.

Beyond just having data, it is important to have the right kinds of data and to have quality data. Crime analysts often must work with data that are less than desirable. For example, sex offender residency data are often based on the last address provided by sex offenders as they register. We know sex offenders move often, may not have a permanent residence, and may stay in a different address than that given to authorities because of residency restrictions. As such, this is not the best measure for this analysis, but may be the best data available.

It is also critical that analysts work with quality data. Police agency data can often be messy – containing numerous errors and missing data. This is often particularly a problem in address data used in mapping. The following is an example of how an address such as 2801 South University Avenue might show up in data:

2801 South University Avenue	2801 South Univ Avenue
University and Asher	2801 South Univ. Avenue
2801 S University Avenue	2801 South University Av
2801 S. University Avenue	2801 South University Av.
2801 S Univ Avenue	2801 S Univ Av
2801 S. Univ Avenue	2801 S. Univ Av
2801 S Univ. Avenue	2801 S Univ. Av
2801 S. Univ. Avenue	2801 S. Univ. Av
2801 S Univ Av.	2801 S Univ. Av.
2801 S. Univ Av.	2801 S. Univ. Av.

This does not even take into account all of the possible misspellings of address or incorrect addresses such as 280, 281, 201, 2881, etc. While mapping programs are getting much better at interpolating the address using fuzzy logic, it still often falls on the analyst to make sure the data are of as high a quality as possible. Some of the issues can be commonly fixed with "find and replace" commands in Excel. The more frequently crime analysts work with data from their agency, they pick up on the common problems in the data. Because of this, it is recommended to keep a running list of the problems you consistently notice in the data. This will save you time as you progress and hopefully reduce the amount of time you spend cleaning the data. If the agency is open to change, crime analysts can also be a great check on the accuracy of the data, making suggestions for changes to the input programs that can ensure greater accuracy.

When working with police agency data, crime analysts typically work with calls-for-service, crime, and arrest data. Each type of dataset represents a variation of what police agencies deal with on a daily basis. Calls-for-service reflect types of calls officers are dispatched to, and may also include calls that are beyond crime, such as checks on the welfare of a resident, checks for debris on the road, animal problems, and sex offender address checks. These are not necessarily crimes but require the police to respond to a call. Crime data are just that, crimes occurring in the police agency's jurisdiction. Crime data are not always homicide, robberies, and burglaries but also entail prostitution, forgery, and others. Even status offenses like underage drinking and possession of alcohol are crimes requiring police response. Arrest data provide police agencies a way of tracking known crime incidents and if an arrest was made. The difference between crime data and arrest data often involves the type of crime reported as a part of the Uniform Crime Reporting (UCR) system, discussed below. For crimes such as homicide, all that is needed to be reported is that a crime occurred – no arrest is necessary. For more minor crimes, such as drug possession, an arrest is required for it to be reported.

Overall, police agency data provide a wealth of primary data crime analysts have at their fingertips. The different types of datasets provide varying characteristics about incidents, offenders, suspects, and arrestees. This provides the opportunity for crime analysts to take all of this information and make sense of it to provide ongoing updates to the agency. Also, similar types of data collected by the police agencies are often reported to the federal government to track trends and patterns across the United States. These show up in the Uniform Crime Reports and the National Incident Based Reporting System, discussed in the following sections.

UNIFORM CRIME REPORTS (UCR)

As discussed in Chapter 3, the official collection of data related to crime began in the early 1800s when the government in England began collecting data on crime in 1805, followed by the French government in 1825. In the United States, some cities and states published crime data as early as the late 1800s. The federal government attempted to collect crime data nationwide as early as 1907; but it was not until a push by the International Association of Chiefs of Police (IACP) in the 1920s that a plan to collect national crime data was developed. The IACP produced monthly reports on crime for several years before it was taken over by the FBI in 1930. Since then, the FBI has produced a monthly, then quarterly, and finally a yearly document of the breakdown of crime at the local level. In 1930, 400 law enforcement agencies from 43 states reported data to the FBI. Currently, there are over 18,000 law enforcement agencies from all 50 states reporting data to the FBI. The document was originally called the *Uniform Crime Report*, but the name was changed to *Crime in the United States* in 1958. This data collection method is still known as the Uniform Crime Report (UCR). The key part to UCR data is that reporting to the FBI is voluntary. This means that, while most police agencies do report their crimes, some do not. And there are varying levels of the quality of data reported. This is a problem for the UCR/NIBRS.

Originally, there were seven categories of crimes collected by the IACP and then the FBI. These were murder and non-negligent manslaughter (later changed to criminal homicide), forcible rape, robbery, aggravated assault, burglary, larceny-theft, and motor vehicle theft. Congress added the crime of arson in 1979. These crimes are known as Part I crimes.

1   Homicide
2   Forcible rape
3   Robbery
4   Aggravated assault
5   Burglary
6   Larceny-theft

7   Motor vehicle theft
8   Arson.

There are also 21 less serious crimes and status offenses that are classified as Part II crimes. These are:

Other assaults	Forgery and counterfeiting	Buying, receiving, or possessing stolen property
Embezzlement	Fraud	Carrying or possessing weapons
Vandalism	Sex offenses	Prostitution and commercialized vice
Drug violations	Gambling	Offenses against the family and children
Drunkenness	Liquor laws	Driving under the influence
Vagrancy	Disorderly conduct	All other offenses except traffic violations
Suspicion	Runaways	Curfew and loitering laws (persons under age 18)

UCR data that are reported to the FBI are available online (ucrdatatool.gov). Users can download crime by city, county, state, and across the United States. The website allows users to select out by agency size and by state based on population coverage. The UCR data website makes the users' life easier by providing the overall counts by offense but also the crime rates (based on population). Downloading and analyzing this type of data is known as secondary data analyses. Secondary data analysis refers to data that were collected by another person or agency for a different purpose. Since UCR data are reported from law enforcement agencies voluntarily, unless stated otherwise by state laws, law enforcement agencies are simply passing along data they collected. Because of this, limitations arise with analyzing UCR data.

At the time it was created, the IACP and FBI recognized there were limitations to the UCR. It was, however, a strong step forward in understanding crime and law enforcement in the U.S., and remained so for many years. The limitations of the UCR have been the subject of many debates and publications over the years. The four most general limitations are discussed below, especially as they relate to data analysis, to give analysts some insight into the potential problems of using UCR data in local crime analyses.

Problems of reporting

The greatest issue for both agency data and for UCR and NIBRS (discussed below) is that we do not have information on all crimes. There is what is known as the "dark figure of crime" that is cause for concern. These are crimes that are never discovered by the police or reported to them. For example, a drug dealer who is robbed is not likely to report the crime to police. Crimes against children and juveniles are less likely to be reported to the police (Finkelhor and Ormrod, 2001). We know that only a fraction of all drug use and prostitution are ever reported. Many of these are called "victimless crimes." As such, the people involved in the crimes are not going to report them. Unless the police discover them or someone else turns the people in, they are never discovered. These are just a few examples of unreported and underreported crimes, but this issue should be considered by crime analysts when conducting analyses.

Closely related to this limitation are those crimes that are discovered but never reported to the police. Most crime comes to the attention of the police through citizen complaints. Many people are victims of crime but choose not to report it to the police. There are many reasons why someone would not report a crime, including fear of reprisal, embarrassment, a relationship with the offender, the possibility of self-incrimination ("someone stole my drugs"), and a perception that the police will not or cannot do anything about it. The severity of the offense also comes into play, but in a different dynamic. For the most part, more serious offenses are discovered and/or reported to the police (murder has the highest discovery/reporting rate). However, some serious offenses such as rape have relatively low rates of reporting due to the reasons listed above.

We also know that officers sometimes do not file an official report of a crime or misclassify events. Mosher (2012) reports that the social distance between the complainant and the offender can influence whether the police record a complaint as a crime. He argues that if an upper class white person complains to the police that the member of a minority group has assaulted him or her, there is a greater likelihood that an official crime report will be filed than if the assault occurred between two minority group members. He also proposed that the more deference shown to the police by a complainant, the more likely an official report will be filed (this more often occurs in domestic violence situations).

These are some of the reasons that Kitsuse and Cicourel (1963), followed by many other researchers, argued that the UCR (and most official data) is more a measure of police practices than a measure of crime in society. Because of these issues, crime analysts should be careful when comparing crime rates across different agencies. Such comparisons are made all the time because these are the best data we have; but you should know the hazards and limitations when doing so.

Lack of information

There are also problems with the UCR even for those crimes that are reported. One of the biggest issues in conducting crime analyses and research is the lack of detailed information about crimes that have been committed. There is basic demographic information, such as the offender's sex, age, and race, but more information about the crime is needed. For example, there is no information describing the relationship between the offender and the victim in UCR data. More importantly for crime analysis, there is no information about the crime itself, such as the day the crime occurred, the time of day, or the location of the crime. A crime analyst working for the police agency would likely have access to these data, but comparing different jurisdictions would not be possible unless agency data for all the desired agencies were obtained – which defeats the purpose of having UCR data. These limitations, and the next one, are specific reasons for the implementation of NIBRS. NIBRS contains much more detailed information about the crime, the offender, and the victim, and is discussed below.

Hierarchy rule

The UCR also has a rule that only the most serious crime will be counted. This is called the "hierarchy rule." This creates problems for crimes involving multiple offenders, multiple victims, or multiple crimes in one criminal episode. For example, say a person assaults and rapes a woman and then takes her phone. The person may very well be charged with aggravated assault, rape, and robbery. However, for the purposes of UCR, only the rape would be counted.

Consistent definitions

There is also the issue that police officers will sometimes misclassify a crime. For example, an officer might take a complaint and classify something as a theft when the reality is that the person lost the item. The reverse can also be true, where an officer does not file an official report (say for missing property) when a theft did in fact occur.

At the U.S. level, this is an even bigger issue for UCR. This is because different agencies and different states define crimes differently, meaning they do not always match in the UCR. As an example, according to Schneider and Wiersema (1990), the UCR would classify an incident where something was stolen from a car as a theft, but under California law at that time, the same incident would be classified as a burglary. Another example is the classification of aggravated assault. Many police agencies use what is called "the three-stitch rule" for aggravated assault. That is, there has to be an injury that results in a doctor/hospital visit before it is considered aggravated. Otherwise, it is classified as a simple assault (Part II). Because one police agency was going through accreditation, the chief directed that all offenses be classified strictly by UCR definitions. The result was a very high increase in aggravated assaults for that city – a problem for the police. After the accreditation the chief directed that crimes go back to the way they were classified previously. In this instance, the crisis of aggravated assault in the city – a problem for the police agency – was "solved" the next year, making the police look better.

Bruce and Desmond (1998) conducted a classroom experiment to show the issues of properly classifying crime. Groups of students in their class were given a set of crime scenarios to classify. All but one group received the UCR crime definitions. The other group was given crime definitions taken from a state criminal code. The scenarios also included multiple victims, offenders, and offenses. Bruce and Desmond found that each group produced different crime figures. Even though all but one group had the same definitions, they all classified crimes slightly differently. Although one could argue that trained officers or those who classify crimes for an agency would be more experienced and consistent in classifying crimes, we know this is not the case. Different officers and other personnel will classify crimes differently; and different jurisdictions will classify crimes differently. This creates a problem in the reliability of UCR data.

NATIONAL INCIDENT-BASED REPORTING SYSTEM (NIBRS)

As stated above, the IACP and FBI knew there were these problems with the UCR when it was developed. The decision was made that some information was better than no information at all, so the UCR was created, even with its understood issues. Police agencies and research alike continued to point out the problems of UCR over the years. Responding to continued criticism, the U.S. Bureau of Justice Statistics (BJS) and the FBI created a task force in 1982 to study improvements in the UCR. This resulted in a conference held by the BJS in 1984 where law enforcement personnel and researchers came together to discuss how to make the UCR a richer source of data. The results of this conference and other discussions were released in 1985 in the *Blueprint for the Future of the Uniform Crime Reporting Program*, which effectively created NIBRS. A decision was made in these meetings that, for a variety of reasons, it would not be advisable to make wholesale changes to UCR or to stop it completely and start a new reporting system. So the decision was made to create the National Incident-Based Reporting System (NIBRS) and have it run alongside UCR until a time (or maybe never) when it would be reasonable to close UCR and switch to NIBRS. The BJS then funded the South Carolina Law Enforcement Division to conduct a pilot demonstration of this program in 1987. The NIBRS program officially started by collecting its first data in 1991. The 1991 data covered Alabama, North Dakota, and South Carolina.

NIBRS is a reporting system used by police agencies that provides a wealth of incident, victim, offender, and arrestee characteristics. This is a departure from UCR data that reports aggregate counts. Imagine many of the descriptive characteristics available in police agency data, just reported by thousands of law enforcement agencies across the United States.

NIBRS collects an extensive list of crime incident data based on 46 Group A offenses and 11 Group B offenses (see Appendix B). Group B offenses only contain arrestee data because most Group B offenses are only known once an arrest is made.

NIBRS data can be downloaded through the National Archive of Criminal Justice Data (NACJD). A nice perk of the NACJD website is that it maintains and updates a list of studies utilizing not only NIBRS data but also other secondary data sources. This provides you with an idea of how NIBRS data have been analyzed and gives you a place to start if you want to design a project using NIBRS data.

NIBRS was designed to improve the UCR in a number of areas, such as including the type of information gathered for each offense, ending use of the hierarchy rule by permitting up to ten offenses to be recorded for each crime incident, and reducing the opportunity for errors in calculating and tabulating information (Major 1992; Reaves 1993). Not only does NIBRS offer greater incident inclusion, incident characteristics are also reported. For instance, suspected use of drugs or alcohol, time of incident, location of incident (street, residence, bar, university, etc.), use of a weapon, multiple offenders, suspected hate crime, and gang involved crimes are all a part of the NIBRS system. Additionally, NIBRS reports demographic characteristics, including age of the victims, offenders, and arrestees. Other measures include victim–offender relationship, level of injury, type of victim (individual, business, financial institution, etc.), and estimated quantity of drug.

The greater detail collected on crime incidents provides better opportunity to understand the dynamics related to crime. For example, Addington (2007) compared homicide characteristics cleared quickly to those cleared over a long period of time or not at all. This research can help understand the temporal aspect of case clearances related to homicides. The research conducted using NIBRS data can help crime analysts think outside of the norm in trying to better understand crime in their jurisdictions.

While NIBRS builds from UCR in capturing greater details on crime incidents, there are limitations. The downside to NIBRS data is the limited coverage of agencies reporting data. As of 2012, there were only 32 states certified to report NIBRS data; which excludes numerous agencies, including some of the largest police agencies in the U.S. In 2016, there were 15 states that report all of their crime data via the NIBRS system (Arkansas, Delaware, Idaho, Iowa, Michigan, Montana, New Hampshire, North Dakota, Rhode Island, South Carolina, South Dakota, Tennessee, Vermont, Virginia, and West Virginia). The range of populations reporting 2013 NIBRS data had a high of slightly over a million for Fairfax County PD in Virginia and as low to a few thousand, such as Hamlin, West Virginia (1,136) and Marmaduke, Arkansas (1,147). Fairfax County was the only reporting agency serving a population over 1 million. NIBRS tends to be reported by a greater number of smaller law enforcement agencies, so caution needs to be made from analyses.

Keep in mind, NIBRS data are also crimes reported to police; so, while there are great descriptors of crimes, offenders, and victims, this information must be known by police. Law-enforcement based data will continue to have problems due to the nature of crime. One way to overcome this issue and try to obtain a better estimate of crime is through surveys. The National Crime Victimization Survey (NCVS) is the United States' primary source reflecting criminal victimization.

NATIONAL CRIME VICTIMIZATION SURVEY (NCVS)

The NCVS, formerly known as the National Crime Survey (NCS), focuses on experience of victimization by surveying persons and households. This survey has been collecting data since 1973. As discussed many times in this chapter, a limitation of police agency data is that the data only represent crimes known by police, and miss the unreported crimes. The NCVS is administered twice a year to collect nationally representative data from about 90,000 households comprising around 160,000 persons 12 years and older (www.bjs.gov). The focus of the survey is to obtain data on the frequency, characteristics, and results of criminal victimization. The self-report survey asks questions pertaining to victimizations experienced in the prior six months.

As the NACJD (www.icpsr.umich.edu/icpsrweb/NACJD/NCVS/) describes, there are four primary objectives of the NCVS:

1   Identify detailed information about victims and consequences of crime,
2   Estimate the number and types of crimes not reported to law enforcement (i.e. the dark figure of crime),

3   Provide uniform measures of selected types of crimes,
4   Permit comparisons over time and types of areas.

Information about the victims includes demographic characteristics such as sex, race, education level, income, extent of injuries, relationship with offender, and self-protective actions taken based on the victimization. The NCVS also collects offender characteristics related to the victimizations and crime characteristics like the time, place, and use of weapon. The survey helps obtain counts and knowledge on underreported crimes like domestic violence, rape, and sexual attacks. The survey separates crimes into two categories: personal or property. Personal crimes include rape, sexual attacks, robbery, aggravated assault, simple assault, and purse-snatching/pocket-picking. Property crimes contain burglary, theft, motor vehicle theft, and vandalism. With the victimization data collected yearly, this facilitates being able to examine trends and variations in victimization. More importantly, the NCVS allows for an estimate of the dark figure of crime that can be compared to official crime data to identify differences in the two data sources.

With survey data, there is always a question about the response rate. The 2014 NCVS had a household response rate of 84 percent and 87 percent of persons eligible to self-report victimization. The questionnaires are available on the Bureau of Justice Statistics website (www.bjs.gov). The BJS also has a NCVS Victimization Analysis Tool (NVAT) that allows users to examine and construct tables on NCVS data. Users can get an initial feel and understanding of the NCVS before conducting further analyses.

Based on the nature and scope of data collected by the NCVS, it is often compared to UCR figures to determine differences between the data sources (e.g. Steffensmeier, Zhong, Ackerman, Schwartz, and Agha 2006). Not surprisingly, self-report victimization data from NCVS has higher estimates than UCR on the actual amount of crime occurrence.

The data sources discussed up to this point relate to crime data, but those are not the only ones that crime analysts will use or need to be aware of for analysis. Many crime analysts are tasked with understanding community and population characteristics as they relate to crime. Official crime data and victimization survey data only provide one part of the picture. Analysts must understand the greater community or neighborhood characteristics that could contribute to crime.

COMMUNITY AND PEOPLE DATA

Crime analysts are often tasked with writing reports that include information about population characteristics of their community. What if your city, county, or jurisdiction does not have this type of data readily available for you to use? One of the most common data sources of community data is the U.S. Decennial Census. Depending on your age, you might have received a form to fill out concerning the 2010 Census. The Census attempts to count every resident in the United States, and is conducted every ten years (www.census.gov).

At this point you might wonder what about other data representing social disorganization or characteristics of the communities in which people reside. As discussed in Chapter 3, social disorganization is one of the most cited community-level theories applied to crime. The Census provides measures utilized to test propositions of social disorganization. Measures you have read about and discussed in class related to community-level correlates to crime include: vacant households, median income, population living below the poverty line, minority, population 15–24 years old, female-headed households, and unemployed. These measures are not an inclusive list, and are often utilized to reflect disadvantaged communities. Similar to the other types of data sources discussed in this chapter, Census data are available online (factfinder.census.gov). There are also options for interactive maps with data available for users interested in analysis (www.census.gov). This provides ease of access to the data for users, with many point and click options to select specific variables and geographies.

Census data are assigned geographic identifiers, state, county, zip code, place, tracts, and block groups, among others. As crime analysts, you will be mostly concerned with smaller geographic areas such as block groups and tracts. Tracts range in size but typically have a population between 1,200 and 8,000, with an ideal population of about 4,000. Block groups are divisions of census tracts with populations between 600 and 3,000 persons. Since block groups encompass a smaller population, there are more block groups across a city than tracts. Block groups provide analysts with the ability to identify greater variation across their jurisdiction than tracts. Often census tracts and block groups are proxies for neighborhoods and communities because they are the smallest geographies that do not have suppressed data (the Census does not report data if there are fewer than ten people in a geographic region because it may reveal information about the people). Crime analysts can download the data to supplement crime data to increase the understanding of the context in which crime occurs.

A downfall of the Decennial Census is that it is only conducted every ten years; by the time the data are collected and made available at smaller units of analysis (tracts, block groups), the data are often outdated. Because of this, there has been an increase in the use of the American Community Survey (ACS) since it is a yearly survey of people across the United States. The ACS is also conducted by the U.S. Census Bureau, and its measures are comparable. The ACS contains similar measures of the census but is based more on estimates than trying to count every resident in the United States. About 1 in 38 U.S. households per year are sent an invitation to participate in the ACS (www.census. gov). ACS provides users with the ability to utilize community and population data for years when the U.S. Census may not be the best estimate of the community characteristics.

Crime analysts need to be familiar with numerous data sources so they can better analyze crime in their jurisdiction. This often involves using more than one data source. Police and government agencies generally ask for crime rates or counts in relation to community characteristics. The U.S. Census and ACS provide analysts with the means to include data representing their communities. One recent improvement with ACS data is the ability to download some of the most common social measures attached to geographic files. You no longer have to download multiple variables, merge them, then join them to spatial files. ACS streamlined this process for users and makes it easier for newcomers to become familiar with the data.

CONCLUSION

Crime analysts should continually strive to get the best data possible for their analyses, even if it means working to obtain or develop datasets of difficult measures. Do not just use arrest data and Census data because it is easy. Make the extra effort to get data that can be theoretically supported in the findings. Many of the data sources will require cleaning or recoding to make the data usable for your analyses. This is common and part of the process. This chapter brings to light some of the more common types of data crime analysts deal with or report. Of course, once you start downloading and using the different types of data, you will gain a better understanding of the data source.

BIBLIOGRAPHY

Addington, L.A. 2007. Hot vs. cold cases: Examining time to clearance for homicide using NIBRS data. *Justice Research and Policy*, 9: 87–112.

Block, R. 1994. STAC Hot spot areas: A statistical tool for law enforcement decisions. In *Proceedings of the Workshop on Crime Analysis through Computer Mapping*. Chicago, IL: Illinois Criminal Justice Information Authority.

Bruce, A.S. and S.A. Desmond. 1998. A classroom exercise for teaching the problems of offense classification and tabulation associated with the UCR. *Journal of Criminal Justice Education*, 9(1): 119–129.

Finkelhor, D. and R.K. Ormrod. 2001. Factors in the underreporting of crimes against juveniles. *Child Maltreatment*, 6(3): 219–229.

Hipp, J.R., J. Petersilia, and S. Turner. 2010. Parolee recidivism in California: The effect of neighborhood context and social service agency characteristics. *Criminology*, 48(4): 947–979.

Kitsuse, J.I. and A.V. Cicourel. 1963. A note on the use of official statistics. *Social Problems*, 11: 131–138.

Major, V.L. 1992. UCR's blueprint for the future. *FBI Law Enforcement Bulletin*, 62(November): 15–18.

Mosher, C. 2012. The myth of accurate crime measurement. In R.M. Bohm and J.T. Walker (Eds.), *Demystifying Myths in Crime and Criminal Justice*, 2nd ed. London: Oxford University Press.

NIBRS. 2012. *Uniform Crime Reporting (UCR) Program: National Incident-Based Reporting System (NIBRS)*. Washington, DC: U.S. Department of Justice.

Reaves, B.A. 1993. *National Incident-Based Reporting System: Using NIBRS Data to Analyze Violent Crime*. Washington, DC: Bureau of Justice Statistics.

Schneider, V.W. and B. Wiersema. 1990. Limits and use of the uniform crime reports. In D.L. MacKenzie, P.J. Baunach, and R.R. Roberg (Eds.), *Measuring Crime: Large-Scale, Long-Range Efforts* (pp. 21–48). Albany, NY: SUNY Press.

Steffensmeier, D., H. Zhong, J. Ackerman, J. Schwartz, and S. Agha. 2006. Gender gap trends for violent crimes, 1980 to 2003: A UCR–NCVS comparison. *Feminist Criminology*, 1: 72–98.

QUESTIONS AND EXERCISES

1   What are the major differences between the UCR, NIBRS, and NCVS for the crime of robbery? Discuss these, and decide which you think would be the best to use when preparing a presentation for a community group on robbery in their neighborhood.

2   Discuss the problems associated with using UCR data for crime analysis. As a crime analyst, what could you do to overcome these problems for a specific project you were working on?

3   Find and download the UCR data for your city (or your home city) for all Part I crimes.

4   Use the Census data finder to download three social characteristics (e.g. homes owned, median income, and number of residents) for the area of your city where you live (or where you grew up).

Describing crime events

In practice, the job of a crime analyst is describing crime events. Whether you are doing simple counts of crimes in a table, displaying characteristics on a map, or conducting complex multivariate analyses, you are still describing crime events. This chapter deals with describing crime events one characteristic at a time or describing the relationship between two characteristics (variables). Then, Chapter 8 deals with more advanced bivariate and multivariate analysis; followed in Chapter 9 by a discussion of making inferences from small groups (samples) to a population. Later chapters will address geospatial techniques.

Describing characteristics one and two at a time are accomplished by univariate and bivariate statistical analyses and/or displaying their distributions in tables, graphs, or maps. This chapter begins with setting up frequency tables of characteristics and displaying them in graphs. Univariate statistical procedures such as calculating the measure of central tendency (the average), dispersion (how much the data are spread around the average), and form (how the data are arranged) are the foundation of these analyses. Bivariate analyses can range from simple cross tabulation tables (crosstabs), where the frequencies of two characteristics are displayed, to more advanced bivariate analyses of the statistical significance and strength of a relationship.

TYPES OF DATA

To be able to conduct statistical analyses, it is important to understand the type of data you have. Some statistical procedures demand that your data meet certain requirements such as normality of form or being of a certain level of measurement. Form is discussed later in this chapter and in the chapters that follow. The different levels of data are discussed in this section.

Understanding the level of measurement of data is critical to your analyses. If you use the wrong data with a particular analysis procedure, you could get flawed or misleading results. This could be detrimental to your agency, and could get you in trouble if you provide bad information on a critical project. There are four levels of measurement of data. Each of these have particular characteristics that make them appropriate for certain analyses and are essential in drawing appropriate conclusions.

Nominal level data typically relate to things that do not have numbers associated with them. This is something like race or gender. Neither of these naturally have numbers associated with them; but we need them to have numbers so we can use them in calculations. So, we just assign numbers to them. For example, we could assign 0 to male and 1 to female in data that we are examining. A critical element of nominal level data is that it cannot be ordered. In this instance, it makes no difference if we assign 0 to male and 1 to female or 0 to female and 1 to male. There is nothing that establishes any order. Conversely, as you will see with ordinal level data, it has ordering. For shirt size, small, medium, and large have an ordering. Assigning 1 to small 3 to medium, and 2 to large would not make any sense. But with nominal level data, the ordering is arbitrary. You can even start wherever you want with the numbers. For example, you could assign 23 for male and 47 for female. It is just a number to represent the category.

Ordinal level data can use higher level statistical procedures than nominal level, but is still categorical data. For ordinal data, a characteristic (variable) does have order, but you cannot tell the interval between the categories or the interval is not consistent. For example, in the discussion of shirt size above, you can tell when you go to the store that a medium shirt is larger than a small shirt. But can you tell how much larger? Typically not. Additionally, we know that the difference between a small and a medium for one brand may not be the same as the difference for another brand. You always hear about clothing sizes that "run large." That means the interval between sizes is not consistent. This will become important for interval level data. Another common place where ordinal level data shows up in crime analysis is where you have categories of different sizes. Take value of a home for example. Say you have the following categories in your data:

$100,000 and above
$75,000 to $99,999
$50,000 to $74,999
Less than $50,000.

Here, it looks like you have pretty consistent intervals of $25,000. The issue is the highest and lowest categories. All we know about the lowest category is that it is less than $50,000. The lowest value of the house could be $49,999 (an interval of 1) or you could have a house that has no value (an interval of $50,000). And there is no real way to know with the categories you have how much the most expensive home is, so you do not know the interval of the highest category.

There is a controversial area of ordinal level data. That is, if you have survey data that use a Likert scale (strongly disagree, disagree, neutral, agree, strongly agree). Many people choose to use this kind of data as interval level. The argument is that the numbers associated with the categories are interval (1, 2, 3, 4, 5; all have an interval of 1). The problem is, yes the numbers have a consistent interval, but the underlying concept does not. Say the question was, "I always root for the Tampa Bay Buccaneers." If you are not a big National Football League (NFL) fan, the difference between neutral and either disagree or agree might be very small (you might have to think about it for a minute to decide which to choose). If, however, the Buccaneers were your favorite team or you hated them, then you may be at the far end of the scale. So the interval between agree and strongly agree if you looked at it on a line scale might be very different from the interval between neutral and agree. That is why you should use ordinal level measures with Likert kinds of responses.

With interval level data, we begin to get to characteristics that have numbers naturally associated with them. For data to be considered interval level, they must meet *all* of three requirements: the data must be ordered, there must be equal intervals, and there can be no true zero.

The ordering for interval level data makes it consistent with ordinal level data. Dates are an example of an interval level variable. They can be ordered. The 2nd of November is later in the month than the 1st of November; but earlier in the month than the 10th of November.

Also, the difference between one day and the next is 1 day. This is important for you to understand. Notice above that the dates were the 1st, 2nd, and 10th. Obviously, the interval between the 1st and 2nd is 1 day. But what about the difference between the 2nd and 10th? For data to be interval, you do not have to have equal intervals between cases in your data. The intervals are established by the concept/variable itself. Dates have a natural one-day interval, regardless of the data. In this example, the difference between November 2nd and 10th is based on one-day intervals of November 3rd, 4th, and so on. When you are establishing the level of measurement for your variables, look at the variable itself; do not look at your data, it may only confuse you.

The final characteristic is that there is no true zero. Here, we are talking about the absence of the characteristic. An interval level variable could have a 0 as one of the categories; but, unless it represents an absence, it is not a true zero. Say you have the variable time in your data set. If something happened exactly at midnight, I would have a time of 0:00:00. That does not mean there is an absence of time; it just means the starting point for this variable is 0. On the other hand, if you were counting police officers, you could have an absence. For example, if your variable was the number of officers who had been killed in the line of duty in a year, you could have 0 officers killed. That is an absence of the number of officers killed in a year.

You also need to remember that you must have all of these characteristics for the data to be interval. Take patrol district numbers as an example. You have districts that are numbers (0, 1, 2, ... 16, etc.). You can also have a 0 district. Interval right? Wrong. While these are numbers with a 0, and you could make an argument of an equal interval, they are not ordered. Is there some characteristic other than its number and maybe geography that separates District 2 from District 4? No; so it is not ordered.

The highest level of data is ratio level. The only difference between ratio level data and interval level data is that ratio level data have a true zero. Exactly how specific you want to be about this true zero is up to you. Typically, things that you can count can have a true zero. For example, the number of crimes committed in a neighborhood in a given month could have a true zero (no crimes committed in a month). Other times, it is not as easy. For example, a tire that is flat could certainly be considered to have 0 air in it (an absence of air). But the reality is that there is air in the tire, just not enough to hold the tire up. Even when counting crimes, you could make the argument that no place has an absolute absence of the ability to have a crime there. So really, there is no true zero for crime. Our advice is not to overthink it. If it appears to have a true zero that you can justify, call it ratio level. Because crime analysts do not use statistical analyses that are only appropriate for ratio level data, it does not matter anyway. Any data that are interval or ratio would use interval level analysis procedures.

CRIME ANALYSES PEOPLE CAN UNDERSTAND

Crime analyses are of little value if the people who need the information cannot understand what you are trying to relate to them. Complicated analyses and formulas often do not go over well with the consumers of crime analyses. That does not mean you need to dumb it down. What it does mean is that you need to be able to present it in a way that is clear and makes sense. In addition to the maps that will be discussed later in the book, other key ways of displaying your results are in tables and graphs.

Tables

One of the clearest ways to present information is through tables. Tables can display several characteristics of a variable, and/or be set up so you can compare several variables or data points, such as shown in Table 7.1.

Table 7.1 shows the reported crime frequency and rate for the U.S. for 1995 to 2014. This table would be good in a report or presentation for at least two reasons. First, it can show how crime has changed over the past 20 years. Specifically, it can show that the numbers and rates of crime have generally dropped. If you were to add data on your city, you could then compare what is happening in your city with the national trends.

Tables do not have to be this extensive however. For example, sometimes a sex and race breakdown of those arrested is good information that can be put in a table. For example, in Table 7.2, the percentages of people arrested for crimes are broken down by race. Again, since this is for the U.S. as a whole, it provides a benchmark of the racial breakdowns of arrests. Providing additional information of the racial breakdown in your city would allow comparisons to be made that could help show what the police department is doing to address overrepresentation of minorities in arrests.

When building tables, it is important to not make them too complicated. You do not want a table of raw data that runs on for pages, or is so small in font that you can hardly read it. Table 7.1 is almost at the point where it has too much information to be displayed in a way that is understandable. Summary tables are what you are looking for. When conducting crime analyses from raw data, it is a simple matter in Excel to convert the raw numbers to percentages, rates, or univariate measures such as means (see below) and use them in the tables. It is also important to understand the difference

Table 7.1 Crime in the United States by Volume and Rate per 100,000 Inhabitants, 1995–2014

Year	Population	Murder and nonnegligent manslaughter	Murder and nonnegligent manslaughter rate	Rape	Rape rate	Robbery	Robbery rate	Aggravated assault	Aggravated assault rate	Burglary	Burglary rate	Larceny-theft	Larceny-theft rate	Motor vehicle theft	Motor vehicle theft rate
1995	262,803,276	21,606	8.2	97,470	37.1	580,509	220.9	1,099,207	418.3	2,593,784	987.0	7,997,710	3,043.2	1,472,441	560.3
1996	265,228,572	19,645	7.4	96,252	36.3	535,594	201.9	1,037,049	391.0	2,506,400	945.0	7,904,685	2,980.3	1,394,238	525.7
1997	267,783,607	18,208	6.8	96,153	35.9	498,534	186.2	1,023,201	382.1	2,460,526	918.8	7,743,760	2,891.8	1,354,189	505.7
1998	270,248,003	16,974	6.3	93,144	34.5	447,186	165.5	976,583	361.4	2,332,735	863.2	7,376,311	2,729.5	1,242,781	459.9
1999	272,690,813	15,522	5.7	89,411	32.8	409,371	150.1	911,740	334.3	2,100,739	770.4	6,955,520	2,550.7	1,152,075	422.5
2000	281,421,906	15,586	5.5	90,178	32.0	408,016	145.0	911,706	324.0	2,050,992	728.8	6,971,590	2,477.3	1,160,002	412.2
2001	285,317,559	16,037	5.6	90,863	31.8	423,557	148.5	909,023	318.6	2,116,531	741.8	7,092,267	2,485.7	1,228,391	430.5
2002	287,973,924	16,229	5.6	95,235	33.1	420,806	146.1	891,407	309.5	2,151,252	747.0	7,057,379	2,450.7	1,246,646	432.9
2003	290,788,976	16,528	5.7	93,883	32.3	414,235	142.5	859,030	295.4	2,154,834	741.0	7,026,802	2,416.5	1,261,226	433.7
2004	293,656,842	16,148	5.5	95,089	32.4	401,470	136.7	847,381	288.6	2,144,446	730.3	6,937,089	2,362.3	1,237,851	421.5
2005	296,507,061	16,740	5.6	94,347	31.8	417,438	140.8	862,220	290.8	2,155,448	726.9	6,783,447	2,287.8	1,235,859	416.8
2006	299,398,484	17,309	5.8	94,472	31.6	449,246	150.0	874,096	292.0	2,194,993	733.1	6,626,363	2,213.2	1,198,245	400.2
2007	301,621,157	17,128	5.7	92,160	30.6	447,324	148.3	866,358	287.2	2,190,198	726.1	6,591,542	2,185.4	1,100,472	364.9
2008	304,059,724	16,465	5.4	90,750	29.8	443,563	145.9	843,683	277.5	2,228,887	733.0	6,586,206	2,166.1	959,059	315.4
2009	307,006,550	15,399	5.0	89,241	29.1	408,742	133.1	812,514	264.7	2,203,313	717.7	6,338,095	2,064.5	795,652	259.2
2010	309,330,219	14,722	4.8	85,593	27.7	369,089	119.3	781,844	252.8	2,168,459	701.0	6,204,601	2,005.8	739,565	239.1

(Continued)

Table 7.1 (Continued)

Year	Population	Murder and nonnegligent manslaughter	Murder and nonnegligent manslaughter rate	Rape	Rape rate	Robbery	Robbery rate	Aggravated assault	Aggravated assault rate	Burglary	Burglary rate	Larceny-theft	Larceny-theft rate	Motor vehicle theft	Motor vehicle theft rate
2011	311,587,816	14,661	4.7	84,175	27.0	354,746	113.9	752,423	241.5	2,185,140	701.3	6,151,095	1,974.1	716,508	230.0
2012	313,873,685	14,856	4.7	85,141	27.1	355,051	113.1	762,009	242.8	2,109,932	672.2	6,168,874	1,965.4	723,186	230.4
2013	316,497,531	14,319	4.5	82,109	25.9	345,093	109.0	726,777	229.6	1,932,139	610.5	6,019,465	1,901.9	700,288	221.3
2014	318,857,056	14,249	4.5	84,041	26.4	325,802	102.2	741,291	232.5	1,729,806	542.5	5,858,496	1,837.3	689,527	216.2

Source: Federal Bureau of Investigation, Uniform Crime Reports.

Table 7.2 Arrests by Race, 2014 (%)

Offense charged	White	"Black or African American"	"American Indian or Alaska Native"	Asian	"Native Hawaiian or Other Pacific Islander"
TOTAL	**69.4**	**27.8**	**1.6**	**1.1**	**0.1**
Murder and nonnegligent manslaughter	46.3	51.3	1.0	1.3	0.1
Rape	67.2	29.9	1.3	1.4	0.2
Robbery	42.3	55.9	0.8	0.8	0.1
Aggravated assault	63.7	33.1	1.5	1.5	0.2
Burglary	67.6	30.2	0.9	1.1	0.2
Larceny-theft	69.1	28.0	1.6	1.2	0.1
Motor vehicle theft	66.5	30.7	1.2	1.3	0.3
Arson	73.1	23.4	1.9	1.3	0.2
Violent crime	59.4	37.7	1.4	1.4	0.2
Property crime	68.8	28.4	1.5	1.2	0.1
Other assaults	65.4	31.9	1.6	1.1	0.1
Forgery and counterfeiting	63.8	34.0	0.6	1.5	0.1
Fraud	66.1	31.8	1.0	1.0	0.1
Embezzlement	61.9	35.6	0.7	1.7	0.1
Stolen property; buying, receiving, possessing	65.5	32.2	0.9	1.2	0.1
Vandalism	70.1	27.0	1.8	1.0	0.1
Weapons; carrying, possessing, etc.	57.3	40.7	0.7	1.2	0.1
Prostitution and commercialized vice	53.7	41.8	0.5	3.9	0.1
Sex offenses (except rape and prostitution)	72.5	24.3	1.5	1.6	0.1
Drug abuse violations	68.9	29.1	0.8	1.1	0.1
Gambling	35.8	58.9	0.4	4.4	0.6
Offenses against the family and children	64.4	32.9	1.9	0.7	*
Driving under the influence	83.7	13.0	1.4	1.8	0.1
Liquor laws	80.2	14.5	3.9	1.3	0.1
Drunkenness	80.9	15.7	2.1	1.1	0.1
Disorderly conduct	63.0	33.9	2.3	0.7	0.1

(Continued)

Table 7.2 (Continued)

Offense charged	White	"Black or African American"	"American Indian or Alaska Native"	Asian	"Native Hawaiian or Other Pacific Islander"
Vagrancy	68.7	28.3	2.1	0.8	0.1
All other offenses (except traffic)	67.8	29.5	1.7	0.9	0.1
Suspicion	52.7	44.7	1.4	1.2	0.0
Curfew and loitering law violations	51.4	46.2	1.1	1.1	0.2

Source: Federal Bureau of Investigation, Uniform Crime Reports.

between statistical tables and presentation tables. There is always the temptation to simply cut the table from statistical output and include it in a presentation or report. These tables often contain information beyond what is needed, however, and it is often not in a format that is easily interpretable (see, for example, Table 7.9). When using statistical packages, be sure to take the output provided and put it in a table that makes sense and reads well.

Graphs

For relating some information, graphs (also called charts) are the best method. They take data and place them in a visual format that makes them generally easy to understand. There are many types of graphs. The ones that will be discussed here are pie charts, histograms, and time line graphs.

Pie charts

The most basic type of graph is a pie chart. A pie chart is best used for discrete, nominal level data where there are a small number (generally less than five) of categories. Nominal level data are best represented with a pie chart because of the obvious breaks between categories. The pie depicts N, or 100 percent of the frequencies, so it is easy for people to understand the graph simply by looking at the size of each slice of the pie. For example, Figure 7.1 shows the percentage of arrests by race for a police agency during the month.

This graph easily shows that the majority of arrests were for White suspects, followed by Black suspects and then Hispanic suspects. There were almost an equal number of Asian and those of other races; both of which were very small compared to other races.

It is the simplicity of pie charts that makes them useful in presentations of crime analyses. One caution is using pie charts with different sizes of data close together. Since most pie charts visually represent percentages, they can be confusing if different variables are placed close together. For example, you might not want to place a pie chart of the time of rapes and the race of murderers close together. Visually, it may appear to be making comparisons when that is not the case. If there is a need to place these kinds of variables close together in a report or presentation, it is best to break them up by using some pie charts and some histograms.

Histograms

Another method of displaying nominal level data is with histograms (also often called bar graphs for nominal level data). The data in Figure 7.1 are shown as a histogram in Figure 7.2. In this case, the

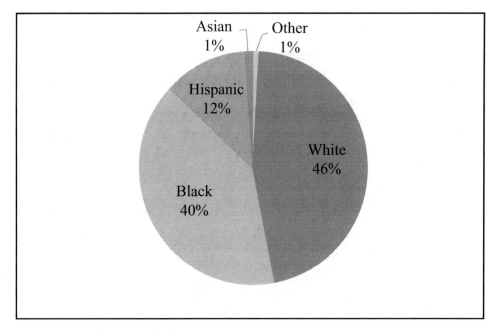

Figure 7.1 Percentage of Arrests by Race for July

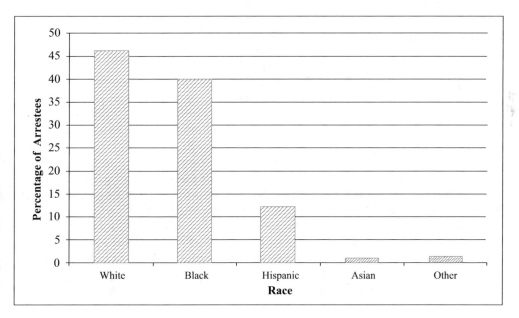

Figure 7.2 Percentage of Arrests for July

bars represent the percentages of arrestees. Note that the bars are separated. This, visually, denotes that this is nominal level data where there is no continuity between the categories. The separated bars also distinguish a particular type of histogram called a bar graph.

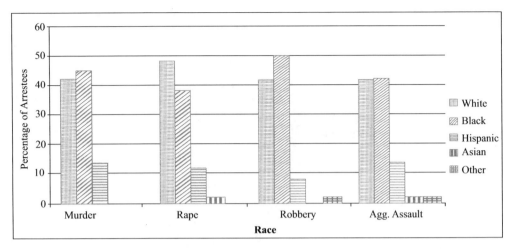

Figure 7.3 Percentage of Arrests by Crime Type for July

It is also possible to use histograms with multiple variables to show comparisons. For example, in Figure 7.3, the arrest percentages by race are displayed for violent crimes.

Here, you can see there are differences in the percentages of arrests for different types of crimes. This is somewhat different from the other graphs in that the data are grouped by arrest type and the bars represent arrest percentages. This allows you to show that there are differences in the arrest percentages for different types of crimes. For example, there were more Blacks than Whites arrested for murder in this month, but there were more Whites arrested for rape than Blacks. You could have also created the graph with the races grouped and the bars representing the types of crimes. These kinds of graphs allow you to present the data in a way that helps the audience understand the point you are trying to make with the crime analyses.

A histogram is also the type of graph used to display ordinal (and occasionally higher level) data. Although not everyone follows the traditional conventions of graphs, you should typically be able to tell the difference between a bar graph being used to represent nominal level data and a histogram being used to represent ordinal level data because, in a histogram, the bars will not be separated (see Figure 7.4).

In Figure 7.4, you can see how crime frequency varies by the size of the town. As expected, there is a general link between the size of the town and the crime rate, where larger towns have a higher rate. You might think that the crime rate in rural areas is higher than expected. In this case, that is not a result of many crimes but more the small population that makes a small number of crimes seem somewhat larger. Because the bars are connected, it indicates there is a continuous flow from one size town to the next.

There are conventions and standards that should be followed when constructing a histogram. First, the item being examined is generally placed on the X-axis, which is the horizontal axis. If the responses are nominal, they should be placed in the most logical format; if they are ordinal or higher level, they should be placed in ascending order from left to right. Another convention is to begin numbering the Y-axis (typically a frequency or percentage) with zero and to use equal intervals throughout the scale. You should always have a title and label the X and Y axes so the reader understands what is being represented. If there is more than one set of bars, a legend should be added to show what is represented in each set of bars. As with any other type of graph, if there is anything out of the ordinary, make sure to include it in a footnote.

Line graphs

Often, crime analysts will want to show change over time. For example, you might want to show the number of crimes per month for the year to look at how they changed. You may also want to compare

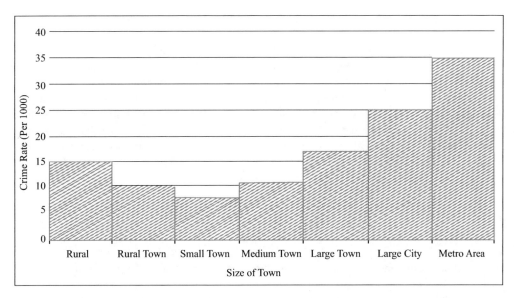

Figure 7.4 Histogram of Crimes by Size of Town

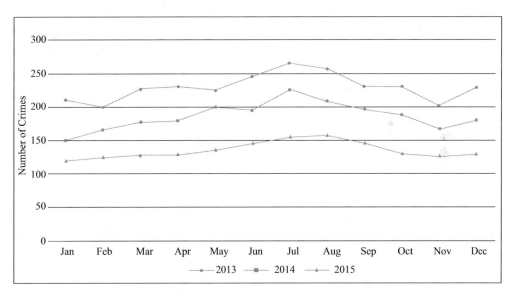

Figure 7.5 Crimes per Month, 2013–2015

the crimes per month this year with those from previous years. You could do this with histograms where the bars represent the months, and different years could be different colors in the month groups of bars. But this may not be the most effective way to make your point. A better way might be with a line graph (often called a trend line). Here, you can show clearly how things change over time.

Take, for example, Figure 7.5. While it shows that crimes have a relatively similar pattern for each month, it clearly shows that crimes have been reduced from 2013 to 2015. If there was a major crime reduction effort in the agency, this would be something that would likely get wide exposure in the city.

As with all other graphs, there are conventions that should be followed when creating line graphs. Similar to a histogram, the item being examined is generally placed on the X-axis, which is the horizontal axis. If the responses are nominal, they should be placed in the most logical format; if they are ordinal or higher level, they should be placed in ascending order from left to right. Also similar to histograms, you should begin numbering the Y-axis (typically a frequency or percentage) with zero and to use equal intervals throughout the scale. You should always have a title and label the X and Y axes so the reader understands what is being represented (in this case, we did not label the X-axis since it was obvious that it was months being displayed; and it allowed us to save space by putting the legend at the bottom of the graph). If there is more than one line, a legend should be added to show what each line represents. As with any other type of graph, if there is anything out of the ordinary, make sure to include it in a footnote.

SUMMARIZING DATA: UNIVARIATE ANALYSES

Using tables and graphs are great ways to relate information to an audience. However, when you have a lot of data, sometimes frequencies, or even percentages, can get overwhelming. In those cases, it is often advantageous to use summary measures that explain the data as a whole. For example, you may want to relate to your audience the central point of the data (e.g. an average), how spread out the data are (high to low, etc.), and if the data are somewhat evenly spread out or if there are extremes in the data. These three pieces of information correspond to the univariate measures of central tendency, dispersion, and form.

Measures of central tendency

Measures of central tendency address the central value or the most typical value of a variable. It is (or should be) tied to the level of measurement of the variable. There are three common measures of central tendency, corresponding to each level of measurement (interval and ratio are combined). These are the mode for nominal level data, the median for ordinal level data, and the mean for interval and ratio level data.

Mode

The mode (symbolized as Mo) is used primarily for nominal data to identify the category with the greatest number of cases. It is most appropriate for nominal level data because it is simply a count of the values – which is all that can be accomplished with nominal level data. It is also often good to know the most fre-quently occurring value of any type of data so your audience knows what occurs most often. The mode is the most frequently occurring value, or case, in a distribution. It is the tallest column on a histogram or the peak on a line graph. Because it is the most frequently occurring value, the mode is easily identified.

There is no formula or calculation for the mode. To obtain the mode, you simply count the scores and determine the most frequently occurring value. Take the data in Table 7.3.

This is a simple listing of the number of officers who took vacation last year. The data are arranged by the number of officers, not the month. Here, you can see that it was most common for 5 officers to be on vacation in a month. This information could be used for a first attempt at determin-ing a plan to have additional officers available. While you may want to gather more information and try to plan by month for the number of additional officers needed, this gets you close as a start.

Table 7.3 Number of Officers on Vacation

7	6	5	4
6	5	5	4
6	5	4	3

For simple data sets, all you need to do to calculate the mode is to count the data and determine which has the highest frequency. For larger data sets, you will want to use the Data Analysis function in Excel. To do this, the data need to be in a column. Using the example in Table 7.3, put each of the numbers in a column in Excel (they do not have to be in order). You then need to establish the upper limits or categories for the data (more on this below, but for now, just type in 7, 6, 5, 4, 3 in a separate column). Then go to the Data Analysis menu item.[1] From there, select Histogram. Where the dialog box asks for Input Range, select the cells that contain the data. Where the dialog box asks for the Bin Range, select the 7–3 you typed in. Select OK and the frequency table will be displayed in a new worksheet.

Now let's take a somewhat more complex project, but one that is much closer to what you would do as a crime analyst. Let's use the data from Table 7.1. We will select the number of rapes over the 20-year period. To do this, you will need to put the values into some ranges (for a data set like this, you would not want the actual values because there would be many frequencies of 1). For this data set, let's use 80,000–83,999; 84,000–87,999; 88,000–91,999; 92,000–95,999; and 96,000–99,999. You will need to type the upper limit number (83,999, 87,999, etc.) into Excel. This will be the Bin Range. Then you can follow the steps outlined above, as shown in Figure 7.6.

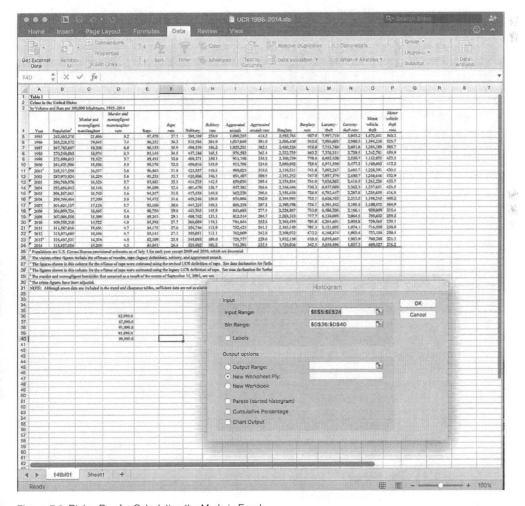

Figure 7.6 Dialog Box for Calculating the Mode in Excel

The result will be a frequency table as shown in Table 7.4. This is a good place to remind you that statistical tables and presentation tables are not the same. The top table in Table 7.4 is a statistical table. If you show that to your superiors or a community group, you will likely get a lot of questions that are not related to sharing this information. If you want to present these data in a table, do something like the bottom table in Table 7.4.

From here, it is a simple matter to determine that the mode for this data is the 92,000–95,999 category with a frequency of 7. This means that more yearly rapes fell into the 92,000–95,999 category than any other category of the data. Note that the mode is not the best measure for these data. They are interval/ratio level data, so using the mean would be more appropriate. The mode is used here for illustration, and could also be helpful if you are trying to show general categories of the most frequently occurring numbers of rapes.

Table 7.4 also presents an opportunity to talk about another part of the mode that sometimes confuses people. The mode is the "category" of the most frequently occurring value, not the frequency. In Table 7.3, the mode was 5, not the frequency of 4. In Table 7.4, the mode was 92,000–95,999, not the frequency of 7.

One last point to be made about the mode. Unlike the other measures of central tendency, distributions are not confined to having just one mode. For example, in Table 7.3, if there had been four 4s, the distribution would have had two modes (discussed further below in the discussion on form). If there had also been four 6s, then the distribution would have had three modes.

Median

If the data are at least ordinal level, the median (symbolized by Me) is the best choice for examining central tendency. The median is the exact midpoint of a distribution. For the simplest distribution of 1, 2, 3, the median would be 2 because it is the exact middle of the distribution.

Table 7.4 Frequency of Rapes in the U.S., 1995–2014

Bin	Frequency
83,999	1
87,999	4
91,999	5
95,999	7
99,999	3

Number of Rapes	Years Occurred
80,000–83,999	1
84,000–87,999	4
88,000–91,999	5
92,000–95,999	7
96,000–99,999	3

This example also shows why the median should be used for ordinal level data. Remember that ordinal data have no equal intervals. Something can be said to be larger/smaller, faster/slower, etc., but not by how much. The median only looks at a number that is above or below the middle, not by how much. For another example, take the following two distributions:

1, 2, 3, 3, 4, 4, 5
1, 1, 1, 3, 10, 50, 100

Each has the same number of values, 7, although each has very different numbers. In this case, the modes would be different: 3 and 4 in the first; 1 in the second. The median for both of these distributions, however, would be 3, the middle value in the distribution. This also demonstrates a limitation of the median. A median of 3 in the first distribution is representative of the data. A median of 3 in the second distribution is not representative of the data. On the other end of level of measurement, the median may be used instead of the mean if the distribution is skewed (see the discussion on form below). The mean is influenced by extreme scores, like those in the second distribution in the example we just looked at. As another example, if you were to calculate the mean for the number of crimes in a month for four neighborhoods with values of 2, 3, 4, and 50, the mean would be 14.75. Obviously, 14.75 is not a good measure of the central value in this distribution. The median of that distribution would be 3.5, which is much more like the central value.

For small distributions, it may be possible to simply count the numbers to determine the middle value. For larger distributions, the formula for the median should be used. Calculation of the median for ungrouped data is relatively simple. All that is needed is the N for the distribution (the total number). If the N is not given, simply count the number of values (use the number of rows minus the header row in Excel). The N is then placed in the formula:

$$\frac{N+1}{2}$$

If the data from Table 7.3 were used, the calculation of the median would be as follows:

$$\frac{N+1}{2} = \frac{12+1}{2} = \frac{13}{2} = 6.5$$

You would then take this number and count up in the distribution to the 6½ value. Note that calculating the median often does not fall with even numbers. It is necessary then to take an average of the two values (in this case, the 6th value and the 7th value). For this example, you would have to take the average of 5 and 5, so the median would be 5. This is the point that cuts the distribution in half. This also happens to be the same value as the mode.

Now calculate the median for the data on Rape in Table 7.1. To do this, we will use the Median function in Excel. This is a simple matter in Excel. Simply select the Formula Builder from the menu or Formula Bar. Select the Median function, then select the range of values. In this example, the median number of rapes would be 91,511.5. Notice, however, that this value does not make a lot of sense here. This is because the values are interval/ratio, so the median does not provide much information. It would be better to use the Mean.

Mean

The most popular and best understood measure of central tendency is the mean (usually symbolized by $\bar{X}$. That is because the mean is simply the average score, and most people know how to calculate the average. The mean should only be used with non-skewed interval/ratio level data. If

X	f	fx
7	1	7
6	3	18
5	4	20
4	3	12
3	1	3
	12	60

$$X = \frac{\Sigma f x}{N}$$

$$X = \frac{60}{12}$$

$$= 5$$

Figure 7.7 Calculating the Mean

it is used with lower level data, it may give erroneous results. For example, take a data set on race that has the categories (1) Caucasian, (2) African American, (3) Hispanic, (4) Other. What would a mean of 2.78, calculated from the data, mean? That the average race of the people was somewhere between African American and Hispanic? No; it really means nothing. Similarly, getting a mean for ordinal data overestimates the intervals between the values. It is appropriate for interval/ratio level data.

The formula for the mean is shown below.

$$\bar{X} = \frac{\Sigma fx}{N}$$

Where fx is calculated by multiplying the value (X) times the frequency for each value. If we were to take the data in Table 7.3, the calculation would be as shown in Figure 7.7.

This means that the average number of officers who took vacation in a month last year was 5. For this data set, the mode, median, and mean are all the same (5). This means this is a very symmetrical data set (which will be discussed further below in the discussion of form).

While calculating the mean is not a difficult process, especially using the functions in Excel, it can be time-consuming for large data sets. Fortunately, Excel also has a Mean function that can be used easily. To do this, simply move to an empty cell (I always use the cell just below the column I am getting the mean for) and insert the Average function from the Formula Bar. Then select the cells you want to use to calculate the mean. When we do this for Table 7.1, we find the mean is 90,985 rapes per year. This is slightly lower than the median number of rapes (91,511.5.), but it is a more accurate measure of the central value of the distribution because the mean is more appropriate for the data in this figure.

Measures of dispersion

In addition to knowing the central value in a distribution, it is important to know how spread out the values are. This is because two distributions can have very different values that can be important. Take, for example, the following two sets of data on bimonthly crimes in two neighborhoods.

Which neighborhood would you rather live in? Both have the same mean (75). For Neighborhood 2, you know what you get each month. It is the same crime rate (and thus perhaps the same chances that you will be a victim). For Neighborhood 1, the crime rate varies quite a bit. One month, you have 0 chance of being a victim. In one month, there is a much greater chance. And all but one month has a higher chance of being a victim than in Neighborhood 2. Therefore, the spread of values is important.

Neighborhood 1	0	80	100	85	90	95
Neighborhood 2	75	75	75	75	75	75

There are different measures of dispersion that can be used for analyzing the spread of values in a distribution. Most of these are for use more by statisticians than those wishing to convey information to a non-technical audience. The measures of dispersion that will be discussed in this chapter are the range and the variance/standard deviation. Although there are measures of dispersion designed for each level of measurement, measures of dispersion for nominal and ordinal level data are not particularly helpful since there is no true "dispersion" in data that have a small number of categories (particularly if the categories are arbitrary as in nominal level data). That is why the variance/standard deviation is the most common measure of dispersion, since it is designed for interval/ratio level data.

Range

The simplest measure of dispersion is the range. The range is simply the difference between the highest and lowest values in a distribution. For example, if the number of officers in agencies in a state had a low of 2 officers and a high of 400 officers, the range would be 398 (400–2). The range is useful in that it is easily calculated; but it does not always provide the best information when used as a single value. For example, if you did not know the data, what conclusion could you make from the statement "The range of officers in the state is 398." For this reason, the range is often written as the two numbers, such as "The range is 2 to 400 officers."

To calculate the range in Excel for a large data set, you can use the AutoSum function in the toolbar. Simply select a cell below the column you are interested in finding the range for; select AutoSum and then Minimum. Select the cells in the column and press enter. This gives you the lowest value for the column. For the Rape column in Table 7.1, the minimum is 82,109. Similarly, move to the next empty cell, select AutoSum and Maximum, then select the cells and press enter. For Table 7.1, this is 97,470. Then you can just subtract the high from the low using Excel or a calculator (in this case 15,361), or you can just list the two values (82,109–97,470). Again, you can see that the single value range in this case is not all that helpful. The two numbers at least give you the high and low values.

Variance/standard deviation

A much more common, more sophisticated, and more complex measure of dispersion is the variance and standard deviation. The variance is a mathematical representation of the spread of values around the mean. The standard deviation is the square root of the variance. The variance is mostly used for mathematical and statistical calculations. As a result of the calculations of the variance, the value produced is not particularly helpful for information about the data because it is not on the same scale as the data. Taking the square root (the standard deviation) puts the scale back to that of the data; so the standard deviation is more often used to indicate the dispersion for interval and ratio level data. Neither of these analyses are appropriate for nominal or ordinal data.

The variance (represented by s^2 for samples or σ^2 for populations) measures the average of squared deviations of scores around the mean (the difference between the mean and each score). The formula for the variance is:

$$\sigma^2 = \frac{\Sigma(X - \bar{X})^2}{N}$$

You can see from this formula that it is really just the formula for an average, $\frac{\Sigma fx}{N}$; but the top value is the sum of each value subtracted from the mean and the sum squared. This gets you the average of the squared deviations around the mean. Squaring this value is necessary because, as a result of the formula for the mean, the deviations from the mean would always equal 0. Squaring this value just leaves the "distance."

There are two ways to calculate the variance in Excel. The first is to set up columns to calculate the parts of the formula. This will be demonstrated for the values in Table 7.3, as shown in Table 7.5. To set up this calculation, list the values in a column (X). In the f column, all values will be 1. To calculate the $(X - \bar{X})$ column, simply subtract the mean obtained above (5) from each value. You note that the sum of these values is 0. To calculate the final column, simply square each value in the $(X - \bar{X})$ column. It is a simple matter, then, to use the formula to calculate the variance.

In this case, the formula and values would be as below:

$$\sigma^2 = \frac{14}{12} = 1.1667$$

While this demonstrates how you would go about calculating the variance, and helps in understanding it, it is much simpler to use Excel to calculate the variance for larger data sets. To do this, use the formula function in Excel. Simply select an empty cell below the column you wish to examine. In the formula builder or function, select Var.P (the population variance). Then select the cells you want to use in your calculation and press enter. For the data on rape from Table 7.1, the variance is 20,607,878. You can see this number is not all that interpretable when the values range from (82,109–97,470). That is why we use the standard deviation.

Table 7.5 Excel Calculation for the Variance

X	f	$(X - \bar{X})$	$(X - \bar{X})^2$
7	1	2	4
6	1	1	1
6	1	1	1
6	1	1	1
5	1	0	0
5	1	0	0
5	1	0	0
5	1	0	0
4	1	−1	1
4	1	−1	1
4	1	−1	1
3	1	−2	4
Σ	12	0	14

Once you know the variance of a distribution, it is a simple matter to calculate the standard deviation. You simply take the square root of that value. This puts the standard deviation back in the scale of the values of the distribution. In the two examples above, the standard deviation would be 1.080 for the data in Table 7.3 and 4,539.6 for the data in Table 7.1.[2] Notice here that the standard deviation for the data in Table 7.3 does not change much. That is because the numbers are so small, so squaring them in the formula for the variance does not change them much. There is a substantial difference between the variance and the standard deviation for the data in Table 7.1, however. The value of the standard deviation is more interpretable because it makes more sense for the dispersion of data that have a range of 82,109–97,470 to be 4,539.6. The standard deviation is also helpful in that any score can be interpreted in terms of the number of standard deviations from the mean, which is called the Z score. This will come into play in the discussion of the normal curve and inferential statistics in Chapter 9.

Measures of the form of a distribution

The final univariate statistical analysis ties together the measure of central tendency and the measure of dispersion of the data. This is the form of the distribution. There are three measures of the form of a distribution: the number of modes, the symmetry (skewness), and the kurtosis.

Number of modes

In addition to establishing the mode(s) of a distribution, it is also important to understand the number of modes. Ideally, a distribution will only have one mode. This is the first step in establishing whether the data are a normal distribution (which is desired for higher order analyses discussed in the next two chapters).

Finding the number of modes in a distribution is easy, but you need to have a frequency table. This is easily constructed in statistical packages, and can be accomplished in Excel, as discussed above. Once you have the frequency distribution, you can examine the values to see how many potential

X	f
7	1
6	3
5	4
4	3
3	1

modes their might be. Using the data from Table 7.3 and the frequency distribution in Figure 7.7, we can determine the number of modes.

Using these frequencies, we can see that there is really just one mode in this data set. It is the value 5 with a frequency of 4. You can also see this if you were to create a polygon of the distribution, as shown in Figure 7.8.

Here, you can see that the data starts off low (frequency of 1 for value 3), then climbs smoothly to the peak (frequency of 4 for value 5), and then drops smoothly to the same low value (frequency of 1 for value 7). This is essentially a normal curve, which is a good thing that will be discussed in later

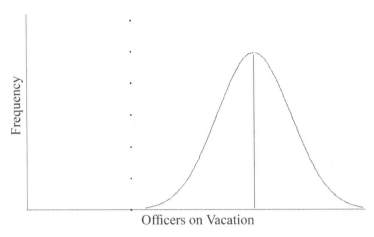

Figure 7.8 Polygon of Data from Table 7.3

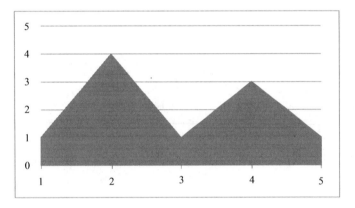

Figure 7.9 Bimodal Distribution

chapters. But what if we had the same frequencies, but they were arranged differently? Determining the *number* of modes is somewhat different from determining *the* mode. It is common to count only the highest frequency in a distribution as the mode. For determining the number of modes in an analysis of form, it may be more beneficial to examine all high frequency values in a distribution rather than finding the single highest value. Consider, for example, the distribution in Figure 7.9. Even though there is only one highest value, there are two peaks in the distribution.

Are we now considering this a bimodal distribution? After all, the "secondary peak" is only a frequency of 1 less than the mode. This is a decision you may have to make as a crime analyst; and your decision could influence any higher level analyses you may undertake.

Skewness

The next type of the form of the distribution is the degree of symmetry (skewness) of the distribution. The symmetry has to do with whether the peak of the distribution is in the center (as in Figure 7.8) or if the peak is to one side or the other. The skewness of a distribution has three categories: symmetrical, positively skewed, and negatively skewed.

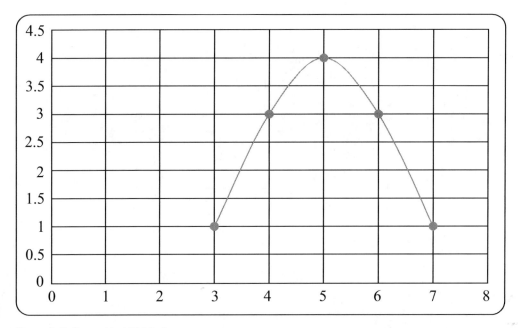

Figure 7.10 Symmetrical Distribution

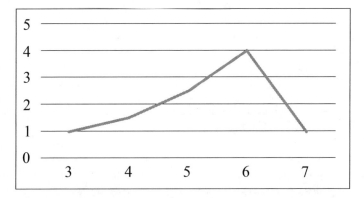

Figure 7.11 Negatively Skewed Distribution

A symmetrical distribution has mirror-image sides such that the distribution could be split at the mean/median and the sides folded over each other for a perfect match. In Figure 7.10, it is easy to see the symmetry in the distribution. The frequencies displayed in this distribution are very balanced: Categories 3 and 7 have the same frequency, as do 4 and 6. Category 5 has the highest frequency.

While this is ideal, this rarely happens when you have real data. There is almost always some skew to the data (where the data are skewed to one end of the scale or the other). The critical determination, then, is if the skew is such that the data are not suitable for higher-order analyses.

If there is no point in the distribution where it could be divided into two perfectly matching points, it is said to be skewed. If the tail of the curve is to the left of the graph (the tail of the graph points to the end of the scale where the 0 is), it is said to be negatively skewed. If the tail of the curve is to the right of the graph (the tail of the graph points toward the end of the scale with larger numbers), it is

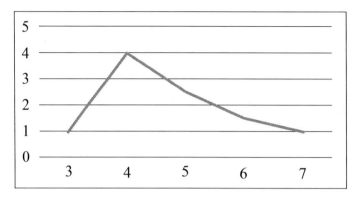

Figure 7.12 Positively Skewed Distribution

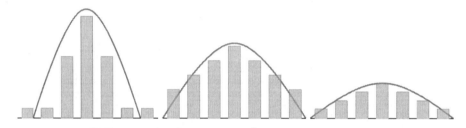

Figure 7.13 Examples of Leptokurtic, Mesokurtic, and Platykurtic

said to be positively skewed. A negatively skewed distribution is shown in Figure 7.11 and a positively skewed distribution is shown in Figure 7.12.

To obtain the value of skewness of a distribution in Excel, use the SKEW function in the formula builder. To do this, move to an empty cell below the column you want to examine. Select SKEW from the formula builder, then select the cells you wish to examine, then press enter. For the data on rape in Table 7.1, the skewness is −0.5194. This is an acceptable level of skewness.[3]

Kurtosis

The final type of the form of a distribution is the kurtosis. Kurtosis can easily be displayed with a histogram. The kurtosis is the extent to which the frequencies of categories cluster around the measure of central tendency or are clustered in the tails of the distribution (a distribution with a larger variance). If most of the values in the distribution are very close to the measure of central tendency, the distribution is said to be *leptokurtic* (as shown in the leftmost curve of Figure 7.13). If most of the values in the distribution are out in the tails, the distribution is said to be *platykurtic*, as shown in the rightmost curve of Figure 7.13. If the values in the distribution are like those in Figure 7.10, the distribution is said to be *mesokurtic*, as shown in the center curve of Figure 7.13. It is desirable to have a mesokurtic distribution in research.

Calculating the kurtosis of a distribution is the same in Excel as calculating the skewness. Follow the procedure used for SKEW except replace it with KURT. In data for rape from Table 7.1, the kurtosis calculated in Excel returned a result of −0.9382. This is very close to the threshold of −1. If it were greater than −1 (for example, a −1.9382) this would be considered a platykurtic distribution. Since it is within the −1 to 1 threshold, the distribution is considered mesokurtic.

EXAMINING TWO VARIABLES: BIVARIATE ANALYSES

While it is critical to be able to display and examine one variable at a time, it is often important to be able to examine the joint distribution of two variables. For example, you may want to look at the relationship between offense seriousness in a city and the race of the offenders committing the offenses. You could do this by hand calculating the values of each offense by the race of the offender; but a better way is to use tables and bivariate statistical procedures. These are often called crosstabs (cross tables in traditional statistical analysis). Excel uses pivot tables to do the same thing (although with somewhat more work). We will demonstrate here how to create a pivot table to show the relationship between race and offense seriousness.

Bivariate tables

In this instance, race is dichotomized into White (0) and NonWhite (1) because of the limited dispersion of NonWhite persons arrested in the data. There are six levels of offense seriousness:

1	Multiple Violent Crimes
2	Violent Crimes
3	Sex Crimes
4	Drug Crimes
5	Computer Crimes
6	Property Crimes

We want to display the joint frequencies and percentages of these different types of crimes. To do so, we will use a pivot table.

To begin, select the columns of data containing the offense seriousness and the race of the offender. Select "Insert," then "Recommended Pivot Table." This creates a new worksheet with a pivot table structure, as shown in Figure 7.14.

Notice there is a window called a PivotTable Builder on the worksheet. This is where you will format the table to look like what you want.

The next step in this process is to make the rows and columns contain the data you want. Although it is not absolute, as a general rule when building tables, you want to have your dependent variable in the rows and your independent variables in the columns. This helps ensure that the statistical analyses that may rely on the table have the proper order of the variables. In this case, we want to move offense seriousness to the rows and move race to the columns (offense seriousness cannot influence race, but the race of the offenders may have an influence on offense seriousness).

Next, we want to add the data. To do this, drag Race to the Values box. This will display the race of the offender by each offense seriousness types. As you can see from Table 7.6, there were 3,200 White offenders for property crime and 2,280 NonWhite offenders. You can also easily see the breakdown of race for the other offense seriousness types.

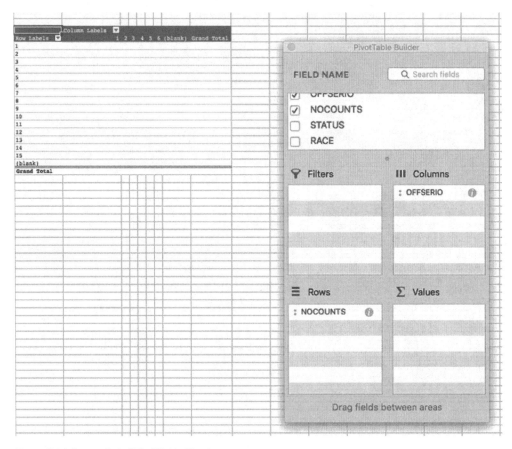

Figure 7.14 Screenshot of Pivot Table Structure

Table 7.6 Table of Offense Seriousness by Race

Row Labels	Count of Race		Grand Total
	Column Labels		
	0 (White)	1 (NonWhite)	
1 (Multiple Violent Crimes)	540	373	913
2 (Violent Crimes)	285	140	425
3 (Sex Crimes)	1054	832	1886
4 (Drug Crimes)	3409	1873	5282
5 (Computer Crimes)	1181	904	2085
6 (Property Crimes)	3200	2280	5480
Grand Total	9669	6402	16071

Although there are many ways you can make the table look better for presentation, we will focus here on the analysis aspects of the table. The only other item we will add to the table is the percentages. This is because percentages are often better at relaying the material to the audience. From Table 7.6, the audience can understand that there is a difference in the number of Whites and NonWhites in property crime; but the magnitude may not be intuitive. To overcome this, we can calculate the percentages for each cell. To do this, drag Race to the Values box one more time. Next, click on the *i* button next to "count of Race2." This will bring up a box called "PivotTable Field." In the Field Name, change the name of the column to "Percent." To make the data a percentage instead of a count, click on the "Show data as" tab. In the dropdown box that is labeled "Normal," click on the down arrow and select "% of column." The table displayed will look like that in Table 7.7.

Now you can see that 33.10 percent of the offenses of White offenders were for property crimes and 35.61 percent of the offenses for NonWhite offenders were for property crimes. You can also add columns in the same manner as above to examine the percent differences between White and NonWhite offenders by offense seriousness (% of row) or the percentage of a particular cell of the total (% of grand total), among other items that can be displayed in a pivot table.

If you need to add this kind of information to a report, you should construct a presentation table. Presentation tables are different from statistical tables (like that in Table 7.7). They should have design and layouts that are more visually pleasing and may help the audience understand what is being presented.

Bivariate analyses

Whether or not you construct bivariate tables to examine or display your data, the foundation of examining two variables is bivariate analysis. Tables may be more likely to be used for nominal and ordinal level variables, but are less likely to be used for interval/ratio level variables.

The foundation of a bivariate analysis is examining the association between two variables. Bivariate analysis of association, also called measures of association, consists of four types of analyses: existence, strength, direction, and nature. Not all of these analyses can be conducted at all levels

Table 7.7 Count and Percentage of Offense Seriousness by Race

Row Labels	Column Labels						
	0 (White)		1 (NonWhite)				
	Count	Percent	Count	Percent	Total Count of Race	Total Percent
1	540	5.58%	373	5.83%	913	5.68%
2	285	2.95%	140	2.19%	425	2.64%
3	1054	10.90%	832	13.00%	1886	11.74%
4	3409	35.26%	1873	29.26%	5282	32.87%
5	1181	12.21%	904	14.12%	2085	12.97%
6	3200	33.10%	2280	35.61%	5480	34.10%
Grand Total	9669	100.00%	6402	100.00%	16071	100.00%

of data. For example, since nominal level data have no ordering, there is no valid way to determine direction. Since this is not a statistics text, we will focus here only on the existence and strength of the association. You should consult any quality statistics text if you want more information on the direction and nature of associations.

Existence

At the most basic level, an association is said to exist between two variables when the distribution of the categories of one variable differs from the distribution of the categories of the other variable. The greater the difference, the stronger the association. Determining if this difference is "real" or could have occurred by chance is the process of determining the *existence* or *statistical significance* of a relationship.

There are two common bivariate measures for examining the existence of a relationship (χ^2 for nominal and ordinal data and Pearson's *r* for interval and ratio data). The most common measures of existence for inferential analyses are *t*-tests and *Z* tests, as discussed in Chapter 9. There are also multivariate measures of statistical significance that are associated with multivariate statistical procedures. They are discussed in later chapters.

Criminal-justice related research has long used a 0.05 level as the "golden rule" when identifying significant measures; however, variables that are above the 0.05 significance value should not be excluded from interpretation so quickly. Yes, higher significant values introduce a greater likelihood of the relationship being artificial or by chance; but to say you are 90 percent confident in the effect an independent variable has on a dependent variable is still important. Research is starting to report "marginally" significant variables at the 0.10 level, but 0.05 is still the most common. We suggest you use 0.05 as a common rule of thumb, but truly examine the significance values of all variables included in the analyses to determine your interpretation.

One of the most common measures of the existence of a relationship is chi-squared, symbolized by χ^2. Chi-squared is most often used with nominal level data and with ordinal level data that is partially ordered (typically less than 5 categories). In testing for the existence of a relationship, chi-squared examines the difference between the observed and expected frequencies in a distribution. Differences between the observed and expected frequencies can be the result of one of two instances. Either the difference is due to chance, or the values are so different that it cannot be said that the difference is due to chance.

To be able to get the expected frequencies for the chi-squared test, copy the pivot table from Table 7.6, move to a blank space in your Excel worksheet, select "Paste Special," and select "values" from the menu. Then delete all but the row, column, and grand total headings and the total frequency cells for the rows and columns. Now you can replace those cells with the expected frequencies. The expected frequencies are what would be expected if there was truly 0 difference between the distributions. To calculate these, select the cell for Level 1 Seriousness by White race (where the 540 frequency was). Now we will build the formula for the expected value. To do this, type =, then select the column total (9669), type *, select the row total (913), type /, select the grand total (16071), then press enter. You will need to do this for each cell, selecting the column total and row total for each column and row for that cell. When you finish, you should have a table that looks like Table 7.8.

To calculate the chi-squared, enter the CHISQ.TEST formula in Excel selecting it from the Formula Builder. Then select the cells containing the observed values (in the original data table in Table 7.6), type a comma, then select the cells containing the expected values (in the table you just constructed). When you press return, you will get the value for the chi-squared. Here, you get a somewhat strange value (1.64428E−16). To make this understandable, right click the cell, select "Format Cells," and select "number." You may also want to give it several places after the decimal so you can see the

Table 7.8 Table of Expected Values for Offense Seriousness by Race

Expected

	0	1	Total
1	549.30	363.70	913
2	255.70	169.30	425
3	1134.70	751.30	1886
4	3177.88	2104.12	5282
5	1254.43	830.57	2085
6	3297.00	2183.00	5480
Grand Total	9669	6402	16071

value beyond two decimal places. In this case, what we see is a value of 0.0000. This means that there is a difference between offense seriousness and race that is greater than the common 0.05 cutoff for statistical significance. We can therefore have some confidence that there is a statistically significant relationship between offense seriousness and race (but see below).

The most common measure of the statistical significance of interval and ratio level data is associated with the Pearson Produce Moment Correlation (Pearson's r). In Excel, there is a formula for Pearson's r (discussed in the next chapter). Unfortunately, there is no significance value associated with this procedure in Excel. But there is a workaround. You can use the Regression function in Excel to find the value of statistical significance. To do this, click on the "Tools" menu and the "Data Analysis." In the dialog box, click in the "Input Y Range" and then select the column of Offense Seriousness. Do the same for "Input X Range," selecting the Race columns.[4] Make sure to click on the labels since there is a heading row. This will also make the output clearer. Then click OK. The output will look like that in Table 7.9.

The important piece of information for examining the statistical significance in this table is in the "P=Value" for Race cell (highlighted in Table 7.9). Here, you can see the value is 0.102183. This is well above the 0.05 cutoff that is desired for statistical significance. We would, therefore, be forced to assume there is no statistically significant relationship between these two variables.

These findings and above on statistical significance brings up issues that must be addressed when conducting tests of statistical significance. First is the level of measurement. In this case, there are two categorical variables (Race is nominal and Offense Seriousness is ordinal). Typically, you want to use a statistical procedure that is appropriate for the lowest level of the data you have. In this case, it would be nominal, so chi-squared would be most appropriate. Using a statistical procedure that is not appropriate for the data will likely lead to erroneous results. That may be what is happening by using Pearson's r with this data. However, we know that chi-squared is very susceptible to large numbers. As you can see in the output in Table 7.9, there are 16,383 data points in this data set. Chi-squared tends to reach a point where it does not change at 120 data points; so having 16,383 almost assuredly means chi-squared will find significance, even if it is not truly there. In cases like this, you will likely want to use a more advanced measure of statistical significance that is appropriate for nominal/ordinal level data but is not as sensitive to large data sets.

Table 7.9 Regression Output for Offense Seriousness and Race

Regression	Statistics
Multiple R	0.012769
R Square	0.000163
Adj R Sq	0.000102
Std Error	1.417948
Observations	16383

ANOVA

	df	SS	MS	F	Sig F
Regression	1	5.371125	5.371125	2.671431	0.102183
Residual	16381	32935.29	2.010579		
Total	16382	32940.66			

	Coefficients	Std Error	T Stat	P=Value	Lower 95%	Upper 95%	Lower 95.0%	Upper 95.0%
Intercept	4.467888	0.014192	314.7957	0	4.440069	4.49570	4.440069	4.49570
Race	0.037109	0.022704	1.634451	0.102183	0.007393	0.816127	0.007393	0.081612

Strength

Each level of measurement has a measure of the strength of the relationship that is appropriate for that level. Most levels of measurement have several strength measures. Excel is limited in the ability to examine the strength of a bivariate relationship at the ordinal level. To demonstrate how to conduct categorical analyses, we will use the example of Lambda in the following paragraph. Addressing the strength of the relationship for interval/ratio level data will be addressed in the discussion of Pearson's *r* in the next chapter.

Lambda is a popular measure of the strength of an association for nominal level data. Lambda is a Proportional Reduction of Error (PRE) measure. This means that we are attempting to reduce the error beyond 50/50 chance in predicting a category of the dependent variable with information about the independent variable. For example, say you were asked to determine whether a person chosen at random was a criminal and no other information was available. In this case, you would simply have to guess because you had no other information about the person. If you were given information about the characteristics of that person, however, you could possibly improve the guess. For example, it is well supported in research that more men than women commit crimes. If you knew that person was a man or a woman, it would improve the prediction over simply guessing. That is the role of a PRE measure – improving the prediction of a dependent variable category (criminal) beyond guessing by using information from an independent variable category.

To illustrate how to calculate Lambda, we will use the pivot table from Table 7.6. To construct the Lambda, we have to calculate the various errors that would occur in predicting categories of the dependent variable (Offense Seriousness).

The first step is to calculate the overall errors that would occur in a prediction. If I knew nothing other than offense seriousness values, I would predict that a person would have an Offense Seriousness of 6 since that is the highest frequency in the Total column (5,480). If I were to predict Offense Seriousness 6, I would still be wrong 10,591 times (not good odds). To improve this prediction, I want to add information about the race of the offender. If I knew the offender was a NonWhite, I would still predict Offense Seriousness 6 since this is the highest value in the NonWhite category (2,280). I would then calculate how often I would be wrong in my prediction by summing the other categories (a total of 4,122 times). I would then do the same for White. This time, I would select the Offense Seriousness category of 4 since it has the highest frequency for White (3,409). I would then calculate the number of times I would be wrong picking White (6,260). We then need to sum the total errors that would be made with information about the race of the offender. This value is 10,382. We can then calculate the PRE measure of Lambda. To do this, use the following formula:

$$\frac{Errors\ without\ IV - Errors\ with\ IV}{Errors\ without\ IV}$$

For the data from Table 7.6, the formula would be:

$$\frac{10591-10382}{10591}$$

The resulting value would be 0.019733.[5] The value of Lambda varies from 0 to 1. In this case, then, we are only able to improve our prediction of offense seriousness by about 2 percent with information about the race of the offender. That is a very low value, and probably would not be helpful.

CONCLUSION

Conducting bivariate analyses without a statistical package can be time-consuming. But it is an important part of crime analysis. Graphs are great, but you will often have to have some support or interpretation of the graphs to have any real influence from your findings. That is where univariate and bivariate analyses come into play. If you have a graph in a report or a presentation, you may have a greater impact if you include information about the central value of the data and generally how the data are arranged (form). Even information about how spread out the data are may help in your presentation. Likewise, if you need to examine two variables, tables are often a great way to display the findings (especially if the variables are categorical). If you feel the need to add a table to your report or presentation, or to examine the relationship between two variables, then understanding if they are statistically significant and the strength of their relationship is important. Take the time to do the bivariate analyses.

QUESTIONS AND EXERCISES

1   Calculate the mode, median, and mean for Murder and Non-negligent Manslaughter in Table 7.1. Use both the calculation and the Excel method for each answer.

2   Calculate the range and standard deviation for Murder and Non-negligent Manslaughter in Table 7.1. Use both the calculation and the Excel method for each answer.

3   Find a journal article related to crime that includes both statistical significance and strength measures (it does not matter which ones). Discuss these in terms of what it means for the findings of the article.

NOTES

1   Note: You must have the Data Analysis tool pack added to Excel; so do this beforehand if you have not done so already. Also, the Data Analysis menu item is in different places in different versions of Excel (typically either Data or Tools).

2   If you wish to use Excel to calculate the standard deviation, you can use STDEVP function for the calculation; or you can take the square root of the variance by using the SQRT function.

3   There are different thresholds that are used for different statistical packages. For some packages, "acceptable" levels of skewness and kurtosis are −3 to 3. For other packages (including Excel) it is −1 to 1.

4   Note: If there are blank cells in your data, Excel will return an error in Regression. You must use a method of data imputation to replace these values as a part of your cleaning process.

5   Note: Make sure you put the Error without IV − Error with IV in internal parentheses in the formula or it will not calculate correctly.

Chapter 8

Examining multiple elements of crime and place

The purpose of this chapter is to provide you with an understanding of how multiple variables in analyses can provide useful information. With so much emphasis put on the ability of a crime analyst to map crime, statistical analyses are often overshadowed. The movement of policing to a philosophy of data-driven decisions means crime analysts need to be able to use a variety of analysis tools. Crime analysts will be expected to conduct higher level analyses as better data are collected and a deeper understanding of crime in a jurisdiction is desired. This chapter discusses the value of correlations and multiple regression. As you progress with a crime analyst's mindset, the ability to identify associations and explain how measures are related becomes important for presenting your findings through written documentation (i.e. report, research brief) or during a presentation (i.e. within law enforcement agency or community meeting).

PEARSON'S *R*

As discussed in the previous chapter, one of the most basic ways to determine if two (or more) variables are linked together is to examine whether they are statistically associated. Measures of strength of an association are mathematical ways to determining how much one variable changes with change in another variable. If two variables always change the same way and the same amount, they are perfectly associated. That almost never happens when examining social characteristics such as crime. Using statistical procedures such as correlations allows us to determine how much of an association there is between the two variables. This can be expressed as how much change in one variable is associated with change in another variable.

Examining associations between variables that are at the interval level is commonly conducted using Pearson's *r*. Pearson's *r* is a bivariate analysis method, meaning it examines the association of two variables at a time. To utilize Pearson's *r*, data have to be normally distributed and interval level (you can also use dichotomized (male/female, 0/1) measures, but this is somewhat more complicated). Pearson's *r* is capable of measuring the existence of an association, the association direction (positive or negative), and the strength of association.

As discussed in the last chapter, the existence of a relationship is the confidence you can have that the results did not happen by chance. When using Pearson's *r*, output will typically have a "Significance," "Sig," or "P Value" associated with it. This is the value of the significance calculation.

A positive association indicates that, as one variable increases, the other variable also increases. For example, say you find in your data that as the number of vacant lots increases in a neighborhood, the amount of crime in the neighborhood also increases. On the other hand, a negative association indicates that, as one measure increases, the other decreases. For example, you could find that, as the median income of a neighborhood increases, the crime rate of the neighborhood decreases. The sign of a correlation offers valuable insight but must be taken in context of the strength and significance of an association.

The strength of the association is the value from the calculation of *r*, as described below. What differentiates Pearson's *r* from other measures of association is that Pearson's *r* requires linearity. Pearson's *r* operates through the least squares line, which measures the amount of spread of the data around a line and the slope of the line. The amount of spread determines the strength of an association. If all values are on the line, there is a perfect association between the two variables. A perfect association would be interpreted as a one-unit increase in one variable will result in a one-unit increase in the other variable (see Figure 8.1). The value of a correlation will range from 0 to ±1.00, with ±1.00 being a perfect association and 0 being no association.

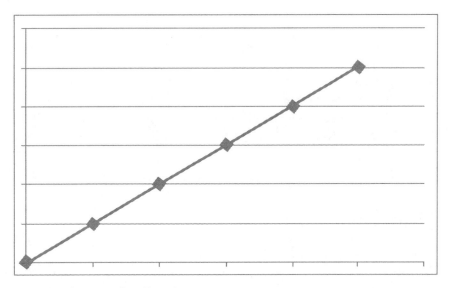

Figure 8.1 Perfect Correlation, Best-Fitting Line

Calculating Pearson's *r*

The following is the formula for calculating a Pearson's *r*:

$$r = \frac{N(\Sigma XY) - (\Sigma X)(\Sigma Y)}{\sqrt{[N(\Sigma X^2) - (\Sigma X)^2][N(\Sigma Y^2) - (\Sigma Y)^2]}}$$

Looking at the formula, you might be wary of wanting to calculate a Pearson's *r* between two variables. Yes, there are multiple mathematical operations being conducted; but if you follow the example below, you will see that it is not as bad as you might think. In the Table 8.1, you are concerned with

Table 8.1 Data for Pearson's *r* (sample data)

CGAs:	Crimes:			
X	Y	XY	X^2	Y^2
7	10	70	49	100
12	19	228	144	361
5	9	45	25	81
24	37	888	576	1369
33	49	1617	1089	2401
19	31	589	361	961
$\Sigma X = 100$	$\Sigma Y = 155$	$\Sigma XY = 3437$	$\Sigma X^2 = 2244$	$\Sigma Y^2 = 5273$

the number of crime generators and attractors (CGAs), indicated by X, and the corresponding crimes, indicated by Y, based on police district. There are six police districts that have varying numbers of CGAs and crimes that occur within the districts. As you see, you are really just taking the X and Y values and doing different things to them (multiplying X and Y together, squaring X, and squaring Y). Then, you just sum those values.

Once you have this information, it is a simple matter of putting it in the formula and calculating the Pearson's r.

$$
\begin{aligned}
r &= \frac{6(3437) - (100)(155)}{\sqrt{\left[6(2244) - (100)^2\right]\left[6(5273) - (155)^2\right]}} \\
&= \frac{20622 - 15500}{\sqrt{\left[6(2244) - (10000)\right]\left[6(5273) - (24025)\right]}} \\
&= \frac{5122}{\sqrt{\left[13464 - 10000\right]\left[31638 - 24025\right]}} \\
&= \frac{5122}{\sqrt{(3464)(7613)}} \\
&= \frac{5122}{\sqrt{26371432}} \\
&= \frac{5122}{5135} \\
&= 0.997
\end{aligned}
$$

The calculations result in a Pearson's r value of 0.997. This indicates that there is a very strong association between the two measures since the highest value of a correlation is ± 1.00. Additionally, there is a positive association between the two measures, suggesting that as the number of CGAs increase, the number of crimes increase in police districts.

Fortunately, you do not have to calculate a Pearson's r on your own; Excel does this for you. The procedures for conducting a Pearson's r in Excel are provided next.

With the data from Table 8.1 open in Excel, select an empty cell where you will want the results displayed. Under the "Formulas" tab, there is the option for "More Function." Click that, then go to the "Statistical" sub-choice and scroll down, you will see "PEARSON" (see Figure 8.2). This is the formula you are searching for to run an association test between two measures.

Now, all you need to do is to select the data (see Figure 8.3). In the formal bar, you should see =PEARSON(). You may also see "Array 1" and "Array 2." For "Array1," the prompt screen is asking you to put in the independent variable values (CGAs) and for "Array2" you select the dependent value range (crimes). To do this, highlight the cells you want to have for your dependent variable, then type a comma to let Excel know you are putting in the independent variable, then highlight the cells you want to have for your dependent variable. When you hit "OK," or press the return button, you can see the formula result showing 0.997, which is the same value that you calculated by hand.

For those of you who have taken a statistics course before, you have probably heard, "correlation does not imply causation." Just because two measures are related, does not mean that one causes the other. For example, during summer, ice cream sales peak and also homicides peak. Does this mean that increases in ice cream sales result in more homicides? No. It could be because there are more activities during summer months that take people away from their homes (i.e. concerts, sporting events, vacation) and school is not in session. Summer has hotter months so ice cream sales would be

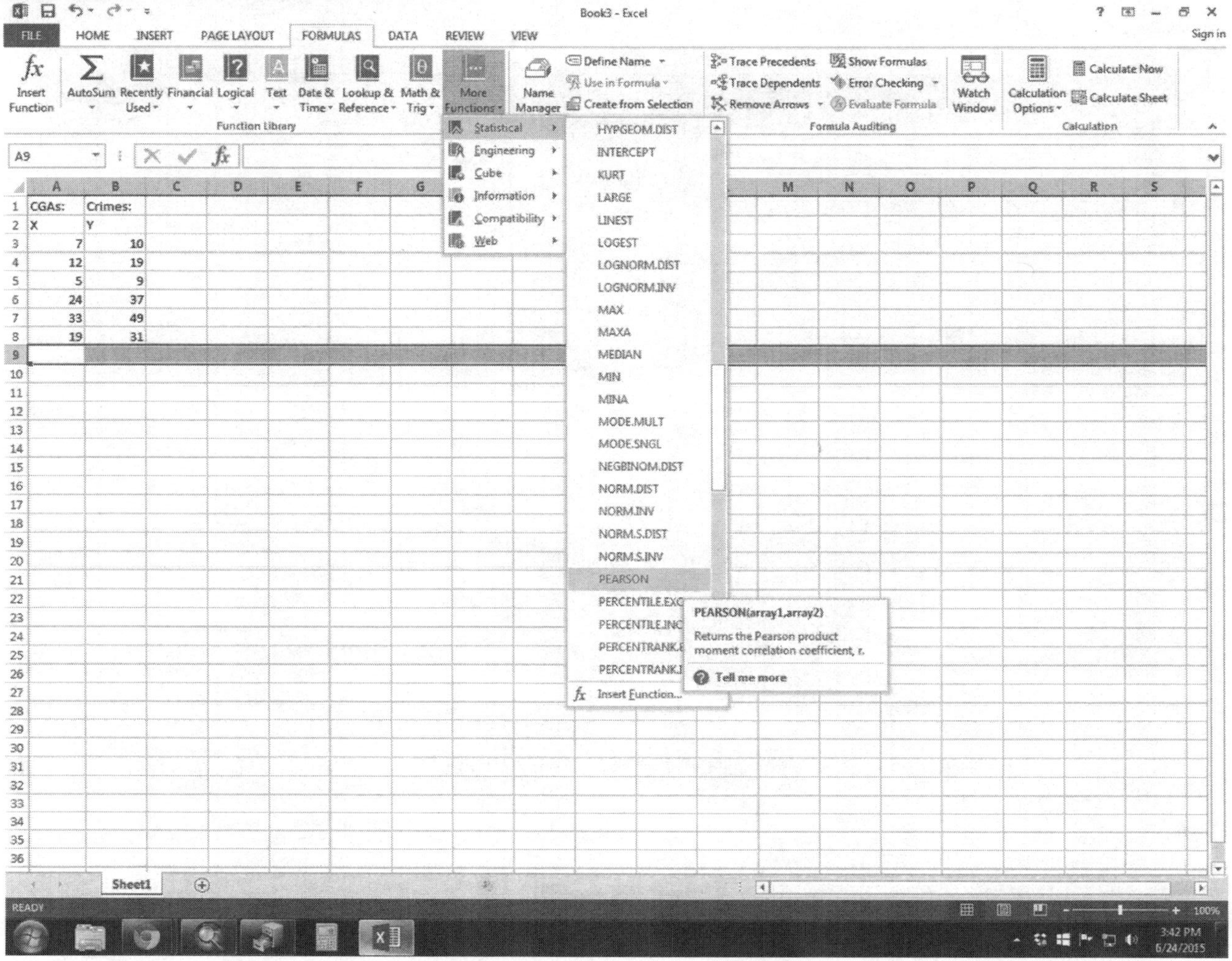

Figure 8.2 Pearson's r Function in Excel

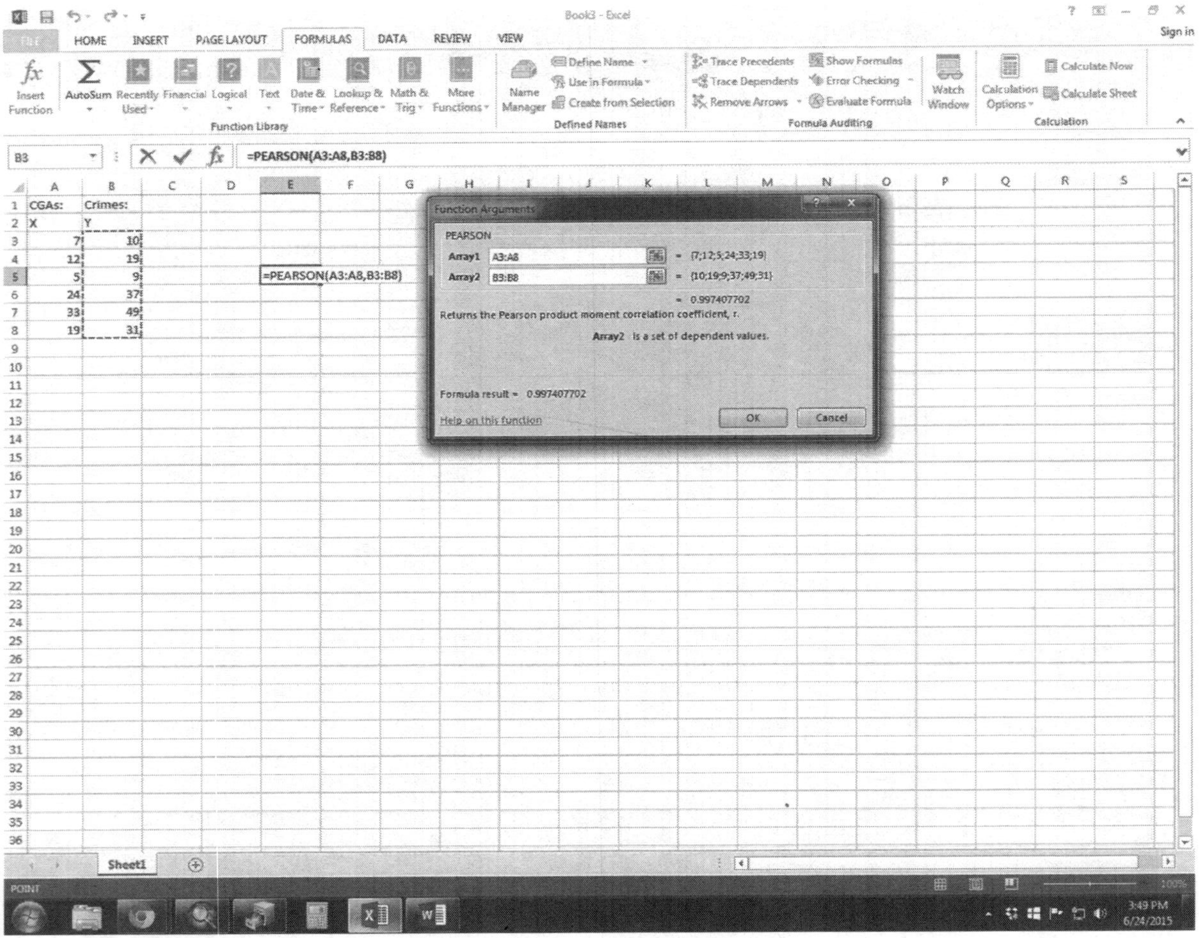

Figure 8.3 Pearson's r Prompt Screen

expected to increase versus winter when temperatures are colder. Just because ice cream sales and homicides are correlated does not mean that increased ice cream sales cause increased homicides.

If you noticed, there is only the option of inserting two measures at a time to calculate Pearson's r. But what if you have multiple independent variables that you want to determine their level of association with the dependent variable? You could calculate each association one by one. You could also use the correlation function in the "Data Analysis" package. The instructions for adding this package into your Excel program is included in Appendix C. Now let's add additional variables to the data from above. We will add the number of parolees and the number of parks per police district, both of which you believe to influence the amount of crime. This gives you three independent measures and a dependent measure. To conduct this analysis, select all of the cells for your data, then click on "Data Analysis," find "Correlation" and click OK. As you can see in the screenshot in Figure 8.4, the variable names were included in the input range for the data. Because this was done, you have to "Check" the "Labels in first row" box so Excel can take those names into account when running the analysis. Then choose the output preference you want (just highlight empty cells) and click OK.

An easy way to double-check to see if this one worked correctly is comparing the value of CGAs and crimes to the prior analysis, and both equal 0.997. When looking over the output table in Figure 8.5, you can see that parks had a negative association with every other variable included in the analysis. That is, as the number of parks increase in police districts, the number of CGAs, parolees, and crime decreases. Next, parolees had a correlation value of 0.967 with CGAs and 0.976 with crimes. This indicates that, when the number of parolees increases, the number of CGAs and crime also increases. This example shows that all the measures are strongly related to one another.

A potential issue that can be identified in a correlation matrix is multicollinearity. Within social science research, especially criminal justice, independent variables are often correlated to some degree, which is multicollinearity. When you have high values of correlation, like in the example above, there could be multicollinearity issues because, if two independent variables are highly correlated (above 0.700), they can influence significance tests and coefficient values. In this case, parolees and parks had a Pearson's r value of −0.734, so they are associated at a level that indicates they are multicollinear. Therefore, the true association between either one of them and crime or CGAs may be distorted. Issues of multicollinearity between independent measures can affect regression analyses. Imagine a wash-out effect. Two independent measures are so highly correlated that when you put both in a regression model, their individual effect is washed-out because there are two measures in the model measuring essentially the same thing. While the correlation value gives insight into multicollinearity issues, it is not enough evidence to justify it as a severe issue. Within Excel, you can test for multicollinearity but it is another add-on that costs extra (www.spiderfinancial.com/products/numxl). Depending on your use of regression in your analyses, you may want to invest in this add-on (it has more than just collinearity tests). This extension allows you to test for multicollinearity using the Variance Inflation Factor (VIF) and Condition Number. We will not go into multicollinearity methods of evaluation, but it is an issue you should consider when you find high correlation values among independent variables.

The ability to include multiple variables at once allows you to not only examine the association of independent variables with the dependent variable, but also the associations between independent variables. Analyzing multiple correlations at once, similar to Figure 8.5, is referred to as a correlation matrix. This is a valuable analytical tool when trying to determine associations between different measures.

Once you have the Pearson's r value, you can calculate the coefficient of determination (r^2). This will give you the proportion of the variation in the dependent variable that is accounted for by variation in the independent variable. For example, the Pearson's r was 0.997 between CGAs and crime. All you have to do is square the value to obtain the coefficient of determination, 0.994. You can multiply this value by 100 for a percentage value, 99.4 percent. This indicates that 99 percent of the variation in crime can be explained by variation in CGAs in police districts. This is an incredibly strong association for social science; and this was high because the data were made up for this example. Do not expect to obtain such high

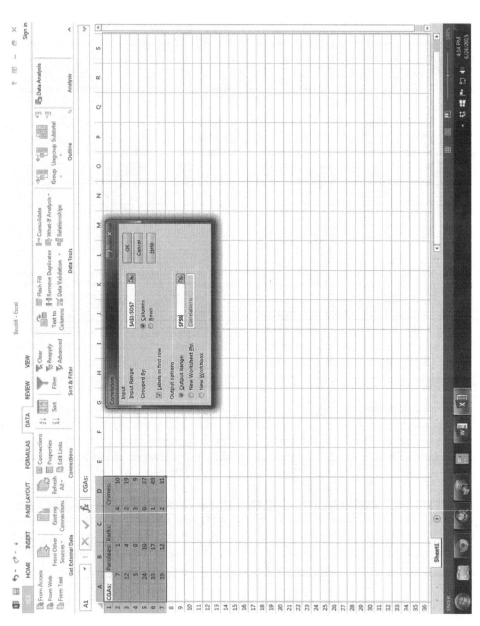

Figure 8.4 Correlation in Data Analysis for Multiple Independent Variables

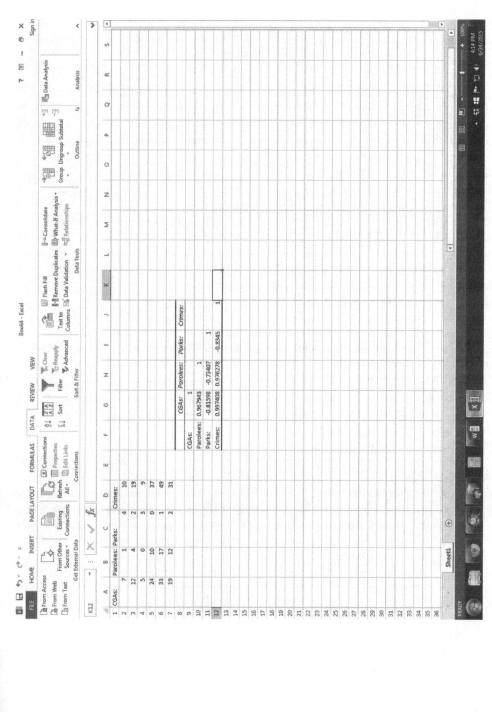

Figure 8.5 Correlation Matrix from Correlation Function in Data Analysis

values with real-world data. To further help you understand not only correlations, but higher level analyses, the next section will use real-world data since you have a basic understanding of the process.

In Excel, when conducting a correlation analysis, the p-value is not provided for the relationships, so you do not know the significance level. To obtain a significance level of the correlation between two measures, you have to run a bivariate regression in Excel (regression is further discussed below) as was shown in the last chapter. In the output of the analysis, the Multiple R is your correlation value and the ANOVA table provides the significance value of the correlation (f-statistic). For a significant correlation, you want a Significance F value lower than 0.05.

BEYOND TWO MEASURES: MULTIVARIATE ANALYSIS

Up to this point we have discussed two variables (or sets of two variables each) within crime analysis. This is known as bivariate analyses. By now, it should be evident that there is more than one measure that explains a crime phenomenon. Crime is a complex topic, requiring more than two measures to understand the multitude of influences. It makes sense that there are multiple measures that could enhance our understanding of crime. Crime analysts are tasked with identifying these measures. This does not mean to throw everything possible into statistical analyses to determine which ones may show an association. The measures included in analyses should be grounded in theory and application. That is, you should be able to discuss why you expect the measures to be related to one another while developing hypotheses of expected findings. Without taking the time to construct a conceptual design of how your measures are connected to one another, any analyses conducted lack the ability to be translated into the greater picture of understanding the crime aspect.

When analyzing several variables, multivariate analyses are utilized to take into account the combined and individual influence of the independent variables. Multivariate analyses provide analysts with the ability to identify what independent variables are associated with the dependent variable. That is, if two or more variables explain some of the variation in the dependent variable, they have at the very least, an additive effect. Each independent variable explains part of the variation in the dependent variable – its slice of the pie.

Within criminal justice research, regression analysis is one of the most popular multivariate analytical tools. While regression may not be as common in crime analysis, the movement toward more data-driven crime analysis will likely require the use of regression to understand crime in communities/jurisdictions. Regression is essentially a Pearson's r applied to multiple variables.

Similar to Pearson's r, regression utilizes the sum of squares. In regression, the sum of squares of the distance from each point to the line discussed in Figure 8.1 is the smallest possible value; minimizing the distance of all pairs of X, Y and defining the strength and direction of a relationship. Multiple regression predicts scores on the dependent variable using the aggregate predictive scores of the independent variables included in the analysis. You want the independent variables to correlate as highly as possible with the dependent variable to increase the combined predictive power (and you would like for them to have the least correlation with each other as possible to reduce multicollinearity). Imagine looking up at the stars and trying to draw a straight line that would result in the shortest overall distance from the line to each star. The stars are data values of independent variables that are being used to predict the dependent variable (reducing the variance to the smallest value).

Calculating a regression

The basic formula for a regression is one of the most recognized formulas in statistics. It is really just the formula for the slope and intercept of a straight line.

$$Y = a + bX + e$$

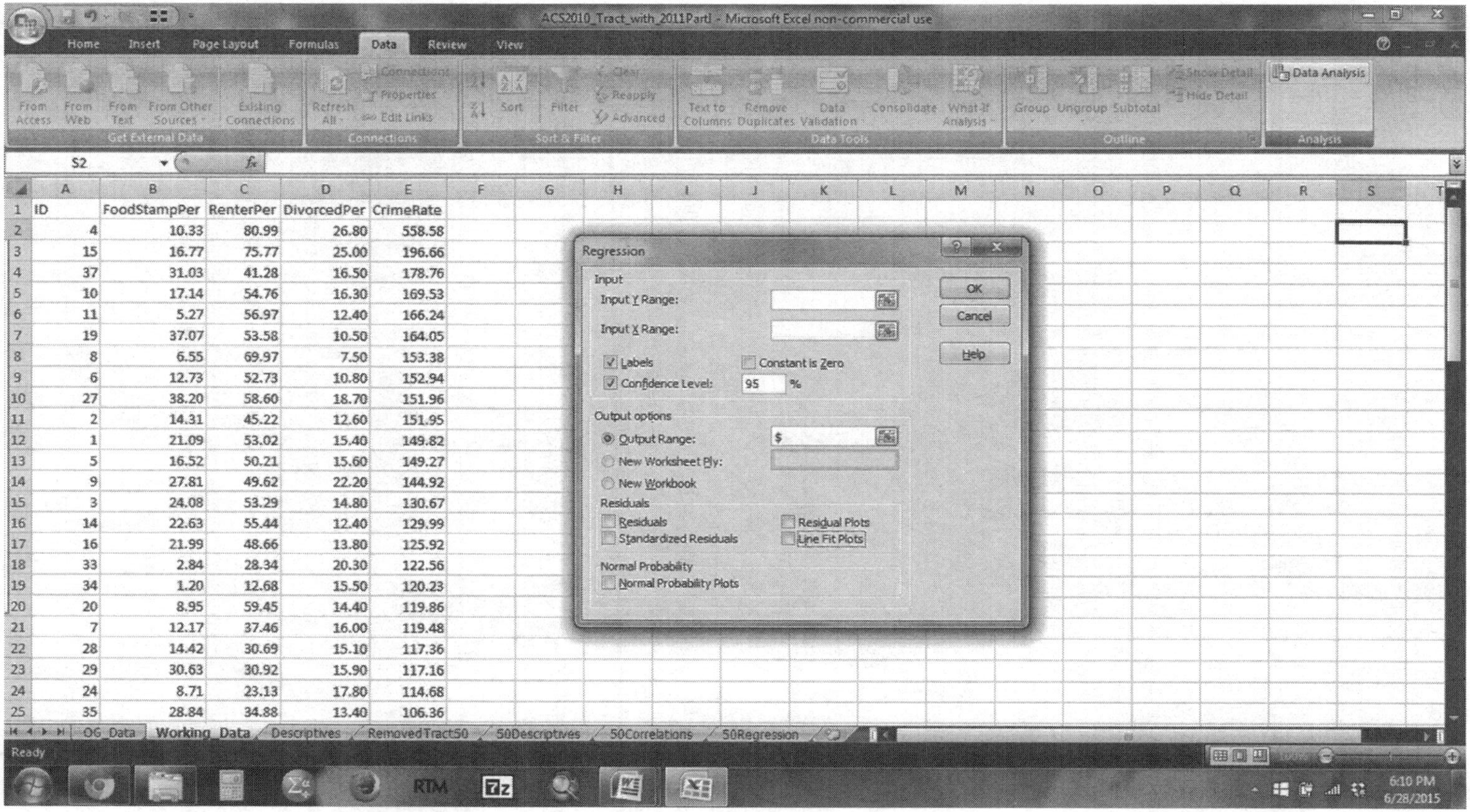

Figure 8.6 Regression Parameters in Excel

In this formula, Y is the predictive value of the independent variable, a is the intercept, b is the slope, X is the value of the independent variable being examined, and e is the error for the model.

This formula will not do a lot for actually calculating a regression model because, in this form, it is really just for two variables. The formula for additional variables is the same, but the number of times there is a bX is the number of independent variables; which complicates the formula. The formula for a model with multiple variables is below.

$$Y = a + b_1 X_1 + b_2 X_2 + b_n X_n + e$$

where each b represents a coefficient for a specific independent variable and each X represents a value of the independent variable in the multiple regression model. The e is the standard error of the model, which is essentially the total error for the whole model.

Regression can also be calculated in Excel. In the "Data Analysis" tool, you have the option of running a regression analysis (see Figure 8.6). To use regression, you would need to fill in the desired input ranges the same way you filled in the Array values in Pearson's r (by highlighting the dependent variable data for Y and the independent variables data for X). In this simple linear regression, you are predicting values of the dependent variable based on the values of one independent variable.

CRIME ANALYSIS EXAMPLE WITH REAL DATA

Now let's look at a multiple regression in Excel using crime data from Little Rock, Arkansas, at the Census tract level. The tract level and block group level are often used as proxies for neighborhoods because of the social data available at those levels. This kind of information is useful for a crime analyst because it provides social context for where crime is occurring. The Census data for this example comes from the American Community Survey (ACS), which provides neighborhood measures at the Census tract or block group level. There are a variety of measures available from these sources that provide social data to examine in relation to crime data (try downloading data at: http://factfinder. census.gov/).

In this example, we will calculate both correlations and regression, showing how the correlation matrix provides valuable insight before the multiple regression and the differences between the analytical techniques. Our dependent variable will be 2011 Part I crime rate per 1,000 residents by tracts in Little Rock ($n = 51$). Our independent variables were downloaded from the 2010, 5-year estimates ACS data. The variables drawn from these data are percent households receiving food stamps, percent of households renter occupied, and percent of population over 15 who are divorced. We are predicting 2011 neighborhood-level crime rates based on 2010 neighborhood characteristics.

Before running a multiple regression, you must first examine your data to determine normality (discussed in the Chapters 6 and 7). That is, you should start with the descriptive statistics of your variables for the analyses. The descriptive analyses provide valuable insight that you need to pay attention to before continuing to higher level statistical techniques. Remember, the unit of analysis is neighborhood, measured through a proxy of Census tract, which can be seen in the "Count" row of the descriptives output in Table 8.2. Review the descriptives table; does anything stick out that could be potential problem(s)?

As you progress through Table 8.2, there should have been a few values that stood out that require greater attention before you continue. The crime rate mean is 101.17 per 1,000 persons with a maximum value of 558.58. This high maximum value could be influencing the variable and causing the kurtosis to be above the desired value (leptokurtic). Additionally, the mean value being greater than the median value (101.17 and 85.62 respectively), indicates a positively skewed measure. These issues

Table 8.2 Descriptives Table Examining Crime Rates in Little Rock

	FoodStampPer	RenterPer	DivorcedPer	CrimeRatePer
Mean	12.13	41.19	13.71	101.17
Standard Error	1.51	2.32	0.66	11.66
Median	7.22	40.41	13.90	85.62
Mode	0.00	#N/A	12.40	#N/A
Standard Deviation	10.80	16.58	4.72	83.24
Sample Variance	116.70	274.74	22.24	6928.11
Kurtosis	−0.44	−0.30	1.09	17.69
Skewness	0.82	0.12	0.17	3.35
Range	38.20	70.86	24.30	556.13
Minimum	0.00	10.13	2.50	2.45
Maximum	38.20	80.99	26.80	558.58
Sum	618.64	2100.66	699.00	5159.46
Count	51.00	51.00	51.00	51.00
Confidence Level (95.0%)	3.04	4.66	1.33	23.41

are supported once you identify the kurtosis and skewness values (17.69 and 3.35 respectively). The kurtosis and skewness values give an indication that there are problems with this variable that may influence the higher level analyses.

A way to examine these issues is to sort the crime rate variable in descending order to see if there is a large jump in values. This will help you identify *possible* outliers before transforming the variables because you do not want to exclude cases from further analyses if it is not required. Look at the portion of the data from Excel shown in Figure 8.7. Once the crime rate variable is sorted in descending order, you can see that one neighborhood had an extremely high crime rate compared to the second highest, 558.58 and 196.66. If you look across the top row, the same neighborhood that has the highest crime rate also has the highest percent of renter occupied households. From our own knowledge, this neighborhood has an environment conducive for criminal activity. This neighborhood could warrant its own analysis based on such a high crime rate.

The last thing you want to do is exclude a case (i.e. neighborhood); but there are occasions when certain influential outliers have to be excluded. You can try to transform the crime rate to bring the measure to a normal distribution. For example, you could use the square root and/or natural log function to transform the dependent variable, crime rate. Doing that in this case would bring the skewness below 2.00; but the kurtosis value is still above 3.00, identifying a leptokurtic distribution.

What if you removed this neighborhood from your analysis? In Table 8.3, you can see that the kurtosis and skewness values are within range once the neighborhood is removed. While we will continue with the neighborhood removed from future analysis, we suggest that you run multiple analyses, determining if the removal of the neighborhood altered the findings. You can compare values along the way as you conduct further analyses.

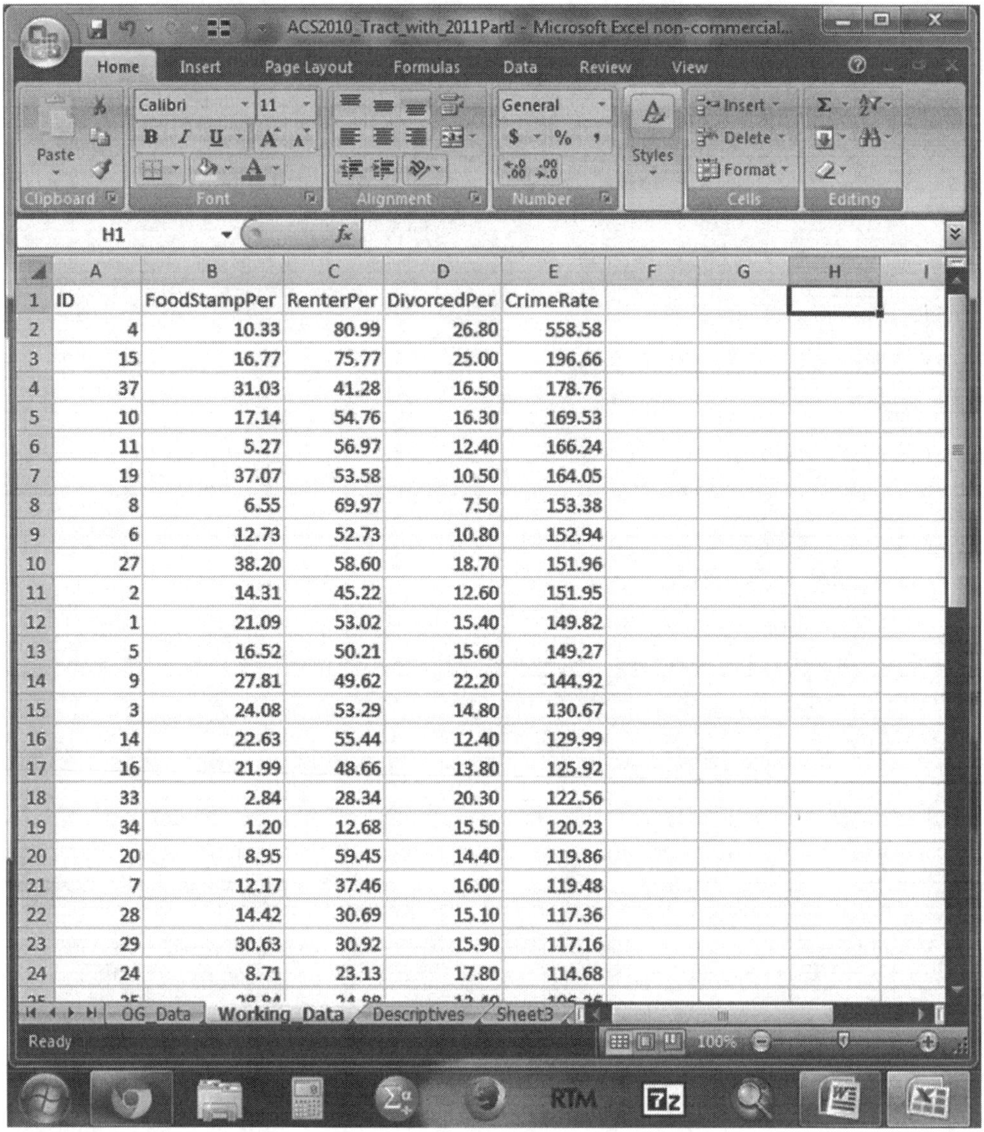

ID	FoodStampPer	RenterPer	DivorcedPer	CrimeRate
4	10.33	80.99	26.80	558.58
15	16.77	75.77	25.00	196.66
37	31.03	41.28	16.50	178.76
10	17.14	54.76	16.30	169.53
11	5.27	56.97	12.40	166.24
19	37.07	53.58	10.50	164.05
8	6.55	69.97	7.50	153.38
6	12.73	52.73	10.80	152.94
27	38.20	58.60	18.70	151.96
2	14.31	45.22	12.60	151.95
1	21.09	53.02	15.40	149.82
5	16.52	50.21	15.60	149.27
9	27.81	49.62	22.20	144.92
3	24.08	53.29	14.80	130.67
14	22.63	55.44	12.40	129.99
16	21.99	48.66	13.80	125.92
33	2.84	28.34	20.30	122.56
34	1.20	12.68	15.50	120.23
20	8.95	59.45	14.40	119.86
7	12.17	37.46	16.00	119.48
28	14.42	30.69	15.10	117.36
29	30.63	30.92	15.90	117.16
24	8.71	23.13	17.80	114.68

Figure 8.7 Crime Rate in Descending Order for Seven Neighborhoods

The next step is to examine the association between the independent variables (IVs) and the dependent variable (DV) (2011 crime rate per 1,000 persons). Table 8.4 shows that all of the measures have a positive association with one another. Examining the values on the crime rate variable in the correlation matrix, the independent variables have values around 0.500 with each of the other independent variables. This indicates that there are fairly strong associations between the independent variables and the dependent variable. The absence of high correlation values between the independent variables (ranging from 0.322 to 0.400) signifies that multicollinearity is not evident (in this analysis). The conclusion that can be drawn at this point is that, overall, as the percentage of households receiving food stamps, renter housing, and percentage of population over 15 years old who are divorced increases, the crime rate also increases.

Table 8.3 Descriptives once Outlier Removed

	FoodStampPer	RenterPer	DivorcedPer	CrimeRate1k
Mean	12.17	40.39	13.44	92.02
Standard Error	1.54	2.22	0.62	7.37
Median	7.06	39.87	13.85	84.72
Mode	0.00	#N/A	12.40	#N/A
Standard Deviation	10.91	15.73	4.37	52.10
Sample Variance	119.01	247.37	19.12	2714.13
Kurtosis	−0.50	−0.52	0.80	−1.21
Skewness	0.80	−0.04	−0.17	0.11
Range	38.20	65.65	22.50	194.21
Minimum	0.00	10.13	2.50	2.45
Maximum	38.20	75.77	25.00	196.66
Sum	608.31	2019.67	672.20	4600.88
Count	50.00	50.00	50.00	50.00
Confidence Level (95.0%)	3.10	4.47	1.24	14.81

Table 8.4 Correlation Matrix of IVs and Neighborhood Crime Rates

	FoodStampPer	RenterPer	DivorcedPer	CrimeRate
FoodStampPer	1			
RenterPer	0.375026152	1		
DivorcedPer	0.400505495	0.322718396	1	
CrimeRate	0.544944881	0.575125689	0.52002174	1

Now that you have examined the descriptives and correlations of the measures included in the research, you can conduct a regression analysis. Follow the same procedures to conduct this regression analysis as explained above in the example. To input the data, select the range of independent variables in your spreadsheet and make sure you have labels checked to indicate the first row is the variable name (i.e. label). This will include multiple variables for the multivariate analysis. Table 8.5 displays the regression output that is given in Excel.

One of the first items you examine in the output is the R square because that gives you the amount of variation explained in the model. In our regression analysis, there was a R square value of 0.521. That means that 52.1 percent of the variation in neighborhood crime rates is explained by the independent variables included in the analysis. The overall model is significant with a value of 0.000, well below the desired 0.05 value. This value is provided in the ANOVA table under the "Significance F" column. If any independent variable had a p-value over 0.05, we might exclude that variable from interpretation (other than noting it was not significant).

Table 8.5 Regression Output from Excel

Regression Statistics

Multiple R	0.722
R Square	0.521
Adjusted R Square	0.490
Standard Error	37.209
Observations	50.000

ANOVA

	df	SS	MS	F	Significance F
Regression	3.000	69306.090	23102.030	16.686	0.000
Residual	46.000	63686.414	1384.487		
Total	49.000	132992.504			

	Coefficients	Standard Error	t Stat	P-value	Lower 95%	Upper 95%
Intercept	−20.284	19.599	−1.035	0.306	−59.735	19.168
FoodStampPer	1.391	0.554	2.509	0.016	0.275	2.507
RenterPer	1.241	0.372	3.334	0.002	0.492	1.991
DivorcedPer	3.365	1.355	2.483	0.017	0.638	6.092

Next, you will most likely care about the significance value of each independent variable. Table 8.5 shows that each independent variable was a significant predictor, at the 0.05 level, of neighborhood crime rates. That is, all of the p-values in Table 8.5 were below 0.05. Because there are multiple independent variables, the significance of each would be discussed in terms of accounting for additional measures (not just a bivariate analysis of one IV and DV). When conducting multivariate regression analysis, you want to account for pertinent measures when possible. By doing so, you do not have omitted variable bias. That is, you did not exclude factors that could influence your dependent variable. As an analyst, you want to account for as many relevant factors as possible that are theoretically driven to test the best model. If not, your findings could be a result of failing to include influential measure(s).

Next, we should examine the strength of the individual variables. In the bottom part of the output, where you see Coefficient, the intercept of −20.284 is the constant value of the linear regression formula. This is where the "best-fitting" line is intercepting the Y-axis. The coefficient values for each independent variable indicate the change in X when there is a 1-unit increase in Y. For example, when the crime rate increases by 1 crime per 1,000 persons, the percent of population that is divorced increases by 3.365. Similar interpretations can be used for each independent variable. Luckily, in this example, all of the independent variables had a positive association with crime rates, evident in both the correlation matrix and coefficient values. If you have a negative coefficient value, it is interpreted as a decrease in which a 1-unit increase in Y results in coefficient value decrease in X. Further, regression analysis allows you to state this is the amount of change in the variable holding the other values constant. For example, the percentage of households receiving food stamps had a significant (p = 0.016) and positive (Coefficient = 1.391) influence on neighborhood crime rates while accounting for the level of renter occupied households and the percent of the population divorced. Multiple regression allows you to identify significant predictors while including/accounting for/controlling for other possible influencers. This is what makes multiple regression different from bivariate analyses.

We can also examine the confidence intervals of the variables. The default for confidence levels in Excel is 95 percent, which you can change. This is where the Lower and Upper 95 percent values can help you understand the values of the independent variables. For each independent variable, the range from Lower to Upper does not include 0.000 as a possible value. For example, for percent of renter occupied households, we can say that we are 95 percent confident that the actual value is between 0.492 and 1.991. If percent of renter occupied households p-value was above 0.05, 0.000 would be within the confidence interval range meaning that the actual value is not significantly different from zero.

Why are all of these numbers important and what can you do with them? Say you wanted to predict the crime rate of a neighborhood but all you had was information on the percentage of households receiving food stamps, percent of renter occupied households, and percent of population over 15 years old that are divorced. You might wonder, how am I supposed to do this? Remember the regression formula:

$$Y = a + bX + e$$

We are going to use this formula to predict the neighborhood crime rate based on the output from our regression analysis. For the sake of this analysis, the neighborhood crime rate we are trying to predict has values as follows: 22 percent food stamps, 45 percent renter occupied, and 31 percent divorced. Now we are going to take these values and put them in the regression formula where Y is the neighborhood crime rate we are trying to predict:

$$Y = -20.284 + (1.397*22) + (1.241*45) + (3.365*31) + 37.209$$
$$Y = -20.284 + 30.602 + 62.768 + 104.315 + 37.209$$
$$Y = 214.610$$

In this example, the neighborhood is predicted to have a crime rate of 214.610 per 1,000 persons. The values obtained in the multiple regression analysis allows you to predict values on the dependent variable.

CONCLUSION

In this chapter, we have discussed two main analytical tools that can be useful in crime analysis. As the push for data-driven crime analysis continues, the analytical capability of a crime analyst will continue to expand to include new techniques. Statistical tools offer a way to support your claims and better understand a crime problem. Correlations and regression might appear to be more research oriented, but to fully understand crime within a jurisdiction, multiple techniques need to be used. This allows for a variety of tests that can identify different relationships, beyond crime mapping. Crime mapping is only one piece of the puzzle. The ability to merge the two into crime analysis offers valuable insight. Correlations allow you to identify the association of two measures and the direction of the relationship. The test indicates how related two measures are; and is an important analysis before conducting multiple regression. Multiple regression extends from linear regression, which examines the prediction of a dependent variable based on one independent variable. In multiple regression, we want to predict values on the dependent variable based on multiple independent variables. By doing so, we can increase the amount of variance explained in the dependent variable when accounting for multiple influencers. Overall, correlation matrices offer insights into relationships found in multiple regression analyses; and, multiple regression analyses identify significant predictors on the dependent variable while accounting for multiple independent variables.

QUESTIONS AND EXERCISES

1   Find three articles that address issues of crime analysis and use regression analyses (hint: look at some of the articles cited in Chapter 3 or do searches for journal articles on crime analysis or environmental criminology). Discuss the data and the analyses. Look for potential problems from the data or the results. Discuss whether you think the authors drew the proper conclusions.
2   Find a data set that contains variables that would be of interest to crime analysts. A good place to start is www.icpsr.umich.edu. See if you can use Excel to conduct a regression analysis of the variables.

Making inferences from one place to another

This chapter focuses on introducing two topics, inferential analysis and hypothesis testing, which are not as often employed by crime analysts. This is not to say that these topics are not important, however. We discuss these topics to provide an overview of key concepts. We will not do calculations of these concepts; but provide the principles to expand your statistical knowledge and assist in advancing crime analysis techniques by providing a foundational understanding. If you are interested in calculating some of these concepts or using inferential analyses, you can find them in any introductory statistics textbook.

MAKING INFERENCES

In previous chapters of the book, you read about data sources and how to examine data. In essence, you have learned how to describe data, either about people or places. You are also able to describe general characteristics related to a data set. Crime analysts typically have access to jurisdiction-wide data, providing a population jurisdictional data set. What if data across a jurisdiction do not exist but you have a sample? Say, for example, you only have good data on 20 of the 99 neighborhoods in the city. Can you draw conclusions about the whole city from a sample of data? In this chapter, we will discuss concepts and assumptions pertaining to inferential analyses.

Inferential analyses are used because collecting data for an entire population is often unfeasible (because of time and/or cost). Imagine a police department that wants to conduct a survey of residents' perceptions of officers. Surveying every resident would be a difficult and expensive task for any agency. This could be hundreds to thousands, to even millions of residents who would be surveyed about their perceptions. With police budgets usually restricted, trying to survey all residents would be almost impossible. This is an instance when a sample of residents across the jurisdiction would be easier to obtain than surveying every resident (population).

To put it in a noncriminal-justice related analogy, imagine the percentage of alcohol in a beer that is printed on the side of the can. A brand that has 4.2 percent alcohol by volume (ABV) in a 12 oz can means that 4.2 percent of the (liquid) weight is alcohol. To test every can for the correct ABV would take a considerable amount of time and increase the costs for the company. A way to test the ABV would be to take a random sample of beer cans and infer the results of those tests to all cans of that type. This method is known as inferential analysis, where a smaller sample is examined and results generalized to the population.

Keep in mind when conducting these kinds of analyses that information gained from your sample is only applicable to the population the sample was drawn from. For example, you would not want to take a sample of the perceptions of the police and only sample people who own houses costing more than $500,000. You could not, in that case, make inference to the population of the city because you only really sampled one population (rich homeowners). You must be cognizant of your sample when making conclusions about the population. You do not want to make assumptions about a population you did not examine.

With this mindset, inferential analyses are capable of identifying whether sample characteristics vary from population characteristics (or whether two samples differ in their characteristics) with knowledge of the probability of error. The analyses indicate whether the differences between the sample and population are large enough to draw a conclusion that the sample differs on a characteristic of the larger population (or the other sample). This can be critical when doing an evaluation of a police effort. For example, you make a change in patrol tactics in one neighborhood of the city and also monitor crime in a different neighborhood that has the same characteristics but where you do not change police tactics. You can then compare the changes that occur in the two neighborhoods to determine if the new tactics are effective.

CONCEPTS

The terminology utilized by inferential analysis is not substantially different from terms you are already familiar with in descriptive statistics.

Population: the entire study group. The size of a population can vary from crimes occurring on one street (small) to crimes occurring across the entire jurisdiction (larger) to all crimes in the world (largest).

Sample: a subset of a population. A sample is used for inferential analyses. The point of inferential analysis is to determine whether a sample can be interpreted as belonging to the population or another sample or if the sample differs from the population or other sample.

Parameter: a characteristic of the population. For example, the average age of residents in a jurisdiction.

Statistic: a characteristic of the sample. This is what crime analysts can use to draw inferences to the population parameter. For example, the average age of residents in one neighborhood in a jurisdiction as a representation of the average age in the jurisdiction.

Inference: analyzing the sample to make conclusions about the population. Basically, inferring the findings from the sample to the population.

Estimate: a finding from sample analyses as an indicator of the population parameter. It would be expected that a sample from a population is an accurate estimate of the population. For example, the average age of a neighborhood is likely not the exact average of the jurisdiction average age; but it should be a fairly close estimate if the rules of inferential analysis are followed.

Expected value: the estimated population parameter. Usually, the expected value will be the mean of the population. The expected value only implies that, on average, the value will be an accurate estimate of the parameter.

Standard error: measure of variation of a statistic around the parameter it is estimating. The standard error can be interpreted similarly to the standard deviation in that the standard error measures the variability of sample means around the population mean. The standard error is influenced by the sample size. As a sample size increases, the standard error decreases. A smaller standard error is desired.

ASSUMPTIONS

As with all statistical analyses, there are certain assumptions of inferential analysis that must be met before the results can be considered valid. The most basic of these assumptions are addressed in this section.

The first assumption, and foundation of inferential analysis, is the sample must be extracted from the same population from which inferences are to be made (or both samples you are drawing are from the same population). This is not always easy. For example, say you want to make inferences to high school students about bullying. To save time and money, you survey your introduction class in college. Are college freshmen in the same population as high school students? Some argue yes; they are not far from the same age. But even this argument has problems. Yes, they are close in age to high school seniors, but what about high school freshmen? A lot happens between 14 and 18 that could substantially influence the findings. When drawing your samples, you need to carefully examine what you consider your population and make sure it is the population you are truly examining.

The second assumption, which you should be familiar with from other statistical procedures, is that the sample and population data must be normally distributed. This matters because inferential analyses have assumptions that require normality. If data are not normally distributed, you can still have some assurance through the principles of the normal curve and central limit theorem (see below) that your conclusions can be supported.

The final assumption requires that the sample data are randomly drawn. In any sample of data, we expect there to be error. Error refers to the sample statistic not being a true measure of the population parameter. What you want to have, though, is random error, not systematic error. Systematic error means something is wrong with the data (bad sampling plan, data not input correctly, etc.), while random error is a product of random sampling (see below). This means that some error will be above the mean and some error will be below the mean, cancelling each other out.

These three assumptions must be taken into consideration when utilizing inferential analyses. The assumptions are examined in the four following components: normal curve, probability, sampling distributions, and the central limit theorem.

NORMAL CURVE

A normal curve should sound familiar as the concept was discussed in Chapter 7 and is expanded on here for inferential analysis. With a normal curve, the mean value is 0 with standard deviations of 1. By knowing these values, Z scores from a sample can be used as standard deviations from the mean to determine where the scores fall in a normal distribution. Remember that, in a normal curve, 95 percent of the values of the distribution fall within ±1.96 standard deviations from the mean (or a Z score of 1.96); and 99 percent of the values of the distribution fall within ±2.58 standard deviations from the mean (or a Z score of 2.58). This is key in determining the results of your analyses.

The formula for a Z score is:

$$Z = \frac{\bar{X} - \mu}{\sigma}$$

where $\bar{X}$ represents the sample mean, μ is the population mean, and σ is the population standard deviation.

In statistical analysis, a normal curve is important because, while samples are expected to be close approximations of the population, they are not exact. Populations are (theoretically) always normally distributed; but samples are not always normally distributed. Because of the principles of the normal curve, we can work with samples with the assumption that they approximate the normal curve. That allows us to use all of the principles of the normal curve and central limit theorem in conducting our analyses to establish the probability of a sample characteristic being a true estimate of the population characteristic (parameter). This allows inferences to be made about the population based on the sample data. Understanding the importance of a normal curve in estimating the expected value is addressed below in the discussion on probability.

PROBABILITY

The concept of probability is a common statistical maxim; but it is also used in everyday life. For example, what is the probability of your star coming back from injury in week 8 in your fantasy football season; or, what is the probability of pumpkin-spiced lattes being available in May? The bottom line of much of a crime analyst's job is usually focused on the probability of a person committing crime.

Although possible, this probability is not about a specific person committing a crime or crimes; it is more about the probability of crime occurring at a specific location or in a small geographical area. This is where inferential analysis and probability come into play.

Probability is the likelihood of an event occurring or the number of times an event *may* occur relative to the total number of times an event *can* occur. The range of probability values are from 0 to 1; and results are interpreted as a percentage. A probability value of 0 signifies an event occurring is not possible; and a probability value of 1 indicates that an event will absolutely occur. For most all things, probabilities are somewhere in between. The ability for a crime analyst to use the data available to provide the agency with the probability of crime occurring at a certain location provides valuable insight that can be used for crime prevention, deployment of resources, etc.

In inferential analyses, probability refers to the probability of being right or wrong on a decision to reject or fail to reject a null hypothesis. Most analyses rely on a rule of a 0.05 significant cutoff – the same 0.05 used in Chapter 7 when talking about significant associations. That is, we would be able to say we are 95 percent confident in rejecting the null hypothesis that there is no relationship.

As with other elements of inferential analyses, probability relies on the assumption of random error. Random error, in turn, relies on the way samples are collected. As stated above, a purely random sample (often called a probability sample) is preferred. Random samples are not always possible, however. The next section addresses types of samples and their advantages and disadvantages for inferential analyses.

SAMPLING

The purpose of research, including crime analysis, is to make conclusions and generalizations. Since it is difficult to obtain data on the population as a whole, a sample is often used to make inferences back to the population. The key part to using smaller samples is making certain the samples are representative of the population.

There are some concepts and terminology that are important in sampling as a methodology for research/crime analysis. Knowing these terms will aid in understanding how sampling will influence the quality of any crime analysis.

The overall population is called a parent population. This is the theoretical group from which samples are drawn. The target population is the actual group from which findings are to be generalized. Finally, the study population is the group from which the actual sample is drawn. The difference between these groups is important for crime analysts to understand. For a particular city, the parent population is likely all criminals in the city (which you cannot really get because we do not even know who all of the criminals are). The target population could be all burglars in the city (which is also unknown). The study population may be all burglars arrested in one year within the city. You might ask, why would all burglars in the city be the target population and not the parent population? The reason is that criminals do not always only commit one crime in their lives. A person may mostly deal drugs, but may burglarize a house or store at some point. As a result, this person is a part of the target population of burglars (or potential burglars), which is a part of the parent population of criminals. Taking this a step further, your study population above was drawn from one year of crime data. What if the drug dealer in this example did not commit a burglary this year but did last year and will next year? She is still a part of the theoretical burglar target population, but would not show up in the study population.

Within the study population, there are smaller elements of the sample. The sampling frame is the sampling units in the study population. This is typically the data set that you will be working from. There are two purposes this sampling frame can perform. One is that the sampling frame (the data in the data set) is used as a sample within itself to make inferences to the population. For example, if you have one year of data (or 5, 10, or even 20 years) on burglars, you are making inferences to essentially all years of burglary activity. This is the most common type of crime analysis. This sampling frame can also represent the actual study population and you can draw a sample or samples from the sampling frame. For example, you may not want all data for the city for your analyses, so you may take a further sample of the sampling frame that includes certain neighborhoods you are interested in. When doing GIS work, this would probably be rare since it is fairly easy to examine the whole data set. If you were doing something more complicated, like examining the effects of deploying community policing teams to certain neighborhoods, you may want to "take a sample of your sample." Within the sampling frame are sampling units. When you are using all of the data set for analysis, the sampling units are the same as the sampling frame. If you are taking subsamples, then the sampling units are subsets of the sampling frame. For example, if you are studying neighborhoods within the city, your sampling unit would be neighborhoods within the city. Finally, an element is what information is collected on. In this example, the unit would be a particular burglary arrest (or a particular burglar, depending on what you are studying).

When drawing samples, there are two general types of sampling techniques: probability and nonprobability samples. A concept that is a central part of these two types of sampling types is sampling error. Sampling error is how much a sample statistic is different from a population parameter; for example, how different the average number of burglars for a particular year is from the actual population of all years of burglary. Often this value is unknown. For probability samples, it is not considered a big deal because of the assumption of a random sample and therefore random error; but it is a bigger issue for nonprobability samples. The two general types are discussed here.

Probability sampling

The best method of sampling is known as probability sampling. This is where every element in the sampling frame has the exact same probability of being selected. This is very difficult to accomplish though. We typically do not know the actual population. For example, we only know the burglars who have been brought to the attention of the criminal justice system. There is no real way to know exactly how many burglars there are, so we cannot establish the baseline for probability. When it is possible to account for all elements in the population, or at least a supportable estimate of the number in the population, a probability sampling technique should be utilized. There are four types of probability samples that are discussed in the following.

Simple random sampling

The ideal type of sampling is known as simple random sampling (SRS). In this type of sampling technique, every element in the population has an equal probability of being chosen for a sample. To conduct a SRS, you need a complete list of the population, then use a random number generator or use random sampling software to draw elements at random. SRS is an ideal method because we can assume the sampling error is random, so the sample can be assumed to be an unbiased representation of the population, and generalizations can be made to the population with greater confidence. As stated above, however, SRS samples are difficult to achieve because you must construct a complete list of a population (and a list of all people arrested for a particular crime in the last year or ten years is not a complete list). It should also be noted that SRS only allows for the assumption of representative sampling, not necessarily a guaranteed representative sample. Often, researchers will assume the sample is completely randomly drawn even when there is no way to know if it was or not.

Systematic sampling

Another form of random sampling is systematic sampling. This type of sampling selects out elements in intervals once the sampling frame is listed. For example, if you wanted to survey 10 houses on a street that had 80 homes total. To obtain a systematic sample, the following formula can be used to determine your sample:

$$k = \frac{N}{n}$$

where N is the population size, *n* is the desired sample size, and *k* is the sampling interval. In the example above, *k* =80/10, or 8. This means that every eighth house would be surveyed. Now that you know the sampling interval, where would you start? A house between 1 and 8 would have to be randomly selected so your intervals could be defined. Say the random starting point was 3, then the houses you would survey would be 3, 11, 19, 27, 35, and so on.

Because you are skipping cases based on your interval when using systematic sampling, you should be careful that the interval does not create a pattern in the population. Extending from the prior example, do you see an issue if the interval selected and the random start point resulted in only corner houses being surveyed? Would this be representative of the street? No. These are questions you have to consider when trying to obtain a random probability sampling frame.

Stratified sampling

Stratified sampling is a type of probability sampling technique that separates the population into sub-populations, which are then randomly sampled. This is completed to ensure that desired population characteristics are represented in the sample, particularly when they may be small in number relative to other categories of the same element. After the subpopulations are determined, random or systematic sampling should be used to assure a probability sample. An example of stratified sampling can be demonstrated from police officers. Say there are not enough female officers in the department to conduct a random sample where enough females are selected at random. A way to account for this is to create two subpopulations, female and male, then randomly select a sample for each subpopulation.

Cluster or multistage sampling

Cluster and multistage sampling are two types of sampling techniques that are often utilized together. Cluster sampling divides the population into natural, homogenous groups (clusters), often based on a geographic representation. This type of sampling helps reduce the costs associated with conducting large surveys. From the clusters, a simple random sample of groups is determined. Multistage sampling is an extension of cluster sampling where, once the clusters are determined, the clusters are then subdivided. The subdividing can occur a number of times before a final sample is selected for analyses. For example, if you could not (or did not want to) gather data on the whole city, you could divide the city into quadrants. Within each of these quadrants, you could randomly select neighborhoods (and you could stratify the neighborhoods so you are getting both high crime and low crime neighborhoods). Then, within the neighborhoods, you could select blocks to gather the data from. You should be aware, however, that by further subdividing of units, the chance for sampling error increases, resulting in a less accurate technique than SRS or stratified sampling.

Nonprobability sampling

Ideally, you want to be able to use a probability sampling technique for your analyses, but it is often not possible. The alternative is to use nonprobability sampling techniques. Just remember, when using nonprobability samples, there is no way to know if the sample statistic is representative of the population parameter. Additionally, you do not know the probability of an element being drawn. These issues limit the generalizability of findings, but the sampling techniques can still provide valuable insight into criminal justice topics. There are four types of nonprobability sampling techniques, discussed here.

Purposive sampling

Purposive sampling is a selective or subjective sampling technique in which sampling units are chosen based on researcher knowledge that the sample is representative of the population. For example, if you wanted to examine victim perceptions of how officers handled 911 calls for violent crimes, you might select victims of aggravated assault, because they should be representative of victims of violent crime.

Quota sampling

In quota sampling, the sample is selected to be proportional to the population. This sampling technique is a nonprobability, stratified sample attempting to resemble the population. A common quota sampling method is the proportion of each race in a sample being reflective of the population. For example, say the population of your jurisdiction is 40 percent White, 30 percent Black, 15 percent Hispanic, and 5 percent Asian. If you want to make sure you get a good representation of all race/ethnicities, you might select a certain number from each group that represents their percentage in the population (thereby "oversampling" some groups with lower numbers in the city).

Snowball sampling

Snowball sampling is a nonprobability sampling technique utilized when it is difficult to identify or find subjects. This approach is more common in qualitative research. Snowball sampling operates through identifying or recruiting subjects through another subject. For instance, if you are interested in understanding criminals who sell illegal drugs on the Internet. This population would be difficult to locate on your own, but identifying one subject could lead you to several more, creating a snowball effect.

Convenience sampling

The last type of nonprobability sampling is known as convenience sampling. A convenience sample is just that, a sample of subjects based on the availability and accessibility to the researcher. It is common for academics to sample their classes or university. This makes the process easier, less time-consuming, and less expensive. On the other hand, the ability to generalize the results of a convenience sample is difficult beyond that small sampling group.

CENTRAL LIMIT THEOREM

The final characteristic critical to inferential analysis is the central limit theorem. The central limit theorem states that, with any population, the distribution of the sampling distribution of the means approaches a normal distribution as the sample size increases. A sampling distribution of the means is a statistical procedure where you take many samples and calculate the mean of the sample. If you take the mean of those means, it should approximate the true mean of the population even if the population is not normal. Even if you just take one sample, as the sample size increases, it becomes more representative of the population. Because of this principle, we can assume that a statistic from a sample drawn from a population is an approximation of the true population parameter, if the sample size is large enough and a probability sample was drawn. This is what makes inferences work.

In research, there is no set sample size that is required for the concept of the central limit theorem to be applied, but a minimum sample size of 30 is a common rule. Working with the principle of larger sample sizes having more "power" to approximate the population parameter, a sample size of 120 or more is typically preferred. In the end, it is up to you as a researcher/crime analyst to decide on a minimum acceptable sample size. It is important to conduct diagnostics on the distributions to determine potential issues that you may have to overcome.

CONFIDENCE INTERVALS

How confident are you in passing this class? When you answer this question, there is a level of uncertainty. In any type of statistical analysis, there is a level of uncertainty. At this point, you have seen a statement about being 95 percent confident. In inferential analysis, there is a similar approach of how confident you are that a sample statistic is a true approximation of a population parameter.

Confidence intervals in inferential analyses produce a range of values that reflects where the true population parameter value likely falls. Since there is sampling error when drawing your sample, confidence intervals overcome this by providing a range of values. A common way of interpreting confidence intervals is, there is a 95 percent ($p < 0.05$) chance that the population mean is between these two values (the confidence intervals). You see this most easily in election projections. If you pay attention, you will see under the graphics on TV where there is a projection of who the winner will be, a foot note that looks like ±3. This is the confidence interval (the real results should be within ±3 of what is in the graphic). Remember, you are trying to make inferences from your sample to the larger population. You will not be able to say you are 100 percent confident this is the exact value because you do not know the population, so you have to speak of the uncertainty, or degree of certainty, you have through confidence intervals.

There are two confidence intervals that are most common in research. The most common is 95 percent confidence. This relates in hypothesis testing to a significance value (p) of 0.05. The other common confidence interval is 99 percent, which relates to a p value of 0.01. Why would anyone want to only be 95 percent confident when you can be 99 percent confident? It has to do with the sample size and confidence interval. If you want to be 99 percent confident, the confidence intervals would be wider, allowing for a greater range of values to estimate the population parameter. Also, smaller sample sizes will produce a wider range of values to account for the larger standard error. So, if you want a confidence interval that is fairly close in number (say + or − 3 percent), you would have to have a reasonably large sample size or use 95 percent confidence intervals. If you want 99 percent confidence, you would need an even larger sample size.

HYPOTHESIS TESTING

As we have discussed, inferential analyses may be utilized to examine a characteristic of a sample, drawn from a population, and infer the findings to the population. This is usually accomplished by comparing groups, so you should have a good understanding of the groups. By having an idea of the groups, you can formulate a hypothesis based on what you think the expected relationship would be between the groups. In inferential analysis, there are two ways to do this. The first way is to compare a sample to the population. The second way is to compare two groups and make inference as to whether they come from the same population.

Many news media outlets today are discussing police use of force. Let's say you, as an analyst, are tasked to see if you can identify differences between officers who use force from officers who do not use force. Can you think of possible reasons why some officers are more likely to use force than other officers? What about:

education level
personality traits
training completed
patrol assignment
shift assignment.

There are many possible reasons, but it is part of your duty as an analyst to make logical connections. Formulating a sound statement of an expected relationship, or a hypothesis, then testing that idea is known as hypothesis testing. For example, say you hypothesized that officers who are assigned to patrol known gang territories use more force than officers who do not patrol similar areas. This hypothesis is capable of being tested and either supported or rejected. You can also make inferences from two separate samples; in this case, officers patrolling high gang areas and those patrolling low gang areas. Before you can begin hypothesis testing, you have to carefully develop research and null hypotheses.

Null and research hypotheses

Null and research hypotheses are two concepts that are a crossover point between statistical analysis and research methods. Null and research hypotheses should be developed as a part of setting up your research project (and all crime analyses are research projects). Research hypotheses usually state the goals or purposes of the research. Null hypotheses examine research hypotheses in a way that can be statistically validated or rejected. Null hypotheses are used in analysis because research hypotheses are hard (impossible) to prove. For example, it would be impossible to "prove" (even statistically with acknowledged error) that the burglars in your town are the same as burglars in a nearby town on some characteristic. However, what you might be able to do through statistical analysis is to state with some degree of confidence that the mean of a characteristic of burglars in your town is sufficiently different from those in the nearby town that they may not be from the same population.

An example of a research hypothesis could be:

Police officers who have more education are less likely to use force compared to those officers who have less education.

As we have discussed, it would be difficult to prove this research hypothesis because we do not know about all officers; therefore, we cannot know the population parameter. The null hypothesis is used to overcome this issue. It allows us to set up the research that there is no statistically significant difference. We can statistically support or not support that statement. The null hypothesis that might go with the research hypothesis above would be:

There is no statistically significant difference in the use of force between police officers with higher education and those with lower levels of education.

Types of hypothesis tests

Hypothesis testing is testing of the null hypothesis of no statistically significant relationship (the null hypothesis). There are a number of tests to examine the null hypothesis in inferential analyses. Which test you use depends on the data (level of measurement, assumption of normality, sample size). There are two broad categories of hypothesis tests: parametric and nonparametric tests. A parametric test assumes that the population is normally distributed while a nonparametric test assumes non-normality. We will discuss three tests often utilized in hypothesis testing.

Z test

A Z test is the most common statistical test used in inferential analysis. It is a parametric test. A Z test can be conducted to compare two large samples or a large sample to a population. A Z test is utilized when sample sizes are at least 120. The Z test has requirements that must be met before running the analyses, which are:

1   Sample size at least 120
2   Population must be normally distributed
3   Interval level dependent variable
4   Variances of two samples should be equal
5   Means of two samples are equal

The goal of hypothesis testing is often to violate the last requirement (the means of two samples are equal). If the means are equal, then there are no significant differences between the samples, so finding that there are different mean values allows for rejecting of the null hypothesis. The formula to calculate a Z test is:

$$Z = \frac{\bar{X} - \mu}{\sigma / \sqrt{N}}$$

In the numerator, $\bar{X}$ is the mean of the sample and μ is the population mean. In the denominator σ is the population standard deviation, which is divided by the square root of the N of the population. The results provide you with a Z score you can compare to the standard deviations of a normal curve. As discussed above, 95 percent of the values of a normal curve are between ± 1.96 standard deviations of the mean, and 99 percent of the values are between ± 2.58 standard deviations of the mean. Once you calculate the Z score, you can compare your obtained value to these critical values to determine with what confidence you can reject the null hypothesis or fail to reject. If your values fall between 0 and ± 1.96 or ± 2.58, then you would assume the two samples come from the same population or the sample is a representation of the population. If the values are outside ± 1.96 or ± 2.58, you would assume they did not come from the same population (which is what you want).

t-test

A t-test is used when there are smaller samples (n < 120). The null hypothesis would expect there to be no statistically significant difference between two samples or a sample and the population. The t-test analysis determines whether there is a significant difference in mean values. There are assumptions associated with conducting a t-test, which are:

1   Data are interval level
2   Normal distribution, even though the actual shape of the t-distribution is not exactly normal (even more so with smaller sample sizes)

3   Probability sample
4   Observations are independent

The formula for calculating the obtained value for a one-sample t-test is:

$$t = \frac{\bar{X} - \mu}{s/\sqrt{N-1}}$$

where the sample mean is subtracted from the population mean. The s represents the sample standard deviation. The denominator includes $N - 1$ to make it more difficult to reject the null hypothesis. The smaller the sample size, the more biased estimates there are from the sample to the population. By subtracting 1 from the sample, it increases the critical value. The obtained value from a t-test is compared to the critical value found in most statistics textbooks. If the obtained value is greater than the critical value, you have significantly different samples. You, as a researcher, can decide if you want to use a 0.05 or 0.01 level of confidence. In other words, whether you are 95 percent or 99 percent confident in rejecting or failing to reject the null hypothesis.

The two-sample t-test formula differs from a sample and population one-sample test, and is shown here:

$$t = \frac{\bar{X}_1 - \bar{X}_2}{\sqrt{s_1^2 (N_1 - 1) + s_2^2 (N_2 - 1)}}$$

Another way of thinking about the two-sample t-test formula is the numerator is the between samples mean difference and the denominator is the variability of the samples. The key part about the t-test is it is used for small sample sizes to determine if the obtained value is greater than the critical value.

Chi-square test of independence

A chi-square test differentiates from a t-test and Z test in that it does not assume a normal distribution of the population (which makes it a nonparametric test). Chi-square is used when the variables in the sample are nominal or ordinal level. A probability sampling method should be employed for a chi-square test; but it can work with limitations when using a nonprobability sample. In this test, you compare the observed values to the expected values to determine if you can reject or fail to reject the null hypothesis (just as you did in Chapter 7). The null hypothesis in a chi-square test is that the variables are not independent. This distinguishes chi-square from the prior hypothesis tests.

Chi-square is designed to examine small sample sizes (n < 30) or instances when you know the population is not normal. Since you can compare two measures in a chi-square test, there is only 1 degree of freedom, and the chi-square value would be a Z score squared. If you divide the chi-square value in half, if it is beyond the ± 1.96, you can reject the null hypothesis (only when the *df* = 1). As the number of degrees of freedom increases, the distribution becomes closer to a normal curve.

TYPE I AND TYPE II ERRORS

Hypothesis testing can result in one of two outcomes: accept or reject the null hypothesis. When testing hypotheses, we speak in terms of confidence, meaning that there is the possibility to be wrong. Think about it: if we have a 95 percent chance of being right, we still have a 5 percent chance of being wrong. Because of this, there are two types of error when making a decision about whether to accept or reject the null hypothesis: Type I and Type II. Type I error refers to when the researcher

Table 9.1 Hypothesis Testing Outcomes: Type I and Type II Errors

Decision	True Population	
	Hypothesis is true	Hypothesis is false
Reject Hypothesis	Wrong Decision, Type I Error (probability = α)	Correct Decision (probability = $1 - \beta$)
Fail to Reject Hypothesis	Correct Decision (probability = $1 - \alpha$)	Wrong Decision, Type II Error (probability = β)

rejects the null hypothesis when it is true. Type II error occurs when a researcher accepts the null hypothesis when it is false. Table 9.1 shows the four potential outcomes of Type I and Type II errors.

The probability of having a Type I error can be determined by the significance level of the test. If the significance level of a hypothesis test is 0.05, then you would be correct 95 percent of the time; but 5 percent of the time, a Type I error occurs. The probability of committing a Type I error can be reduced by increasing the significance level (i.e. from 0.05 to 0.01). While the probability of committing a Type I error decreases by doing so, the probability of committing a Type II error increases.

This means the probability of committing a Type II error is also dependent on the significance level (i.e. 0.05 or 0.01). Since a Type II error is defined by the probability of rejecting a false null hypothesis, when the significance level is set low, there is less risk in committing a Type II error. This is because there is a smaller chance of rejecting the null hypothesis.

In general, researchers try to balance between Type I and Type II errors by determining the significance levels that are considered a standard in research (0.05). If you are not comfortable with 5 percent error, 0.01 can be used to reduce it to 1 percent. If you are more concerned with Type II error, you could reduce the chance of a Type II error by lowering the significance value to 0.10 (thereby increasing the probability of making a Type I error to 10 percent). By doing so, this results in a reasonable risk of committing a Type I error while having an adequate level of protection of committing a Type II error.

CONCLUSION

This chapter has introduced you to the concepts of inferential analysis. Even though inferential analyses are not used all that much in crime analysis, you should be familiar with the concepts in case you are required to employ inferential analyses as a part of a project. There are four principles you should remember about inferential analyses. These will help guide you in any inferential analysis you conduct.

1   It is always best to draw a probability sample. This allows you to take the most advantage of the principles of inferential analysis.
2   The larger the sample size, even with a non-normal population, the better able you are to take advantage of the principles of the central limit theorem to support your analyses.
3   Your inferences will not be exact; but you can use the principles of probability to have a level of confidence that your value is within a particular range.
4   This confidence can be used to accept or reject the null hypothesis you established when setting up your project.

With these principles in mind, you can conduct your analyses with some confidence of having valid and supportable findings.

QUESTIONS AND EXERCISES

1   Find a journal article that uses inferential analyses in addressing a crime issue. Discuss the data
     and the analyses. Discuss the sampling method and any problems it might cause. Look for poten-
     tial problems from the data or the results. Discuss whether you think the authors drew the proper
     conclusions and whether they can infer from the sample to the population (or that the samples
     were from the same population).
2   As a part of a small group project, design an inferential crime analysis study to examine something
     in a jurisdiction. Follow all of the procedures talked about in this chapter (developing research
     and null hypotheses, developing a sampling method and drawing the sample, etc.). Discuss how
     difficult this would be in reality and what you would need to do as a crime analyst to overcome
     these issues.

Useful tips and techniques

This chapter is designed to provide you with useful analytical tools that you can use in Excel to further understand your data, and tips for setting up your data to have them in a usable form. This is not an exhaustive list of all that can be examined in Excel, but provides an overview of common techniques and tools that will benefit crime-analysis type work. Remember, depending on the type of assignment or research question, the type of analyses will vary. That is why it is important to learn and utilize as many techniques as you can. This will enhance your abilities as a crime analyst and showcase your ability to tackle a variety of crime research questions that agencies could ask you to answer.

CALCULATING RATES AND CHANGE

Rates are calculated to take into account the population of an agency or city. This is important because City A could have 15 homicides with a population of 75,000 and City B could have 15 homicides with a population of 55,000. By constructing rates, you factor in the population and make a standardized variable that you can compare to other cities/agencies. Crime rates by city are usually calculated per 1,000 persons or 100,000 persons, depending on the city/agency comparison. The formula for crime rates per 1,000 persons is:

$$Crime\,Rate = \left(\frac{number\ of\ crimes}{population\ total} \right) * 1000$$

In Excel, crime rates are calculated with the same formula (make note of the parentheses in the formula). Figure 10.1 shows actual larceny-thefts reported from the San Francisco Police Department during 2008–2012, downloaded from UCR (www.ucrdatatool.gov/). The online data tool for UCR allows you to download the rates; but calculating the crime rates on your own can be helpful when you are not able to download specifically the crime rates. The data from which this formula was drawn are shown in Figure 10.1.

In the San Francisco data, we are calculating larceny rates per 1,000 persons, so the formula for 2008 would look as follows:

$$Crime\,Rate = \left(\frac{25142}{798144} \right) \times 1000$$

If you were to calculate the larceny rates for 2008 to 2012 and add them to the Excel spreadsheet, it would look like Figure 10.2.

Looking over the crime rates for San Francisco, you can see a decrease and then an increase in 2011–2012 in the rates of larcenies per 1,000 persons. A better way of viewing the change in rates from year to year is by calculating the percent of rate change. The percent of rate change formula for yearly change is:

$$Percent\,Rate\,Change = \left(\frac{Present\ Crime\ Rate - Past\ Crime\ Rate}{Past\ Crime\ Rate} \right) * 100$$

Using this formula with the San Francisco UCR data, a new column in Figure 10.3 reflects the yearly percentage change in larceny rates per 1,000 persons.

Calculating the percent in rate change provides you with a definite descriptive number to discuss from rather than generalities. For example, in 2012, there was about a 15 percent increase in the

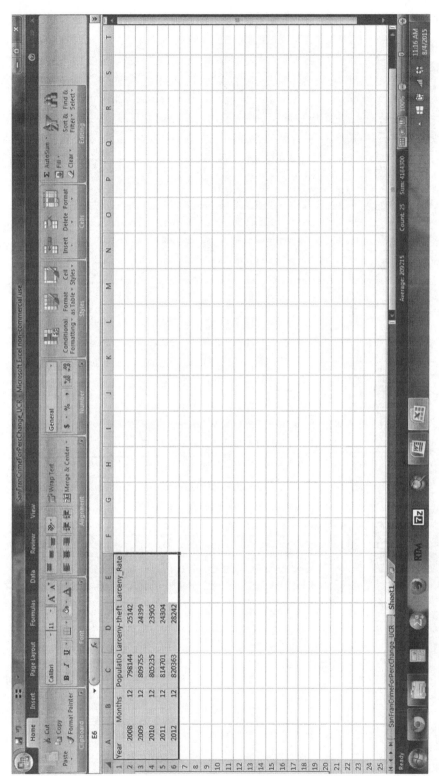

Figure 10.1　San Francisco: Larceny Rates per 1,000 Persons

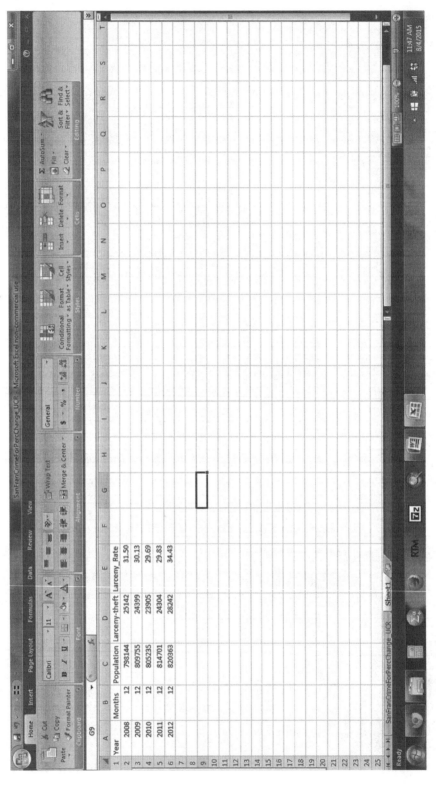

Figure 10.2 San Francisco: Larceny Rates Calculated per 1,000 Persons

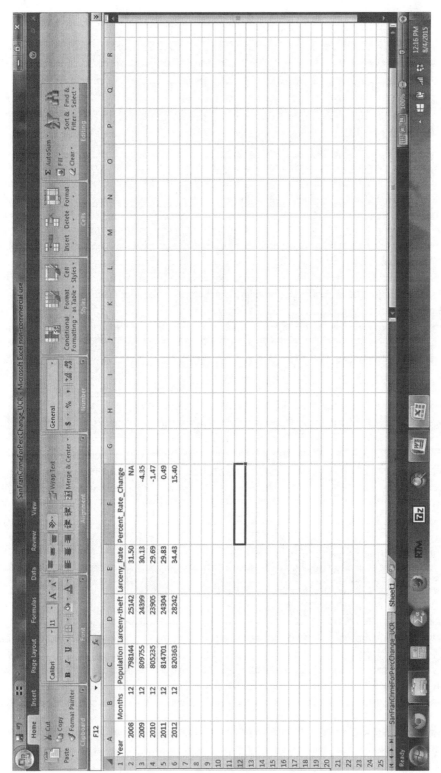

Figure 10.3 San Francisco: Percent Change in Larceny Crime Rates per 1,000 Persons

rate of larcenies per 1,000 when compared to the 2011 larceny rate. You may wonder, why would you just not examine the number of larcenies and calculate the change in total number of larcenies; but remember, crime rates take into account the population. In 2012, there was an increase of almost 6,000 in the population in San Francisco. The population of each year should be considered when conducting analyses.

TEXT TO COLUMNS

Depending on the type of data you obtain, they may arrive in a format that is not useful for analysis. For example, data could be obtained where multiple fields could be in one column, such as having names in one column, and you would like to have first and last names separate. The data should be separated into individual columns so you can work with as many elements of the data as possible. Another common example is when the date and time field are together rather than separate, as shown in Figure 10.4. The first step in separating data is to select the data range you want to split (in Figure 10.4 it is Column A).

Under the Data tab, click the Text to Columns feature (see Figure 10.5).

There are two general ways to separate data: delimited and fixed width. Delimited data are usually separated by a character such as , / : ; or any other type of identifiable character, even a space. Fixed width refers to a break throughout the entire column that is uniform. For example, if you have a 9-digit number and you need to use only the first 3 digits, you could set a fixed width to separate between the third and fourth number.

In the current example of the Date Time column, there is a space between the two characteristics. Because of this, you can select the Delimited option and check the Space box so Excel knows what delimiter to look for in the column, as shown in Figures 10.6 and 10.7.

Once you check the Space box, you will notice a line separating the two features, date and time, as shown in Figure 10.8.

You will want to select that the Date field will be read in as a date, in the correct format, and leave the Time field as general. Once you click Finish, Figure 10.9 shows how the data will appear.

Now you have the data in a format that allows you to use the date either with or without the time in your analyses.

REMOVING DUPLICATIONS

When crime data are obtained, there is the possibility the same incident will appear multiple times. This can happen because the incident has multiple types of classifications. Figure 10.10 is an example of how crime data are often obtained in Excel format and issues that you need to address before starting your analyses. Notice that lines 2 and 6 and lines 4 and 5 in Figure 10.11 have the same INCNBR and most of the same information (such as the time, date, and address), but have a different CODEDESC. If these duplicate crime incidents were left in, the numbers would be inflated, showing that crime is higher than it is in reality. However, you should make absolutely sure before removing duplications that these are true duplications or that you do not want the additional data. For example, often duplications in crime data are because there are multiple crimes committed in a single incident, or there are rows for offender (or multiple offenders), victims, etc. In these cases, you may want to combine the multiple rows into one row so you have all of the data. If they are truly duplicates, or you do not care about the additional people, crime, etc., then remove the extra rows.

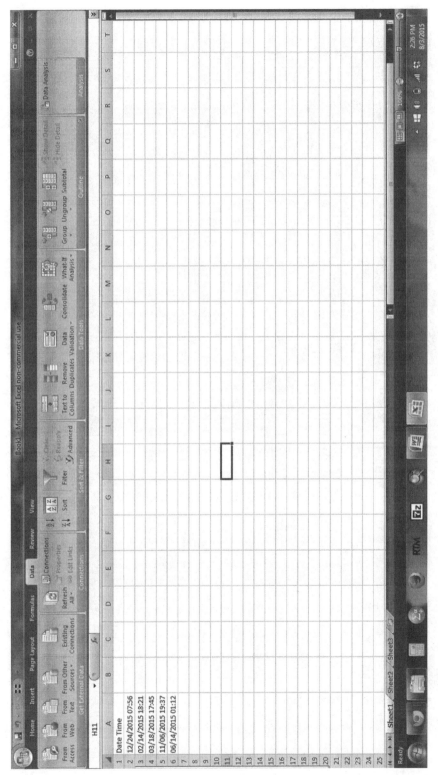

Figure 10.4 Text to Columns

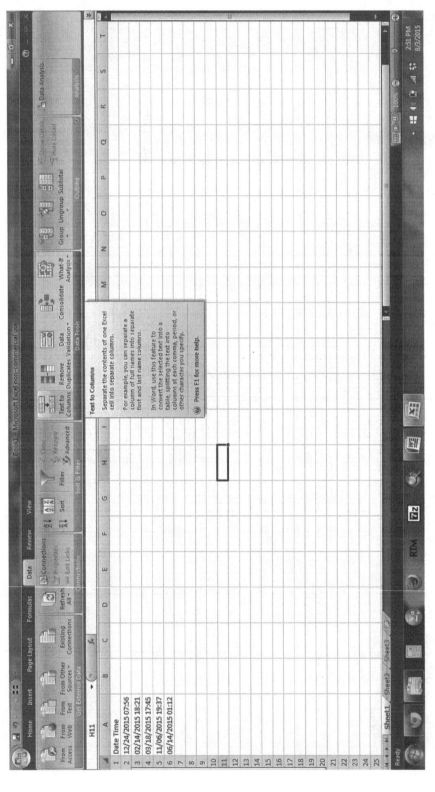

Figure 10.5 Under Data tab, Text to Columns function

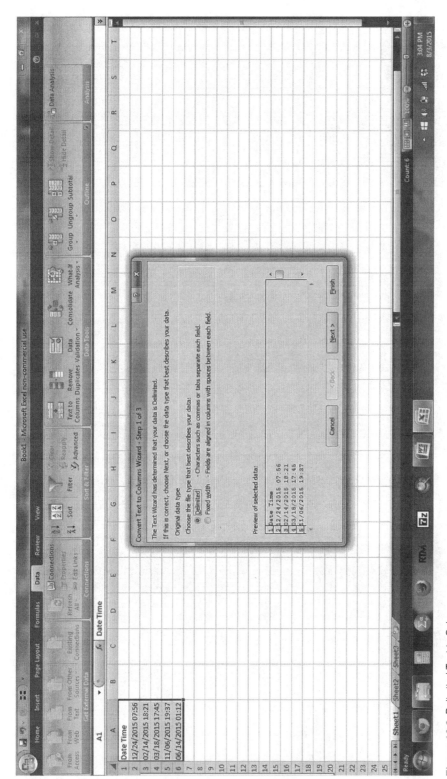

Figure 10.6 Delimited Text to Columns

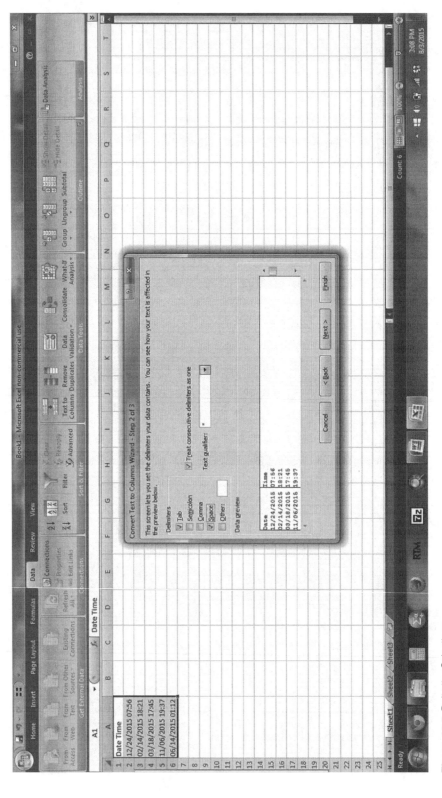

Figure 10.7 Delimiter Selections

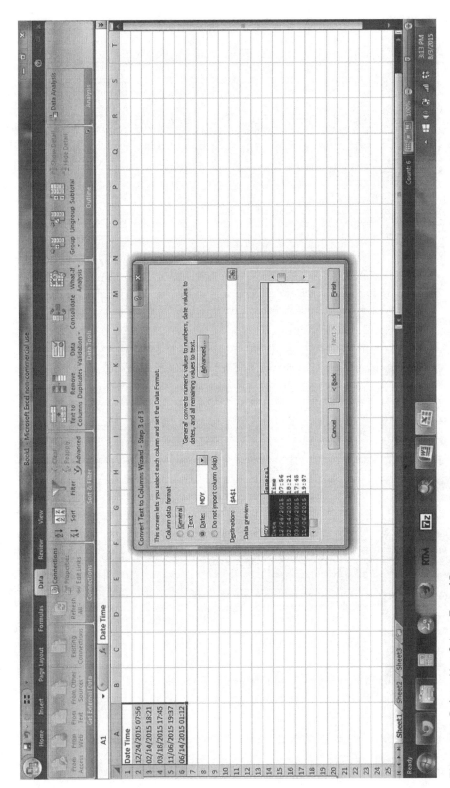

Figure 10.8 Defining New Column Type of Data

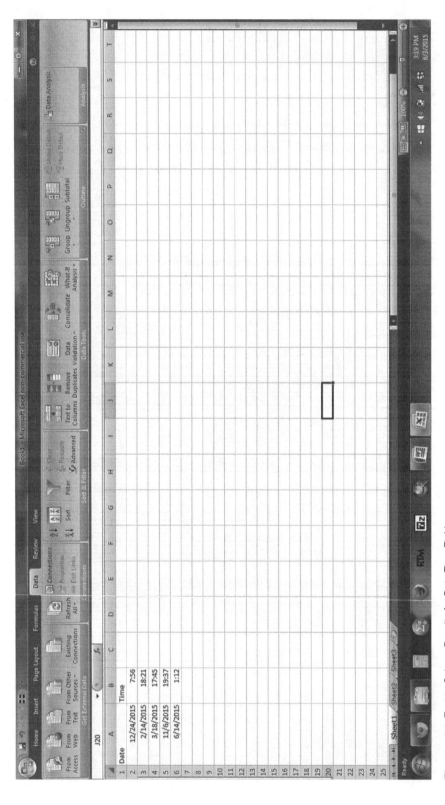

Figure 10.9 Text to Column Results for Date Time Field

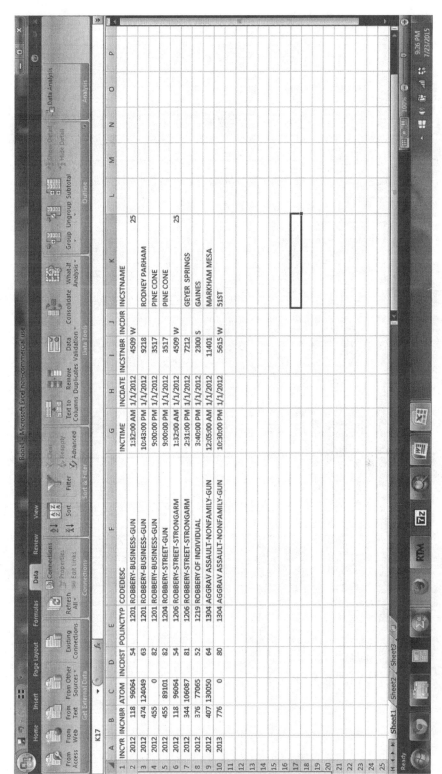

Figure 10.10 Sample Crime Data

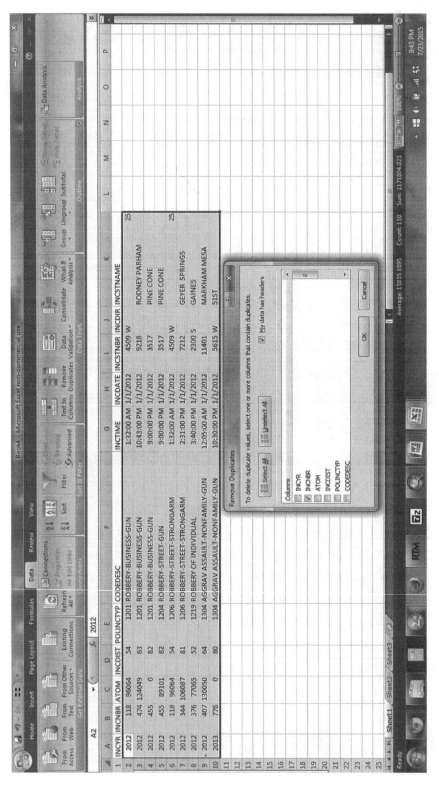

Figure 10.11 Removing Duplications

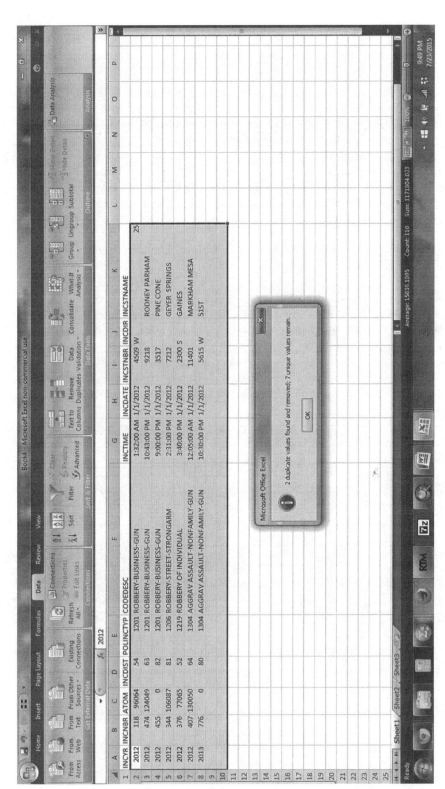

Figure 10.12 Duplication Result Screen

Under the Data tab in Excel, there is the tool to remove duplications. Before being able to use the tool, you need to select the data frame. Once you do so, you can remove duplications based on the variable you have chosen. In this case, we will remove duplications based on the variable INCNBR.

Clicking OK will remove the duplicates, by row, and will prompt you with a screen that identifies how many duplicates were removed and how many cases (crimes) remain in the data set (see Figure 10.12). There are 2 duplicate values that will be removed and 7 will remain, providing you with a more reliable data set to continue further analyses.

This is a simple example of removing duplicates. In reality, you could have just looked at the data and known which records to remove; however, it is not typically this simple. You often have many thousands of records to deal with, and it is not always as clear which records are duplicates. That is why data cleaning is critical to proper analyses, and why the Duplication function in Excel is so helpful.

CONCATENATION

Concatenation is often a term that is used within crime analysis as a step needed before being able to map crime. When data are pulled from a CAD system, the address field is usually pulled in multiple segments. That is, the street direction (N, S, E, W), the street number, street name, and street type (st, blvd, pkwy, interstate [often in all of their forms before cleaning]) are all in different fields in the data. Since these fields are extracted in a number of fields, a crime analyst is required to join these fields into one, usable column so the addresses can be geocoded. Note, however, it is much easier to clean the data when they are in separate columns than when they are together. So, make sure you do your data cleaning before you concatenate.

Using the same sample data discussed in the duplication subsection, Excel has a formula that will concatenate multiple fields into one column. The data displayed in Figure 10.13 are actual data of crimes in Little Rock. In this data, the INCSTNAME contains the address name. You should notice inconsistencies and problems in the data in this column that, as a crime analyst, you would deal with on a daily basis when cleaning data. For example the 25 should be 25th, and there is not a column that provides a street type. While this is not a huge concern, when there are similar street names in a jurisdiction, the difference is identifiable by the type (i.e. circle, drive, loop). Remember that these data are input by humans, so there is always the possibility of error.

The Concatenate function is found in the Formula menu under Formula Builder (or use the icon). Look for the function in the Text portion of the formulas. The formula to concatenate the address for the first incident would be: = CONCATENATE(I2, " ", J2, " ", K2). Can you think of why the " " are needed? There is a space between the quotes. The space inserts a space between each field. If you do not have the quotes and this extra space between them, the address would be run together. Once you input the formula and required cells, you hit enter and the result is shown in Figure 10.14.

The Concatenate function will place the results in column L. You will then need to label the column to finish the process.

FIND AND REPLACE

As a crime analyst, much of your time will consist of data cleaning. Do not be surprised by your bloodshot eyes due to the lack of looking elsewhere other than the next incident in your data set. A bit of advice that will make your life easier as you progress working with crime data is to create a list of

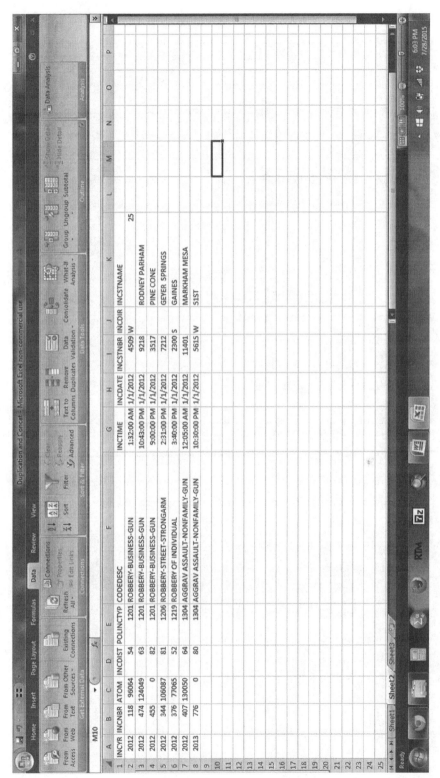

Figure 10.13 Concatenation Data Fields

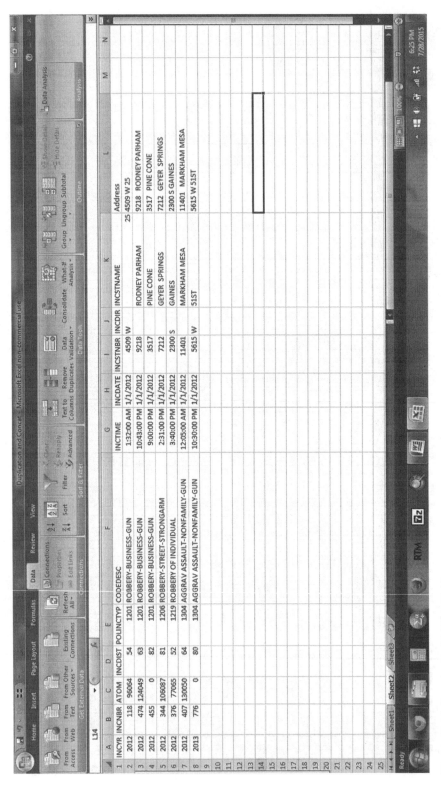

Figure 10.14 Concatenated Address Field

commonly misspelled streets or change in street names that you find in the data. Also, one of the most common abbreviations is MLK, instead of entering Martin Luther King Drive. These are common issues that become time-consuming issues in later spatial analyses, so it is easier to correct these problems in Excel where it is user-friendly.

Excel has the option to Find and Select. Using these functions will save you time from going through individual cases or searching the entire column. By selecting (highlighting a column) and doing a Find then Replace, you can search for common misspellings or abbreviations that need to be changed for later analyses. If you are confident in your skills, you can do a find and replace "all" but you need to be confident knowing that "all" of the incidents that will be found are ones that you want to change.

To use the Find (and replace if that is what you want to do), select the data column that you want to search in (this is very important – and see the note below), then select the Find and Select icon as shown in Figure 10.15. Type what you want to search for in the Find box (and what you want to replace it with in the Replace box if you want to replace). This finds all of the places where your search string is located in the data (and replaces it with what you write in that box).

This function is critical to data cleaning, and can save you hours of work in geocoding if you will be doing spatial analysis later.

One note about the Find and Replace function in Excel. Sometimes, the function is too broad and you wind up changing things you do not want to change. For example, if you do a global search and replace in one column to change st. to Street, it may also change St. Stephens Avenue to Street Stephens Avenue in another column. There are times when it is more effective to cut the data to Word, where there are better Search and Replace functions and macros, make the changes, and then move the data back to Excel.

TEMPORAL HEAT MAP

A common theme of crime analysis is the consideration of the temporal element of criminal activity. Time is a dynamic concept that is an essential part of everyday activities (remember routine activities theory). Victims and offenders have daily routines that contribute to the development of criminal opportunities. Throughout the textbook so far we have discussed different temporal patterns, from hour to day to seasonal. Depending on the time of day and day of the week, certain crimes are more prevalent.

You could look at bar charts or line graphs to examine the time element of crime; but those only tell part of the story. The utilization of a Pivot Table in Excel gives you the ability to look at multiple variables at the same time. For example, you might examine the time of day incidents occurred by day of the week. This is a quick and easy tool for crime analysts to use to help guide their future analyses. This type of analysis is known as a temporal heat map. Once the pivot table is constructed, you can change the coloring (i.e. cosmetics) of the data fields to identify highs and lows more easily.

In the example in Figure 10.16, auto theft data from January to May 2013 were used to display the utility of temporal heat maps as a means for understanding crime problems. Between January 1 and May 31, there were 419 auto thefts. Based on the nature of the crime, when do you think auto thefts are likely to occur? When are automobiles most vulnerable for theft? These are types of questions you should ask yourself while first being assigned a task or problem to identify.

To create a temporal heat map based on the auto theft data begin by clicking on the Insert tab in Excel. There is a Pivot Table option as shown in Figure 10.17.

Before you click on the Pivot Table, the data have to be set up in a manner to be used. For example, since we are examining the day of the week and time of day, we need a column for Day

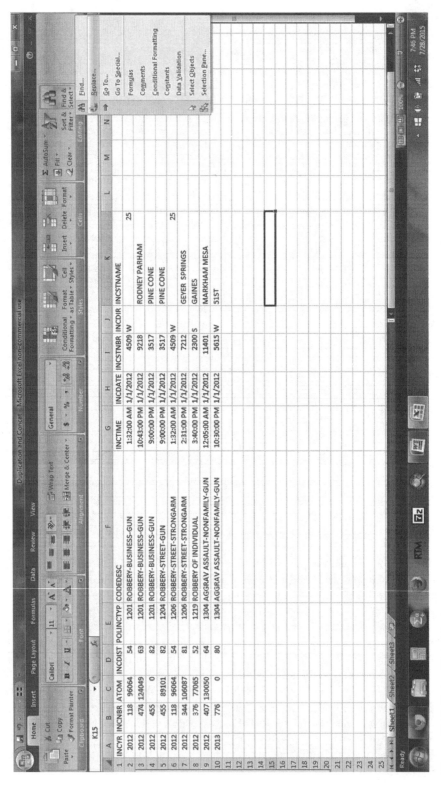

Figure 10.15 Find and Select Feature

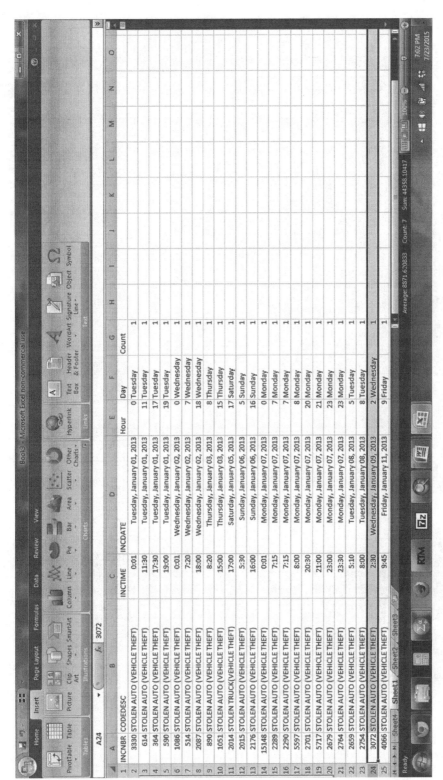

Figure 10.16 Auto Theft Data Format for Pivot Table

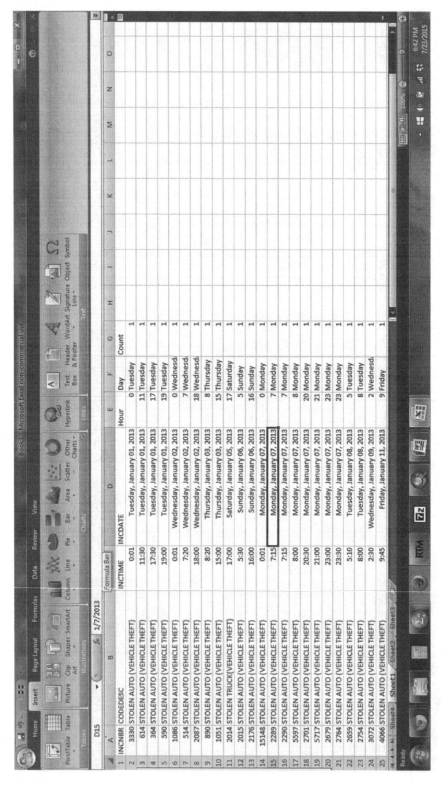

Figure 10.17 Pivot Table for Temporal Heat Map

(i.e. Monday) and Hour (i.e. 0, 1, 2). Typically, when crime data are used, you have a date field such as 01/01/2013. This provides the day but it needs to be parsed out for it to be used in the pivot table. You can do this using the Text to Columns procedure discussed above. Additionally, the time crimes occur are reported in a number of ways but sometimes in a standard format (1:30 PM). To make it easier, converting the time to 24-hour time and only using the hours field allows you to examine day of week by hour of the day; two important temporal characteristics. Figure 10.16 provides a screenshot of how the data were separated to use in a Pivot Table. Looking over the auto theft data, you might wonder what the column Count is for within the data. This column will be used as just that, a count, identifying each auto theft as 1 incident. The use of this column will become more evident when constructing the pivot table.

Once you click the Pivot Table, a prompt screen will appear as shown in Figure 10.18 asking for you to select the data you want to include as part of the table. For this example, you would want to include the Hour, Day, and Count.

After inputting the data range for the Pivot Table, Figure 10.19 displays the new screen that appears for you to select data you want to be displayed for the Temporal Heat Map. You can see from Figure 10.19 that the Hour range was moved to the Row, the Day range moved to the Column, and the Count to the value. As you start to move the variables, you will see your table update and eventually look similar to Figure 10.20.

The shading that is present in Figure 10.20 is not there automatically. To get this kind of shading, you need to select the data from the 10 under Friday to the bottom right corner (5). Then, click on the Home tab then Conditional Formatting. Figure 10.21, shows you what you should see when trying to apply a color scale. The color scale provides the varying colors to identify high (red) and lows (green).

The temporal heat map for auto theft provides useful insight into patterns of crime between January and May, 2013. This heat map has a great deal of information pertaining to the temporal characteristics. In general, there were few auto thefts during late morning hours, while after normal working hours shows a general increase in the number of auto thefts. If the images were printed in color, the temporal heat map would straightforwardly identify the "hot" periods such as, Friday at 22:00 (10 pm) and midnight (Hour 0), along with Monday at midnight.

The auto theft temporal heat map can provide agencies with the ability to target not only specific days of the week, but also certain times of the day when auto theft is prevalent. The ability to construct a temporal heat map is an analytical tool that can provide insight into the dynamic nature of when crimes take place.

CONCLUSION

The tools and techniques discussed in this chapter are common ones that can be used to quicken your data cleaning process, and as supplements to common analytical techniques. As you work with more data and projects that require different approaches, you will continue to expand on your analytical skills. What is often the most helpful is, as you complete a project, to make notes on aspects you had issues with to try and search for a better methodology to overcome that issue. There are numerous extensions that you can add to Excel, and you can use different programs to help with your analyses. Just remember that extensions often cost additional money; therefore, do some searching online and ask other analysts for common solutions to similar problems. The network of crime analysts is a helpful group that tend to be open with what has worked best for them in the past, and they do not have a problem sharing knowledge gained over the years. Just remember, crime analysis is a dynamic field that continues to evolve, requiring crime analysts to add skills to their toolbox.

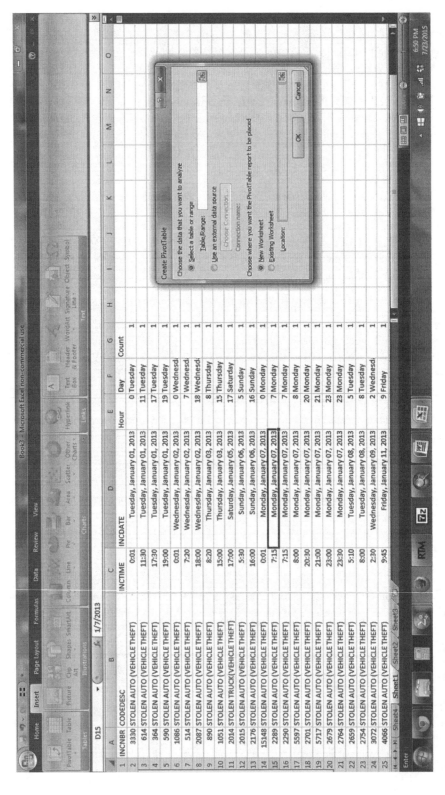

Figure 10.18 Pivot Table Prompt Screen

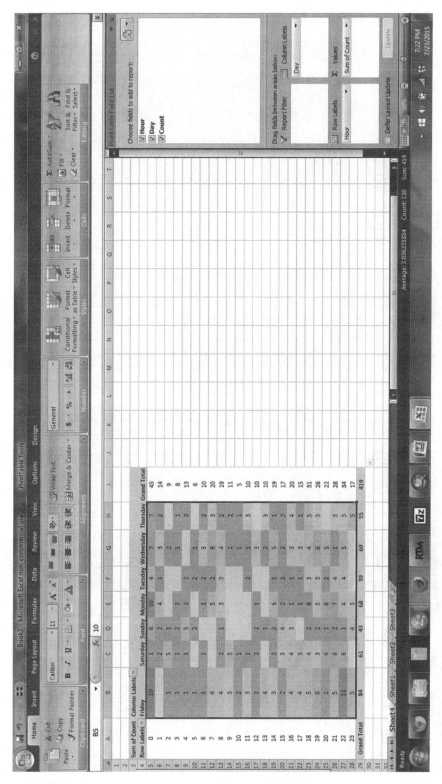

Figure 10.19 Pivot Table Field List

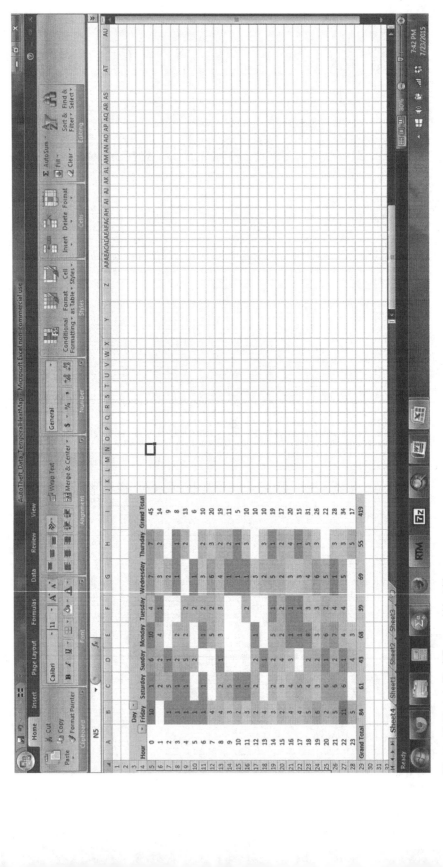

Figure 10.20 Auto Theft Temporal Heat Map

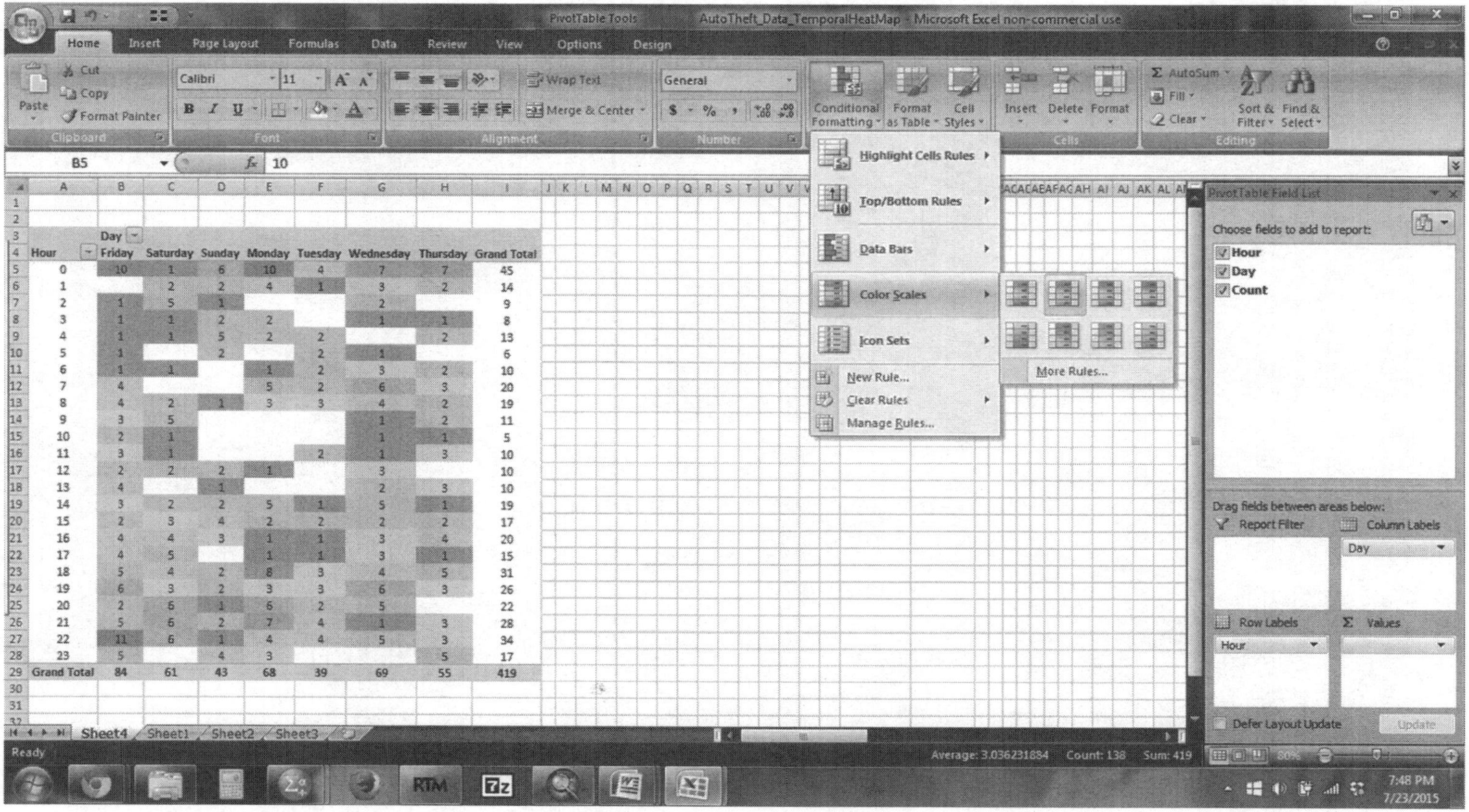

Figure 10.21 Color Scale for Temporal Heat Map

QUESTIONS AND EXERCISES

1   Download ten years of crime data and population counts from the UCR website for your city, or where you grew up. Pick a crime and determine the crime rate and yearly change of crime rate for that crime. What conclusions can you draw from your findings?

2   Use the Find and Replace functions in Excel to replace a crime type for a different term (for example, change homicide to murder or change larceny to theft). Did you encounter any problems in Excel in doing this?

Spatial and temporal applications

Time and space are often central to crime analyses, both individually and in combination. For example, many analyses of crime are based on the time of day of the event (either the exact time, or typically broken down by patrol shift). For any analyses that involve GIS, space plays a central role. Although currently not as common in crime analyses, time and space can also be used together. For example, analyses often involve maps that are broken down by patrol district and patrol shift. While these typically do not analyze the intersection of time and space, there are ways time and space can be analyzed together, such as in agent-based models that factor in both time and space for the agents and environment (see discussion below on time and space intersections). Wartell and Gallagher (2012) stated that crime analysts should "use their knowledge of place, opportunity, and the situational nature of crime when assessing criminogenic factors" and that these should help guide police actions. Each of these methods and more are discussed in this chapter to give you an idea of the ways time and space can be used in the practical work of crime analysis.

TIME ELEMENTS IN CRIME ANALYSIS

The foundation of time elements in crime analysis is that the number of crimes varies by the time of day and the day of the week. In fact, Felson and Poulsen (2003) argue that crime varies more by hour of the day than any other predictor. Typically, the late evening hours (11 pm to 3 am) are peak hours for crimes to occur; but this is not always the case. For example, Drawve, Walker, and Felson (2015) found that juvenile crime (particularly juvenile violent crime) increases in hours right after school is dismissed. It is also common for crimes to be higher on Friday and Saturday nights than other days of the week.

One of the early leaders in using geographic analyses, Amos Hawley (1950), outlined three types of time characteristics: tempo, rhythms, and timing. He proposed tempo is the number of events per unit of time, such as the number of crimes in an hour of one day, the number of crimes in a particular patrol shift, etc. A rhythm, according to Hawley, is the flow of a time pattern. Examples are daily patterns of crime in a week and seasonal patterns of crime. Timing is the intersection of time and rhythms. These patterns of timing are central to routine activities theory; for example the rhythm of shopping patterns and the rhythm of patterns of robbery.

Felson and Poulsen (2003) developed an interesting argument for crime analyses related to time (specifically, when a day begins). They argue that beginning a new day at midnight simply because the chronological clock has turned makes no sense for examining crime. This time is right in the middle of many indicators of higher crime (alcohol use, dark of night, etc.). They argue the day should begin at 5 am, when most of the people up late may be at home and workers are beginning their day. A similar argument could be made for starting the day at 7 am in accordance with many police shifts.

Felson and Poulsen (2003) developed methods of examining time related to crime that would serve as good summary measures for crime analysis and presentation. They proposed creating a "median minute of crime," which is the minute of the day that exactly half of the crimes occurred. For example, if the median minute of burglary was 6:59 pm (assuming their start time of 5 am), then exactly half of the burglaries of that day occurred before 6:59 and half occurred after. Then, they proposed to divide the rest of the day into quartiles. This is accomplished by dividing the first and second halves into their own halves using the procedure for calculating the median minute. This would show how crime is distributed by time throughout the day. It could also show clustering of crime. For example, say the median minute of burglary was 7:15 pm. This shows that half of the burglaries occurred relatively in the daytime and half at night. Examining the quartiles, you might find that the quartile cut for the first half was at 4:58 pm. This would mean that it took a relatively long time for burglaries to occur in the first part of the day, but they were relatively clustered between 5 pm and just after

7 pm. This could be an indication of the "motivated offenders" of school-aged burglars who are just getting out of school and the fact that more homes are occupied after 7 pm (producing more capable guardians). These kinds of analyses could be very helpful for providing information for police patrols and operations.

Seasonality of crime is also an issue that has received attention. Seasonality can be broad time-based cycles (such as summer v. winter), or smaller elements (such as time of day cycles of crime). Seasonality can also be based on something that regularly occurs in time but is based on something else. For example, seasonality of crime can very much be based on when schools are in session or out for the summer. Seasonality has also been linked to cycles of the moon.

Seasonality was first addressed by Quetelet (1842/1969) in France. He looked at crimes during summer and winter and found differences in both violent and property crimes. Anderson's (1987) research found that summer months had higher rates of crime than winter months. Interestingly, most research on seasonality in Europe finds winter months to be most active in crime, whereas research in the U.S. finds summer months to be most active. This is another indicator that crime is largely specific to temporal and spatial influences, which should be kept in mind in doing any crime analyses.

Thompson and Bowers (2013) examined the seasonality of crime using a method that combined time of day and seasonality. They looked at the influence of darkness on robberies. They found a significant relationship between darkness and personal robberies. They attributed at least part of this to greater anonymity of offenders (harder to see their faces in the dark) and a reduction in the number of capable guardians (harder for eyewitnesses to see in the dark, fewer people on the streets).

Most seasonality research has focused on one of two elements – either the effects of heat or cold on behavior or on the social aspects of weather (summertime activities v. staying inside when it is cold). DeFronzo (1984) found that the number of days the temperature was greater than 90 degrees Fahrenheit was significantly correlated with increases in burglary. In combining climate and time, Lab and Hirschel (1988) found a relationship between property crime and temperature during the day, but not at night. Cohn and Rotton (2000) attempted to control for many of the variables thought to interact with weather and seasonality (holidays, school breaks, etc.) in their analysis of seasonality. They discovered that controlling for these interaction variables increased the significance of temperature on property crime.

Seasonality can also have some very social-based reasons for changes. It would seem likely, for example, that robberies would be higher during the summertime. While this has been supported by some researchers, others have robberies higher in the winter months. This may be a result of higher unemployment rates (fewer construction and agricultural jobs). The Christmas season can also play a role, either because there are a greater number of targets (people shopping and more money) or because people are more desperate to get money for Christmas presents. This shows that there are many reasons, including social factors, that can produce fluctuations in crime.

Brantingham and Brantingham's (1995) concept of "edges" (see below) also works with time elements of crime. As we discussed elsewhere, edges are places where there is a noticeable change; such as land bordering a river, houses behind a strip mall, or a major street between business and residential areas. These edges can also be in time, such as when a bar closes at night. The number of people exiting the bar changes, thus changing the nature of interactions on the street.

One problem of crime analyses involving time of day is the number of categories. Even using hours as the basis of time, there are 168 hour categories in a week. As Felson and Poulsen (2003) point out, this creates a situation of too few cases per cell to be useful in many statistical analyses; and it produces tables and charts that are often too large and too cluttered to properly interpret. For this reason, time is often aggregated at higher levels, such as basing time on patrol shifts (which reduces the number of categories to 21 per week).

SPATIAL ELEMENTS IN CRIME ANALYSIS

As demonstrated in over 100 years of research, we know that crime clusters in certain places; and it is not evenly distributed across areas such that some places have a much higher probability of a crime occurring there than other places. As has been stated in many places in this text, the foundation of spatial elements of the examination of crime began with Balbi and Guerry (1829) and Quetelet, and their efforts to examine the spatial distribution of crime in France in the 1800s. This was expanded in other countries soon after. The concept of examining spatial aspects of crime was further expanded by Mayhew in London in 1861. He moved from examining the differences in crime rates within counties to examining the distribution of crime within the city. Following initial inclusion of crime in urban analyses conducted by Park, Burgess, and others at the University of Chicago in the 1920s, Shaw and McKay (1942) firmly placed spatial analyses of crime in the criminological lexicon with their work on the distribution of crime and social characteristics in Chicago.

Brantingham and Brantingham (1995) placed the geography of crime in the context of crime generators and crime attractors (based on nodes, paths, and edges). They proposed that "crime patterns cluster around offender and victim nodes and along the principle pathways between them." When the paths and nodes of people come together (such as in an entertainment district), they can form crime attractors/crime generators that produce increased levels of crime. The fact that crime concentrates is a product of these spatial constructs. According to Brantingham and Brantingham (1995), "the clustering of land uses and the temporal routines of daily life cluster nodes, channel movement and force a convergence of unaccountable individual path potentials into a limited number of actual paths between nodes." These are the elements of sound crime analyses related to space, and can be used to plan for police patrols.

Spatial aspects of crime, and spatial analyses as central to crime analysis are somewhat unique in the interrelationships between variables and data points. For example, it is virtually impossible to disentangle the influence of poverty and/or race on crime within a neighborhood. Even more complex is the interrelationship of data points. Bernasco and Elffers (2010) argue that "in geographically referenced data, all units of analysis are interrelated." The example they use is that "each unit is a certain distance from every other unit in the data" and, therefore, a characteristic of one data point may influence all or part of every other data point. Further, data points that are close by may have more influence than data points farther away. So, although all data points have the potential to influence other data points, the influence is not consistent. As they point out, since most statistical procedures have an assumption of independence of observations, this makes spatial crime analyses particularly challenging.

The spatial analysis of crime has taken substantial steps in both sophistication and in use over the years – moving from simple pins placed in maps on the wall to a whole criminological theory specifically addressing the spatio-temporal aspects of crime. Below are some of the more central theoretical elements of spatial analyses. These are by no means all of what goes into crime analyses based on space and time; but does provide an introduction to what can be accomplished in this area.

Journey-to-crime

An area where crime mapping has allowed police agencies and researchers to examine the spatial nature of crime is in journey-to-crime and distance-to-crime analyses. Journey-to-crime is a process of examining the trips offenders take to locations where they commit crimes. Journey-to-crime is used to determine how far offenders travel to commit a crime. Typically, these analyses use offenders' home residences as the starting point for journeys-to-crime, and measure the distance to where the crime occurred. Because there is no current way to accurately predict the exact route offenders take to commit their crime (they rarely leave their house and go directly to the place where the crime is committed), some research in this area is called distance-to-crime, as we discuss elsewhere in the book.

While the distance-to-crime is generally consistent, there can be aberrations; often based on edges. Brantingham and Brantingham (1975) found that the interior parts of residential areas had much lower burglary rates than the border areas. Most likely because of awareness space – people drive through the border areas, but it almost has to be insiders who burglarize interior areas.

Distance decay

An element closely related to journey-to-crime is distance decay. This function states that offenders will commit crimes close to their home and also close to areas where they work or frequent often. This function is largely based on awareness space.

Verma, Ramyaa, and Marru (2013) used agent-based modeling to examine the extent to which distance decay could be modeled using rules of behavior. In their model, agents were coded to go to particular places (work, school, etc.), but were also able to "explore" their environment (thereby producing greater awareness space). They found strong support for a distance decay function, even when modifications to their original model were made to give the agent more freedom. A primary finding of this research is that "our model is able to show how this awareness space is itself developed by random movements."

Bichler, Schwartz, and Orosco (2010) examined distance decay using a variety of control variables that separated offenses and offenders into subgroups. They found substantial differences in the journey-to-crime within subgroups. They argued that increased ease of transportation and the changes in community growth and land-use patterns may have altered offender behavior in ways that may make some previous findings obsolete. This underscores the importance of crime analysts keeping up with changes in the knowledge base about cities and people to make sure they are using the best methods for analyses.

Near repeat crimes

An outgrowth of journey-to-crime is related to "near repeats," or crime occurring within certain distances (and/or times) to specific locations. Typically, near repeats are analyzed using some kind of buffer zones to examine some aspect of crime occurrence (see Walker, Golden, and VanHouten, 2001, for an example of buffer analysis related to sex offenders). Beyond simple counts, methods of accounting for the crimes within buffers have been proposed that add to the spatial analysis of criminal events.

Murray and Roncek (2008) used buffers around bars to examine the influence they may have on nearby assaults. They argued that Cohen and Felson's (1979) concept of guardianship may be present inside a bar itself; but bar staff may encourage those involved in confrontations to leave the premises. This may result in assaults occurring outside the bar or a short distance away (however, look at the discussion of Roncek and Maier (1991) below of the differences in circular buffer analyses and using a different buffer measure).

McCord and Ratcliffe (2009) used location quotients to compare the characteristics of an area to the larger surrounding area. In using this method, circular buffers are placed around a particular place. The number of crimes within the area is then summed and divided by the area of the buffer. The result of this analysis is a quotient of the total crime per buffer area. This value is an indicator of the crime density in the buffer area. For example, a location quotient value of 2 would indicate the crime density around a particular place is twice that of the area surrounding it.

Intensity value analysis (IVA) was proposed by McCord and Ratcliffe (2009) as an enhancement to location quotient analysis. They argued that a problem of location quotients is that all crime points are assigned the equal value of one, regardless of their distance from the buffer's center. To overcome this limitation, IVA "calculates the intensity of crime points into a single, inverse distance-weighted value based on the aggregate proximity of all crime incidents found within the buffer surrounding each facility." In IVA, crime points located farther from the center of a buffer are assigned lower values, so the influence of crimes that are further away (and therefore theoretically less linked to the facility) have less influence on the analysis.

More recently, Risk Terrain Modeling (RTM) was developed to examine the spatial influence of crime (Caplan, Kennedy, and Miller, 2011). RTM builds on the literature of environmental criminology and hot spots and attempts to predict the distribution of crime based on crime generators and attractors. RTM is further discussed in Chapter 14 as a method of predicting crime.

Street networks and crime

One enduring element in the spatial analysis of crime is the relationship between street networks and crime. Brantingham et al. (2005) proposed that "there are a set of patterns/rules that govern the working of a social system – one composed of criminals, victims and targets, interacting with each other – the movements of whom are influenced by the city's underlying land use patterns, street networks and transportation system." As early as 1285, King Edward I of England attempted to control crime partially through controlling the road network (Plucknett, 1960). In the Statute of Winchester, he commanded that gates to towns be locked from sun down to sun up and that roads be widened and cleared so robbers could not hide near them. Dyos (1957) presented many examples of how nineteenth-century London attempted to address crime by developing and changing street networks. As talked about elsewhere in this book, the early works of Park, Burgess, Shaw and McKay and others at the University of Chicago found a close relationship between mixed-use areas and crime. For example, Burgess (1916) found a strong relationship between delinquency and proximity to business streets.

In the early 1990s, cities began to explore how to control traffic patterns in attempts to reduce crime. This concept was based on decreasing the awareness space of criminals (see also Chapter 3). A primary method used during this time was the increased use of cul-de-sacs in suburban neighborhoods. This kind of closing off of streets matched Newman's (1972) argument of restricting vehicular and foot traffic to reduce crime.

Beavon, Brantingham, and Brantingham (1993) sought to examine the influence of street networks on property crime. Their study was based on the following principles:

1   Street networks physically influence how people move about within a city.
2   Street networks can also influence the way people become familiar with certain sections of a city.
3   Property crime generally occurs within an offender's regular activity space.
4   Property crime should be highest near the areas offenders are most familiar with or frequently travel through.
5   If travel frequency decreases as road complexity increases, then the areas with the most complex roads and the buildings on the least accessible streets should have the lowest amounts of property crime.

They tested these premises by examining the accessibility and traffic flow in two suburbs compared to the amount of property crime, controlling for a measure of target attractiveness. This analysis was based on Brantingham and Brantingham's (1991) work that found cities with grid street layouts were more predictable than areas with winding roads, cul-de-sacs, or dead-ends. Beavon et al. found that accessible streets with higher volume of traffic had a greater likelihood of crime.

COMBINATION OF TIME AND SPACE

Grubesic and Mack (2008) argued that many analyses "treat the spatial and temporal aspects of crime as distinct entities, thus ignoring the necessary interaction of space and time to produce criminal opportunities." They contended that analyses of space and analyses of time are good, but there is a need to examine the space–time occurrence of crime events after controlling for spatial and temporal effects. This is particularly important when utilizing routine activities theory as a basis for analyses (as many crime analyses do). Routine activities theory proposed that crime occurs when a motivated offender and a suitable target converge in space and time in the absence of capable guardians. If the time element is not considered, there is no convergence.

One reason there has not been more use of time and space analyses is because combining analyses of space and time greatly increases the complexity of the analyses. This is not only because of the complexity of the time and space elements themselves, but also because they interact in myriad ways that are often difficult to simplify for explanation and presentation (imagine trying to build a map that shows the spatial elements of crime in a city as they vary by even hour of the day across a year). As a result, analyses often involve more complex methods and statistical knowledge.

Balemba and Beauregard (2012) conducted a chi-squared automatic interaction detection (CHAID) analysis of the factors influencing sexual assault, including time and location. Their findings were that sexual assaults were very complex in their contributing effects, and varied depending on the specific characteristics. For example, a sexual assault was more likely at night when the victim was an adult, the assault was more likely on a weekday when the offender was a stranger, and a kidnapping as a part of the assault was more likely in public space. This shows the complexity of analyses based on time and space, and highlights the need to carefully interpret any findings of space and/or time analysis.

Johnson (2010) examined burglaries in both space and time using a Knox analysis. To conduct this analysis, he compared an instance of a burglary with every other burglary in the area and then computed the time and distance between occurrences. Thus, each burglary represented a pair of occurrences with every other burglary. He found that more pairs of events occurred near each other than would be expected if only looking at the probability of a burglary alone. He also noted that there appeared to be a distance decay function of the data (see above).

Johnson and Bowers (2004) examined the clustering in space of burglaries over time. They proposed that while some crimes in some places may "endure" (that is remain in relatively the same place – such as some drug markets), some move slowly in response to identification of potential targets and to avoid detection. They used the example of burglary, and proposed that burglaries "slip" in geography over time – that is they move incrementally within an area. Their conclusion was consistent with what we know about burglars, that "more professional" burglars target more profitable homes and move when the profits are lower and the risks increase. This is in contrast to impulsive burglars who are likely to target homes nearer to them, even though the profit may be much smaller. Johnson and Bowers proposed that police resources in relation to affluent area burglaries should only be deployed based on data from the current month or no more than one-month prior. After a month, it is likely that the location has "slipped" to a nearby area. The potential that crimes will move slightly in geography

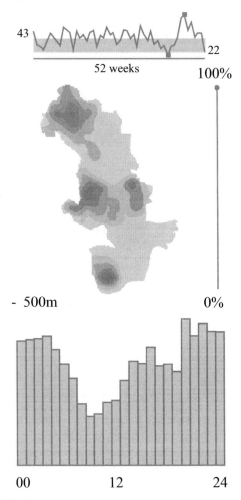

Figure 11.1 Hot Spot Plot of Burglary
Source: Townsley (2008: 67).

over time is something that should be taken into account in crime analyses. This is particularly relevant in the discussion of displacement below.

Thompson and Townsley (2009) found that hot spots (discussed in detail in Chapter 13) of crime tend to shrink and expand at various times of the day. This is something that must be taken into account by crime analysts. If police resources are based on a hot spot zone that is largely taken in the aggregate but shrinks significantly (say, at night), then the resources would be deployed inefficiently and incorrectly during the time of a smaller spatial footprint. Thompson and Townsley also found that when hot spot areas shrink, they become more consistent and concentrated over time. They proposed this was largely due to the nature of routine activities of victims and the business hours of commercial establishments. For example, since the number of establishments that are open in later hours shrinks, it changes the activity patterns of potential victims. This, in turn, shrinks the hot spot.

Townsley (2008) proposed a method of visualizing the space–time dimensions of hot spots. He called this method a hot spot plot. The hot spot plot is shown in Figure 11.1.

In Figure 11.1, there are three graphics. The top graphic shows the trend of crime for the selected area over the course of a full year. The middle figure shows a static kernel density (KD) map of burglaries in the area. The bottom graphic displays the difference in frequency of burglaries in this area over a 24-hour period. In this way, a more complete understanding of the space and time elements of crime in a particular area can be displayed.

LIMITATIONS AND CAUTIONS

There are two issues that are often brought up in any spatial analyses: ecological fallacy and the modifiable areal unit problem (MAUP). Both of these are methodological issues that crime analysts should be aware of in conducting their analyses.

Ecological fallacy was a criticism aimed at early ecological researchers (Gehlke and Biehl, 1934; see also Walker, forthcoming 2018, for a discussion of ecological fallacy in spatial research). Ecological fallacy occurs when the results of an analysis based on aggregate data are inferred to individuals. For example, an analysis of social and crime data based on police beats (say social characteristics of certain criminals) cannot be inferred to individuals within the police beat (you cannot make the assumption that because a person has these social characteristics that are highly correlated at the beat level, he or she must also be involved in crime). This can also occur in terms of place. We know from the discussion in this chapter that crimes concentrate in certain areas, and that some locations have a much higher probability of a crime occurring there than in other places. An ecological fallacy occurs if we have data at a particular geographic area (a Census tract or a police patrol district) and then assume all houses within that area have the same probability of being a crime location.

MAUP is a situation where aggregated data units are often somewhat arbitrarily defined (Openshaw, 1984). There is also an associated modifiable temporal unit problem. MAUP happens when the government or researcher defines a neighborhood based on a well-meaning but somewhat arbitrary boundary. This is particularly relevant when neighborhoods are defined for analyses based on Census boundaries (which typically do not follow what the residents of a neighborhood would define as their area). Analyses based on these arbitrary boundaries run the risk of missing the reality the characteristics being studied may cross boundary lines (this is likely when there are no hard edges such as a waterway or major road); or a hot spot could occur along the arbitrary boundary line.

MAUP becomes a problem because different scales of boundaries will produce different results. For example, the relationship between some social factors and crime at a Census block group level may not be the same as the relationship at the Census tract level, which may not be the same as the relationship at the police patrol district level, and so on.

Since these limitations and issues are likely in all spatial analyses, crime analysts should take them into account when planning and doing analyses. These limitations can be addressed to varying degrees of satisfaction, but recognition of them should be a part of any analyses.

CONCLUSION

Analyses of space and of time are central to crime analyses. These kinds of analyses are based on 100 years of research and theoretical development, which have only grown stronger since the 1990s. These analyses can be complex, however. A strong theoretical and conceptual framework, attention to using the proper methods, and appropriate analysis procedures must be used to prevent erroneous results that can be harmful to an area.

REFERENCES

Anderson, C.A. 1987. Temperature and aggression: Effects on quarterly, yearly, and city rates of violent and nonviolent crime. *Journal of Personality and Social Psychology*, 52: 1161–1173.

Balbi, A. and A.M. Guerry. 1829. *Statistique comparée de l'état de l'instruction et du nombre des crimes dans les divers arrondissements des Académies et des Cours Royales de France*. Paris.

Balemba, S. and E. Beauregard. 2012. Where and when? Examining spatiotemporal aspects of sexual assault events. *Journal of Sexual Aggression*, 19(2): 171–190.

Beavon, D., P.L. Brantingham, and P.J. Brantingham. 1993. The influence of street networks on the patterning of property offenses. In Ronald V. Clarke (Ed.), *Crime Prevention Studies*, Vol II (pp. 149–163). New York: Willow Tree Press.

Bernasco, W. and H. Elffers. 2010. Statistical analysis of spatial crime data. In A. Piquero and D. Weisburd (Eds.), *Handbook of Quantitative Criminology* (pp. 699–724). New York: Springer.

Bichler, G., J. Schwartz, and C. Orosco. 2010. Delinquents on the move: Examining subgroup travel variability. *Crime Patterns and Analysis*, 3(1): 14–37.

Brantingham. P.L. and P.J. Brantingham. 1975. Residential burglary and urban form. *Urban Studies*, 12: 273–284.

Brantingham, P.J. and P.L. Brantingham. 1991. *Environmental Criminology*. Prospect Heights, IL: Waveland Press.

Brantingham, P.L. and P.J. Brantingham. 1993. Nodes, paths and edges: Considerations on the complexity of crime and the physical environment. *Journal of Environmental Psychology*, 13: 3–28.

Brantingham, P.L. and P.J. Brantingham. 1995. Criminality of place: Crime generators and crime attractors. *European Journal on Criminal Policy and Research*, 3(3): 1–26.

Brantingham, P.J., U. Glasser, B. Kinney, K. Singh, and M. Vajihollahi. 2005. A computational model for simulating spatial and temporal aspects of crime in urban environments. *IEEE International Conference on Systems, Man and Cybernetics*, 4: 3667–3674.

Burgess. E.W. 1916. Juvenile delinquency in a small city. *Journal of the American Institute of Criminal Law and Criminology*, 6: 724–728.

Caplan, J.M., L.W. Kennedy, and J. Miller. 2011. Risk terrain modeling: Brokering criminological theory and GIS methods for crime forecasting. *Justice Quarterly*, 28(2): 360–381.

Cohen, L.E. and M. Felson. 1979. Social change and crime rate trends: A routine activity approach. *American Sociological Review*, 44: 588–608.

Cohn, E.G. and J. Rotton. 2000. Weather, seasonal trends, and property crimes in Minneapolis, 1987–1988. A moderator-variable time-series analysis of routine activities. *Journal of Environmental Psychology*, 20: 257–272.

DeFronzo, J. 1984. Climate and crime: Tests of an FBI assumption. *Environment and Behavior*, 16: 185–210.

Drawve, G., J.T. Walker, and M. Felson. 2015. Juvenile offenders: An examination of distance-to-crime and crime clusters. *Cartography and Geographic Information Science*, 42(2): 122–133.

Dyos, H.H. 1957. Urban transformation: A note on the objects of street improvements in Regency and early Victorian London. *International Review of Social History*, 2: 259–265.

Felson, M. and E. Poulsen. 2003. Simple indicators of crime by time of day. *International Journal of Forecasting*, 19: 595–601.

Gehlke, C.E. and K. Biehl. 1934. Certain effects of grouping upon the size of the correlation coefficient in Census tract material. *Journal of the American Statistical Association Supplement*, 29: 169–170.

Grubesic, T.H. and E.A. Mack. 2008. Spatio-temporal interaction of urban crime. *Journal of Quantitative Criminology*, 24(3): 285–306.

Hawley, A. 1950. *Human Ecology: A Theory of Community Structure*. Chicago, IL: University of Chicago Press.

Johnson, S.D. 2010. A brief history of the analysis of crime concentration. *European Journal of Applied Mathematics*, 21(4–5): 349–370.

Johnson, S.D. and K.J. Bowers. 2004. The stability of space–time clusters of burglary. *British Journal of Criminology*, 44: 55–65.

Lab, S.P. and J.D. Hirschel. 1988. Climatological conditions and crime: The forecast is . . .? *Justice Quarterly*, 5: 281–299.

McCord, E.S. and J.H. Ratcliffe. 2009. Intensity value analysis and the criminogenic effects of land use features on local crime patterns. *Crime Patterns and Analysis*, 2(1): 17–30.

Mayhew, H. 1861. *London Labour and the London Poor.* London: Griffin, Bohn, and Co.

Murray, R.K. and D.W. Roncek. 2008. Measuring diffusion of assaults around bars through radius and adjacency techniques. *Criminal Justice Review*, 33(2): 199–220.

Newman, O. 1972. *Defensible Space: Crime Prevention through Urban Design.* New York: Macmillan.

Openshaw, S. 1984. *The Modifiable Areal Unit Problem.* Norwich: Geo Books.

Plucknett, T.F.T. 1960. *Edward I and the Criminal Law.* Cambridge: Cambridge University Press.

Quetelet, L.A.J. 1842. *A Treatise on Man and the Development of His Faculties.* Edinburgh: W. and R. Chambers.

Roncek, D.W. and P.A. Maier. 1991. Bars, blocks and crimes revisited: Linking the theory of routine activities to the empiricism of "hot spots." *Criminology*, 29: 725–753.

Shaw, C.R. and H.D. McKay. 1942. *Juvenile Delinquency in Urban Areas.* Chicago, IL: University of Chicago Press.

Thompson, L. and K. Bowers. 2013. A stab in the dark? A research note on temporal patterns of street robbery. *Journal of Research in Crime and Delinquency*, 50(4): 616–631.

Thompson, L. and M. Townsley. 2009. (Looking) Back to the future: Using space–time patterns to better predict the location of street crime. *International Journal of Police Science and Management*, 12(1): 23–40.

Townsley, M. 2008. Visualising space–time patterns in crime: The hotspot plot. *Crime Patterns and Analysis*, 1: 61–74.

Verma, A., R. Ramyaa, and S. Marru. 2013. Validating distance decay through agent based modeling. *Security Informatics*, 2: 3–14.

Walker, J.T. Forthcoming. 2018. Ecological fallacy. In J.C. Barnes and D.R. Forde (Eds.), *Encyclopedia of Research Methods and Statistical Techniques in Criminology and Criminal Justice.* Hoboken, NJ: John Wiley.

Walker, J.T., J.W. Golden, and A.C. VanHouten. 2001. The geographic link between sex offenders and potential victims: A Routine Activities Approach. *Justice Research and Policy*, 3(2): 15–33.

Wartell, J. and K. Gallagher. 2012. Translating environmental criminology theory into crime analysis practice. *Policing*, 6(4): 377–387.

QUESTIONS AND EXERCISES

1 Discuss why many crimes happen at night; then discuss why burglary is less likely to occur at night than other crimes. Put this in the context of routine activities and activity/awareness space.

2 Construct a crime analysis project to support your arguments in Question 1. What kind of data would you need? How would you want to arrange the data? What analyses would you use? How would you present the findings?

3 Say you found in your data that overall journey-to-crime fit traditional distance decay findings (less than 2 miles from the offenders' homes); however, for juveniles under 18, the average distance was 6.4 miles. What do you think would explain this finding?

4 Get a copy of the street network for the neighborhood where you live from Google Maps. What does the layout of the streets tell you about the likelihood of crime in your neighborhood? What places would be more likely to have a crime occur? What places would be less likely? What could possibly be done to reduce crime in areas where it is more likely?

Crime mapping

A mainstay in crime analysis is the ability to visually depict crime or any type of data spatially. Think about technology today and then think about it 20–30 years ago. The advancements in mapping have progressed rapidly from paper maps and atlases to cell phones that can give you directions anywhere you want to go. Just as technology has impacted society as a whole, police agencies have progressed to analyzing their own data spatially through crime mapping. This chapter focuses on the development of crime mapping and applications of crime mapping. It is designed to provide an overview, common terminology, and analytical methods related to crime mapping.

HISTORY

As already mentioned in several chapters in this book, crime mapping dates back to the 1800s in the works of Balbi and Guerry and Quetelet. Maps at this point were drawn by hand, drastically different from what we are capable of today. The progression of crime mapping in the United States took longer to adopt but is now a mainstay in research and police agencies.

Some of the first applications of mapping related to crime in the U.S. were in the context of the ecological model established by Park and Burgess and Shaw and McKay. They utilized choropleth and pin maps showing juvenile delinquency to identify community/neighborhood characteristics that had an influence on crime/health-related issues. These researchers had a significant impact on the development of our understanding of neighborhoods and crime. While researchers were advancing the understanding of social influencers of where crime occurs, larger agencies such as the New York Police Department were starting to utilize pin maps in the early 1900s.

The growth of crime mapping was influenced by the development of MAPS – Mapping and Analysis for Public Safety – through the National Institute of Justice (formerly Crime Mapping Research Center; CMRC). This assisted in spreading knowledge and what was currently being done by analysts and researchers. MAPS and the researchers' investment in developing crime mapping software aided in the emergence and prominence of crime mapping in police departments.

One of the earlier software programs was MapInfo. It helped bring to light what crime mapping is capable of when it was an emerging analytical tool. This provided a movement away from pin maps to computerized mapping. More common programs now are ArcGIS, QGIS, and to an extent Google Maps/Earth. Additionally, in newer versions of Excel, there is a PowerMap function, allowing users to spatially visualize data. The newer programs provide statistical methodologies to analyze the geography of crime, truly getting at the spatio-temporal characteristics. Advancements in GIS software makes it possible to handle greater amounts of data in a manageable way. If you continue down the crime analysis route, you will be exposed to what all these types of software programs are capable of in relation to crime analysis.

Much of what has been discussed in this textbook is to provide a background and understanding of aspects important to crime analysis before jumping into crime mapping. Crime mapping is an essential tool, but there needs to be a foundational understanding of core concepts, statistics, and applications before learning the hands-on portion. Mapping allows you to visually show and analyze the data points in space; but the successful analysis of spatial patterns of crime requires that mapping tools be guided by the theory discussed in this book that can link crime to place, can explain the spatial characteristics of different types of crime, and can provide explanations for the relationship between crime and certain characteristics of neighborhoods and people. Once you understand the concepts and theory that makes crime mapping work, mapping software provides a means to examine the spatial, temporal, and social/physical characteristics surrounding crime for law enforcement agencies (see Chainey and Ratcliffe, 2005).

SOFTWARE

One of the most widely known and used mapping software programs is ArcGIS by ESRI (www.esri. com/arcgis/about-arcgis). ArcGIS has numerous built-in tools, with additional extensions and tool-boxes that fit about any user's needs. The program is designed to provide users the ability to develop a greater understanding of spatial relationships.

Since many people are trained in using ArcGIS, agencies often pay to use the software since analysts are trained with that specific software. This does create an issue when law enforcement agencies have limited resources and expensive software is not always available for crime analysis. There are other less expensive and free programs that have the same analytical techniques, just not as user-friendly. These are still very valuable programs when trying to better understand local safety issues without financial support for more expensive programs.

QGIS is often utilized as an alternative since it is a free and open-source GIS program (www.qgis. org). QGIS provides guides and tutorials for new users. What makes QGIS a bit more user-friendly is that many of the instructional materials are translated into multiple languages. QGIS has many plugins and features that fit the needs for crime analysts. The learning curve might be a bit steeper given the popularity of ArcGIS; however, since QGIS is open-source, there is a large community of users often willing to help and troubleshoot problems.

Additional programs have started to incorporate mapping functions. Newer versions of Microsoft Excel have some mapping options. Under the Insert tab in Excel, there is a 3D mapping or Power Map tool. This tool allows users to map data and run simple functions such as pin maps and clustering or density maps (i.e. hot spot maps). Numerous agencies likely already have the Microsoft Office Suite; and, with Excel having data analysis extensions, supplementing those with mapping features makes Excel a valuable analytical program for crime analysts. While the spatial applications are limited currently, this could provide a first step for analysts to start to visualize their data spatially.

DATA

In crime mapping, some form of GIS (typically ArcGIS) is used to take real-world environmental features and project them on a map. This application extends beyond criminal-justice related uses and, with other fields utilizing GIS, the amount and quality of data continue to increase. As a crime analyst, there are two main types of data utilized in crime mapping and GIS in general: vector and raster.

Vector data

If you have examined or looked over a crime map before, you have already been exposed to vector data most likely. There are three general types of vector data: point, line, and polygon. These types of data can contain attributes specific to each point, line, or polygon features. Think back to a pin map, where you literally put a pin on a map depicting a crime; now, instead of a pin on a map, there is a point on a map. The point would have attributes detailing the type of crime, time it occurred, address, weapon use, and a number of other potential factors. Examples of point features include:

crime incidents
arrests
traffic incidents
police stations/sub-stations
fire stations
businesses (bars, liquor stores, grocery stores, big box retailers, etc.)
311/citizen complaints
call-for-service
transit stops (bus/subway/train).

In Figure 12.1, the points on the map depict a violent crime. The GIS data for Figure 12.1 are shown in Figure 12.2. This is not the full attribute table, but provides information of the type of violent crime and the address of the incident.

In Figure 12.1, you are also able to identify another type of vector data: line features. Most commonly, lines will represent streets for crime analysis purposes. Street files contain attributes allowing you to create an address locator. This is important because address data (point vector data) you want to visualize on a map needs a foundation to match to, and that is where street files come into play. An address locator is constructed from the street files which then allows you to link your point data to street files. Street files typically contain attributes about the street name, prefix, street number range (left and right side), direction, and other various elements. Other examples of line features include:

streets
highways
alleys
transit routes (bus/train/subway)
hiking/walking/biking paths
rivers.

Figure 12.3 is an example of what an attribute table looks like for street line data. PL_ADD_F is the left boundary while PR_ADD_T is the right boundary. There are two sides to streets that can have varying address numbers. These attribute fields are used in the creation of an address locator.

Generally, anything with an address or XY coordinates can be represented on a map by a point. For example, if you had a list of all the bars in a city, you could display those on a map. Keep in mind, though, this type of data is represented by points only. This can create an issue in some analyses because it does not represent the actual building or object you are trying to display. Say you are trying to represent a school: the point or address locator only provides a single point and does not indicate the whole building. This is what happens when you put an address into your mapping app and the directions take you to a back or side door. You then have to figure out about the building and where the entrance is.

The last type of vector data is polygon features. Similar to how polygons are discussed in other subjects, in GIS and crime mapping, a polygon is a figure enclosed by multiple lines. In mapping,

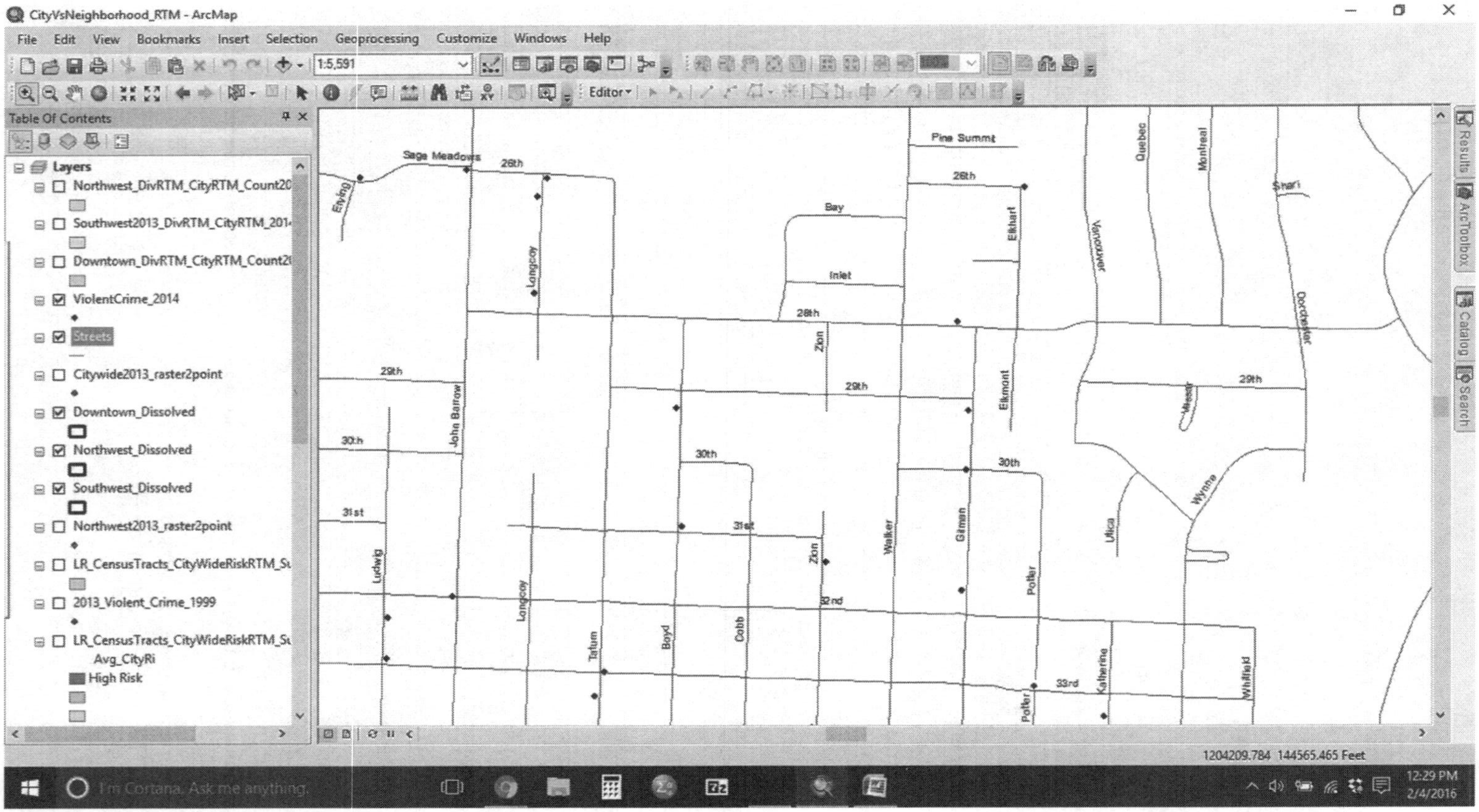

Figure 12.1   Point and Line Feature Examples

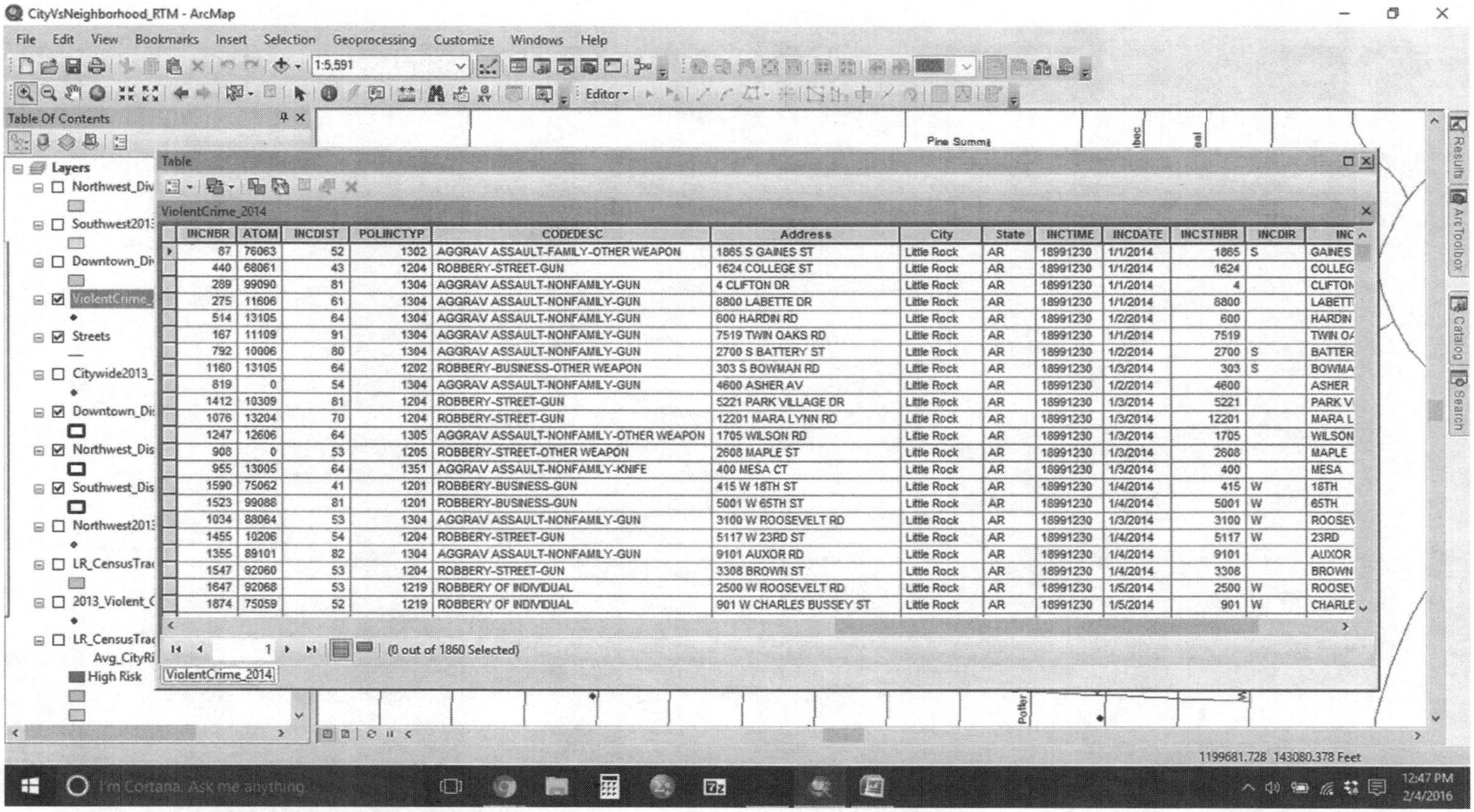

Figure 12.2 Vector Point Feature Attribute Table

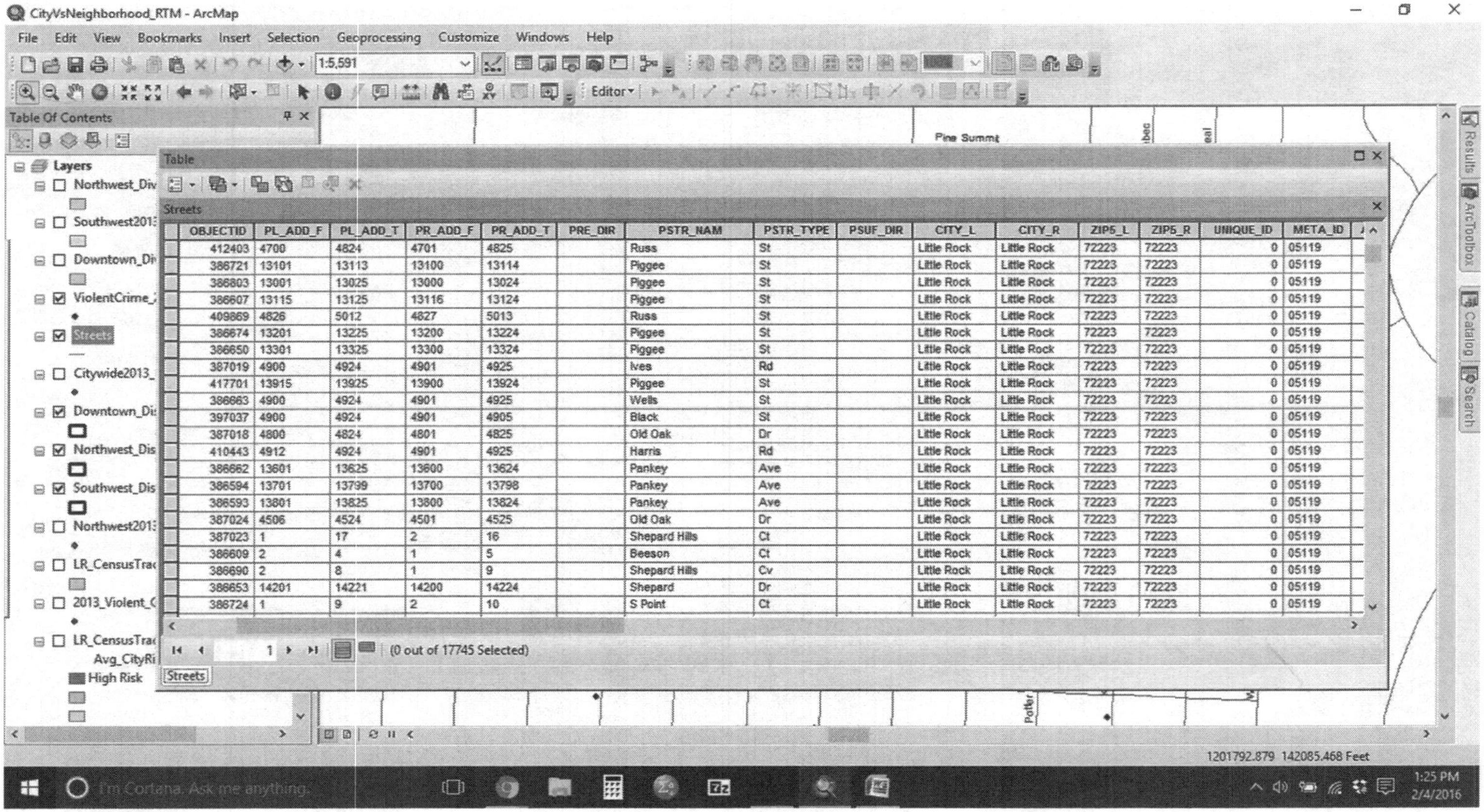

Figure 12.3   Street File Attribute Table

polygons can be countries, states, cities, neighborhoods, parks, and even buildings (among many others). Examples of polygon features include:

lots
parcels
park boundaries
college/school campuses
police districts/divisions
gang territories
zip code tabulations
counties.

Figure 12.4 shows the city boundary of Cincinnati, Ohio (polygon feature) with the streets throughout the city (line features). At the other end of the spectrum, smaller levels of analysis can be useful, such as Census tracts and block groups or police districts. By using Census tracts or block-groups, you can link data from the ACS or Census, such as total population, percent unemployed, percent living below poverty level, among many others.

The Census tracts encompassing Cincinnati, Ohio, are displayed in Figure 12.5. Census tracts separate cities into smaller levels of analysis, and, once Census or ACS data are merged to the tracts, you can examine the overlap of social characteristics and crime. Census tracts and block groups have unique identifiers for each one, allowing you to link data from multiple sources back to the spatial reference. Census tracts and block groups are often operationalized in research as neighborhoods because these are the closest subunits in a city providing social measures (i.e. disadvantage index, residential stability, isolated youth). Again, you should be careful when using artificial or government boundaries to represent neighborhoods because they may not be accurate representations.

Raster data

Raster data are continuous, and are usually represented by unique cells. Imagine a picture you have taken or think in television terminology in respect to pixels. Raster data are a matrix of cells as shown in Figure 12.6. Each cell is unique and contains attribute data per each cell. An easy example of raster data are weather maps you likely see on your local news station. The pixilation look to storm maps represents raster-based data. We will see the use of raster data in Chapter 13 with the LISA analyses.

In relation to crime analysis, a spatial analytical tool is Risk Terrain Modeling (RTM; Caplan and Kennedy, 2016). RTM is discussed in greater depth in Chapter 14; but, in short, RTM constructs a risk assessment for where crime is likely to occur based on place features of the landscape (i.e. bars, restaurants, pawn shops, etc.). After identifying multiple place features risky for crime, multiple raster layers (each one represents one place feature) are combined. Since raster data are grid based, if you have multiple raster layers over the same jurisdiction with the same size of cells, you can add them together. Also, retrospective analysis, such as kernel density analysis, operates using raster data.

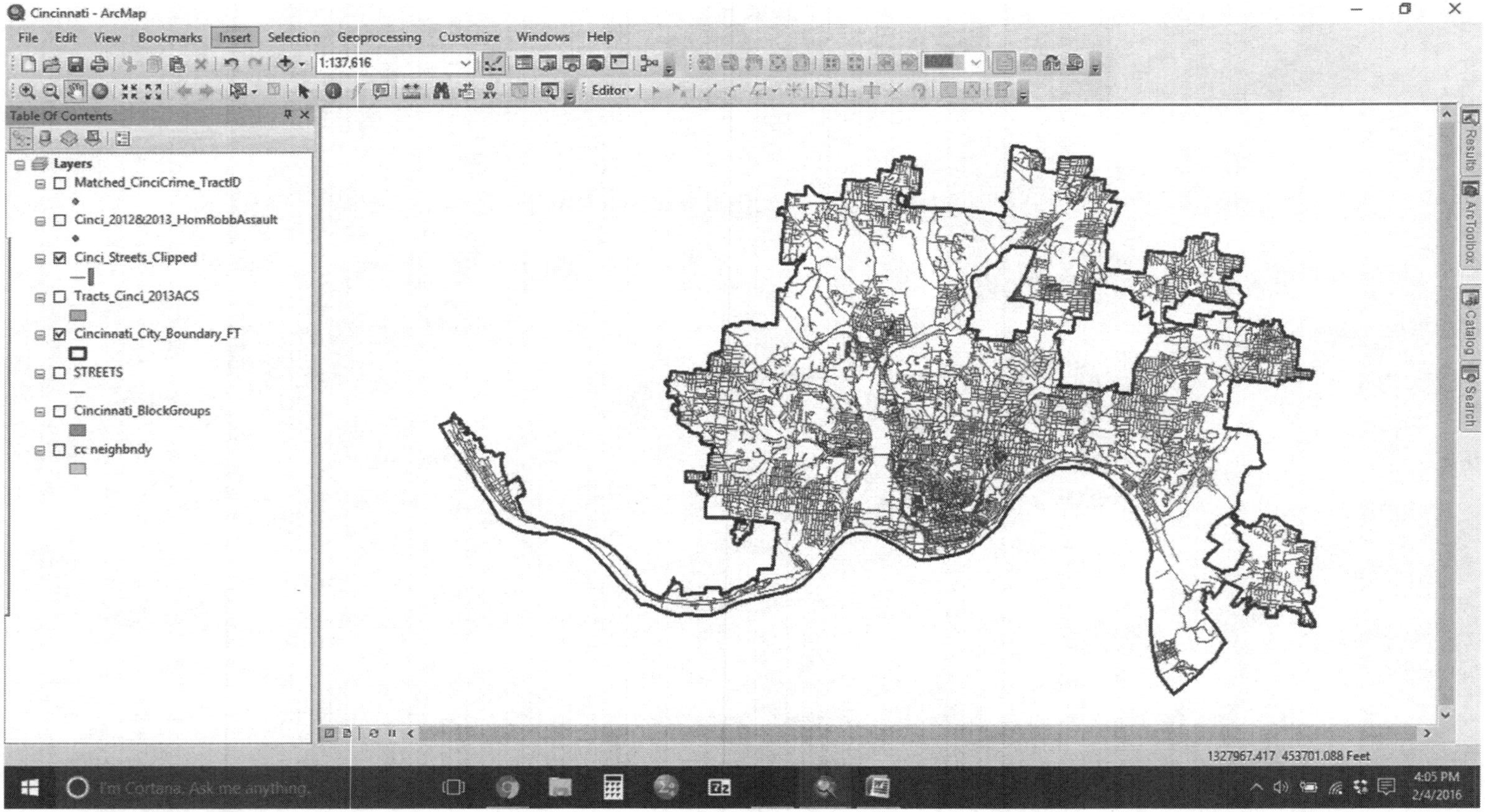

Figure 12.4 Cincinnati Polygon Feature with Streets

Figure 12.5 Cincinnati Census Tract Polygon Features

Figure 12.6 Raster Data Grid

APPLICATIONS

There are numerous applications in crime mapping. This subsection is to only bring your attention to common analyses and concepts. For greater details and depth on crime mapping capabilities, a crime mapping course would teach you those.

Buffers

Buffers are often used by crime analysts to determine how much crime occurs within specified distances surrounding features of the landscape (i.e. schools, bars, strip clubs, movie theaters). A buffer is just that, a circle around points of interest, typically vector data (points, lines, polygons). Buffers range in size from a certain distance (500 feet, 1,000 feet, etc.), to block lengths of cities, to half-miles or larger, depending on the purpose of the analysis.

There are two main aspects of buffers users must decide on when analyzing relationships. First, it should be determined if you will allow a buffer to dissolve. Dissolving a buffer is a process of making the buffer smaller if it "collides" with another buffer. If you do not dissolve buffers, when there are overlapping buffers, as in Figure 12.7, crime can be double counted. Figure 12.7 has three liquor stores with a 1,000-foot buffer around each. In the two bottom buffers, there is overlap of one crime incident. If you do not dissolve the buffers, each buffer would count that violent crime. This can be useful when you are only interested in how much crime occurs around each buffered place; however, the crime counts would differ from the overall number of crime incidents being analyzed.

When buffers are dissolved is shown in Figure 12.8. When the buffers overlap and a dissolve function is used, the overlapping buffers are dissolved so there is no overlap. This results in no double counting of crime incidents.

When utilizing buffers, GIS programs usually let you compute multiple ring buffers. What if you were interested in how many restaurants are within one, two, three, and four blocks of where you reside. First you would identify what the average block length is, then put those increments around your residence. This would identify the number of restaurants in each buffer increment, allowing you to sum as you see fit. This tool can save you time as an analyst and better inform you on descriptive counts around features of the landscape (i.e. schools, residences, buildings, parks).

Buffers are not always utilized to identify how much crime is occurring around certain features. For example, sex offenders usually have living restrictions such as not living within a certain proximity to schools or parks. An easy method would be to put a buffer around the schools and parks then track where known sex offenders reside. This would allow law enforcement agencies to determine if any offenders are in violation of the living restrictions. Another example would be with CCTV (closed-circuit television) cameras. If you knew the range of the cameras, you could put a buffer around each one to determine where there are overlapping areas or where coverage is absent.

Distance/journey-to-crime

Having the ability to map locations of crime generally begs the question at some point of how far the offender traveled to commit the crime. Because of the nature of the question, additional data are needed to determine this distance. The homes of offenders are often used as the starting point to determine how far from their residence they traveled to commit crime. As discussed in environmental criminology, people in general have a greater awareness space around their immediate residence (which provides potential crime opportunities). This is because people spend a majority of time in their home environment and surrounding neighborhood.

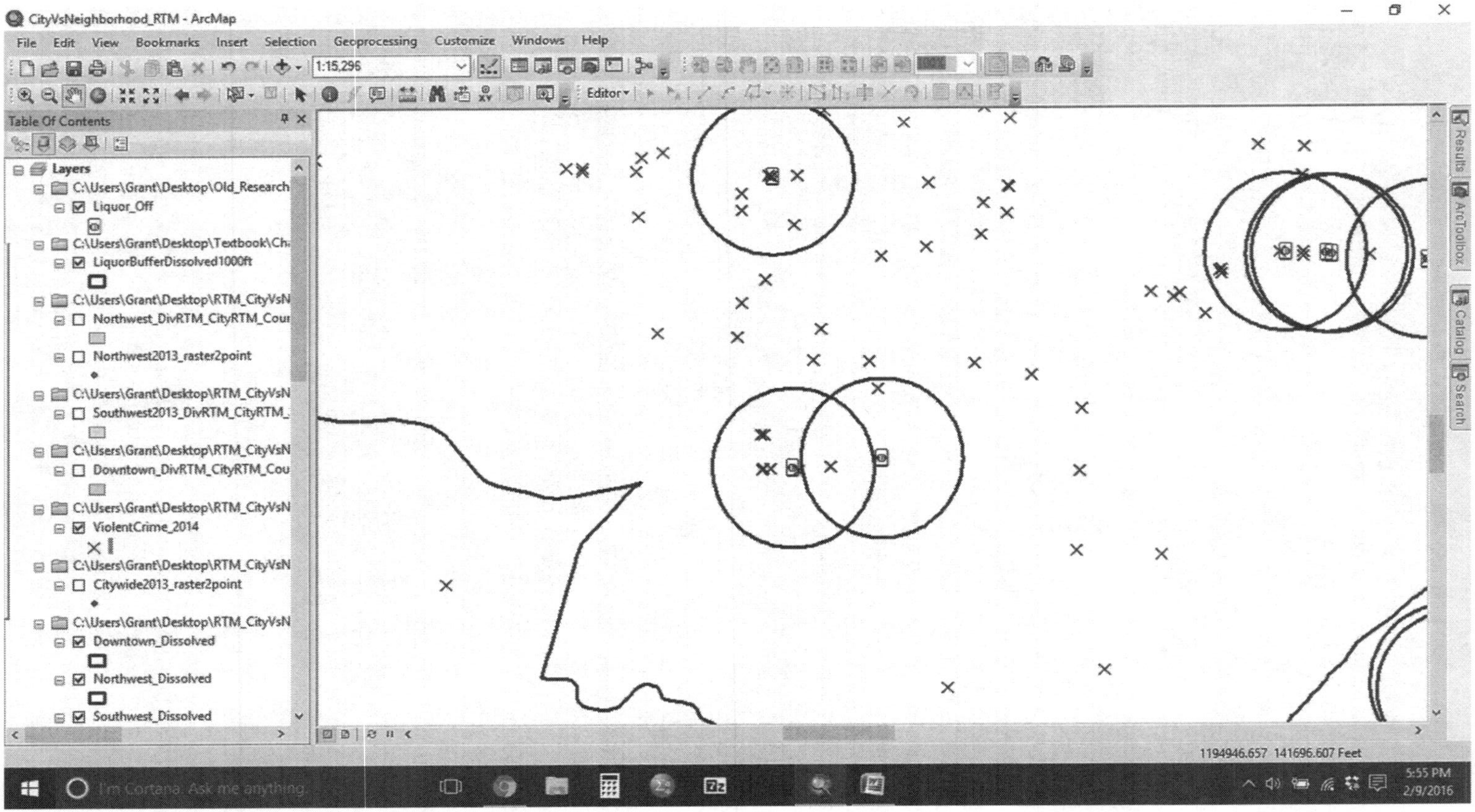

Figure 12.7 Liquor Stores and Violent Crime with 1,000-Foot Non-Dissolved Buffers

Figure 12.8 Liquor Stores and Violent Crime with 1,000-Foot Dissolved Buffers

Imagine you are looking to go to a new coffee shop so you look on the Internet. Part of the search usually entails how far the coffee shop is from you (distance). This frame of thought is similar to how analysts examine distances traveled by criminals. This approach/analysis often assumes offenders were at home when they decided to commit crime. The decision to commit crime could result from many different reasons, and is not always determined when offenders are at home.

Since offender residence data are easier to obtain, often through arrest data, the discussion of where they reside and where crime is committed is referred to as distance-to-crime. Traditionally, this is thought of and discussed as journey-to-crime; however, it is rare we know the true journey offenders took to commit crime. Offenders would have to divulge information about the journey they took to commit crime and where they were when they decided they wanted to commit a crime in the first place. These data are harder to obtain, so a more generalized concept of distance-to-crime is used to not confuse the notion of a true journey-to-crime.

In terms of distances traveled to commit crime, there are attributes that can shape the distances traveled. Think of what characteristics of people, crimes, or places could influence distances traveled. To guide this a bit, if you wanted to commit a crime, imagine the ideal place and then think about the distance from where that location is to your home. Most likely, the distance is not terribly far. At face value, this makes sense because offenders have a working knowledge of the environment. They are aware of who belongs there and where possible targets exist in time and space. Keep in mind that distance to crime analyses examine general patterns in offenders, not one offender at a time. So, distances traveled are discussed in averages or reference the median distance.

Specific crime types also require differing amounts of distances traveled (see Block and Bernasco, 2009). The opportunity to commit crime is not equal everywhere, and certain locations have greater possibilities than others. For example, commercial burglary opportunities will differ from residential burglary based on the type of burglary being committed. Commercial burglary would most likely require a greater distance to be traveled versus residential if residential addresses are used as a starting point. A residence, most of the time, has other residences around it, making residential burglary easier in terms of cost–benefits.

Another consideration is age of offenders. Drawve, Walker, and Felson (2014) made the argument and found support that, as juveniles age (from 11–17), the distance traveled to commit crime would generally increase. The argument here is that older juveniles have a greater number of activities taking them outside residences, they have the ability to drive, and sometimes have less parental supervision. When this occurs, there is a development of a greater awareness for where criminal opportunities exist within juveniles' activity spaces. Usually age is dummied into adults/juveniles or older/younger rather than looking at specific age, as in Drawve et al.'s (2014) study. In that study, categories of younger offenders were more likely to travel less distance to commit crimes than their older counterparts.

There are several problems that exist in analyzing distance-to-crime. We have already discussed the use of home residence as a measurement point to the crime location. This has usually been the basis of journey-to-crime analyses because they are the best available data. Data analyzing distance-to-crime are often arrest data. Arrest data have details on where the crime took place and also where the arrestee resides. There are many crimes, however, that do not result in arrests. In these cases, it is impossible to understand the distance-to-crime. Further, arrests do not always happen at the location of the crime. It is not unusual for the arrest location in crime data to be dominated by the address of the police station or jail. In these cases, it is not known where the crime occurred unless it is a different field from the arrest location.

As methods for collecting data and storing data continue to increase, and accessing the data becomes easier, analysts will have greater flexibility in determining journeys-to-crime rather than just distance. Even if you do not have access to GIS software, there are mapping websites where you can put in two addresses and ask for directions. The results give you a distance based on the street network; and you could record this as the distance. This could be a more accurate measure of distance-to-crime, but it is difficult to undertake if there are hundreds or thousands of cases.

Near repeat

In crime analysis, there is a phrase known as the "near repeat phenomenon," also referred to as repeat victimization. As discussed elsewhere in this book, this is because when a crime occurs in a specific place, the area surrounding the place experiences an elevated level of risk for similar crimes to occur in a certain time period (see Ratcliffe and Rengert, 2008). Brantingham and Brantingham (1975) discussed how residential burglary should, more than other crimes, show a spatial distribution related to the land-use patterning of the study area. Understanding residential burglary spatial patterns allows for a better prediction of where residential burglaries may occur in the future. This speaks to how interrelated crime is in time and space. To ease in the identification of near repeats, Ratcliffe (2007) developed the near repeat calculator, which is free to download.

There are two main concepts linked to repeat victimization: event dependency and risk heterogeneity (Sagovsky and Johnson, 2007). Pease (1998) referred to these concepts as boost (event dependency) and flag (risk heterogeneity). Here, after the initial victimization, the likelihood of further offenses is boosted. Burglars may come back for items that were left at a residence, which "boosts" the risk of being revictimized (see also Chapter 12). Risk heterogeneity refers to a location that is repeatedly victimized because of some enduring characteristic(s) that "flags" it as a suitable target. A property may be flagged for a number of different reasons, such as a lack of security measures or minimal natural surveillance (Sagovsky and Johnson, 2007). It is possible that different burglars flag the same property, so it is possible that it may not be the same burglar committing the repeat burglaries to a residence but a result of overlapping awareness spaces.

Townsley, Homel, and Chaseling, (2003) found near repeat burglaries were located in homogenous areas where there was little to no housing diversity, while few repeat burglaries were found in heterogeneous housing areas. Homogenous housing areas may allow for the near repeat burglaries, and thus stable hot spots to form (Townsley, Homel, and Chaseling, 2003). If offenders are able to gain access to one residence, and the surrounding residences are the same, it provides additional criminal opportunities with little to no additional effort. Think of an apartment complex where every building has the same entry method. Once you learn how to gain access to one, you have tens or hundreds of other opportunities. The homogenous housing area itself creates the criminal opportunities.

This can be viewed as a contagious effect. Once one residence is burglarized, the surrounding residences are at a heightened risk to become burglarized. The burglar could become familiar with that area and, while committing the first burglary, may have found new targets that have equal or greater rewards. Because residential areas are generally clustered within a city, clusters of repeat residential burglaries could form in small geographical areas. This repeat victimization may produce stable victimization areas of burglary consistent with the literature on other crime hot spots (discussed in Chapter 13).

KEY CONCEPTS

Beyond the concepts discussed so far, there are some terms that you should be familiar with when doing GIS crime analyses. Some of the more important of these are briefly discussed here.

Map Projection: The world is a 3-dimensional surface but the maps are produced in 2-dimensions. GIS files are developed based on a coordinate system to preserve properties of how it appears in space. There are different types of projections depending on the area being studied (i.e. county, state, country, world); each preserves different elements to better reflect how the area appears on the surface of the earth.

Map Scale: A scale provides a reference to the size of the study area on a map. Depending on the analysis level, it might be more appropriate to use feet, meters, miles, or kilometers.

Map North Arrow: For a point of reference, professional maps need a north arrow to provide context to the environment (for examples see LeBeau, 1987; LeBeau and Vincent, 1997). In the simplest form, a north arrow gives a sense of direction.

Geocode: Crime data often have to be taken from a spreadsheet form and placed in a GIS software program. Geocoding is the process of taking addresses and linking them to points on a map. Ratcliffe (2004) identified that when geocoding crime data, the minimum needed to match (become a pin on a map) is 85 percent. In general, analysts want to match as many crimes to a map as possible so analyses do not suffer from missing data issues. As analysts work more with their agency data, they will pick up on patterns in the data requiring greater cleaning and where improvements are needed to increase the reliability of the data.

Geographic Profiling: By name alone, geographic profiling is a spatial analytical technique to assist in serial violent crime investigations (see Rossmo, 2000). The technique can be used to support a crime analyst's examination of crime series in hopes of potentially identifying where offenders live, dump sites, and crime sites (among others).

CONCLUSION

Crime mapping is a mainstay in crime analysis. Mapping is not the only type of analyses that need to be conducted. Analysts need to be familiar with the background to why mapping is important. You can always make a pretty map, but what does it mean? The value of a crime analyst is to relay data analysis to officers, administrators, city officials, and the community. The interpretation of the maps is more valuable than the map itself. This is part of the reason for the current textbook. All too often crime mapping is learned without a basis in environmental criminology, relevant statistics, and common applications/terminology, creating a steeper learning curve. As technology continues to advance, the abilities of analysts and the tools available to them will be even greater. Even with these advancements, the value of human capital analysts offer to agencies will be critical in truly understanding relevant issues in their jurisdictions.

REFERENCES

Block, R. and W. Bernasco. 2009. Finding a serial burglar's home using distance decay and conditional origin–destination patterns: A test of empirical Bayes journey-to-crime estimation in The Hague. *Journal of Investigative Psychology and Offender Profiling*, 6(3): 187–211.

Brantingham, P.L. and P.J. Brantingham. 1975. Residential burglary and urban form. *Urban Studies*, 12: 273–284.

Caplan, J.M. and L.W. Kennedy. 2016. *Risk Terrain Modeling: Crime Prediction and Risk Reduction*. Oakland: University of California Press.

Chainey, S. and J. Ratcliffe. 2005. *GIS and Crime Mapping*. London: Wiley.

Drawve, G., J.T. Walker, and M. Felson. 2014. Juvenile offenders: An examination of distance-to-crime and crime clusters. *Cartography and Geographic Information Science*, 42(2): 122–133.

LeBeau, J.L. 1987. The methods and measures of centrography and the spatial dynamics of rape. *Journal of Quantitative Criminology*, 3(2): 125–141.

LeBeau, J.L. and K.L. Vincent. 1997. Mapping it out: Repeat-address burglar alarms and burglaries. In D. Weisburd and J.T. McEwen (Eds.), *Crime Mapping and Crime Prevention* (pp. 289–310). Monsey, NY: Criminal Justice Press.

Pease, K. 1998. *Repeat Victimisation: Taking Stock*. Crime Detection and Prevention Series, Paper 90. London: Home Office.

Ratcliffe, J. 2004. Geocoding crime and a first estimate of a minimum acceptable hit rate. *International Journal of Geographical Information Science,* 18(1): 61–72.

Ratcliffe, J.H. 2007. *Integrated Intelligence and Crime Analysis: Enhanced Information Management for Law Enforcement Leaders*. Washington, DC: Police Foundation.

Ratcliffe, J.H. and G.F. Rengert. 2008. Near-repeat patterns in Philadelphia shootings. *Security Journal*, 21(1): 58–76.

Rossmo, K. 2000. *Geographical Profiling*. Boca Raton, FL: CRC Press.

Sagovsky, A. and S.D. Johnson. 2007. When does repeat burglary victimisation occur? *Australian & New Zealand Journal of Criminology*, 40(1): 1–26.

Townsley, M., R. Homel, and J. Chaseling. 2003. Infectious burglaries: A test of the near repeat hypothesis. *British Journal of Criminology*, 43(3): 615–633.

QUESTIONS AND EXERCISES

1   How has crime mapping advanced and what are its implications for the future?
2   What are the two main types of data in crime mapping? How are they used? What is the importance of an address locator?
3   Search for one of the free crime mapping programs discussed or find one not listed. What are the reviews? If you have your own computer, consider downloading a free program with practice data.
4   Why is distance/journey-to-crime important? Why is distance-to-crime used rather than the traditional idea of journey-to-crime?
5   Why are the homes of offenders used when determining how far they traveled to commit crime?
6   What is "near repeat phenomenon"? Search for recent articles testing the near repeat hypothesis. What did the results find? What crimes were examined?
7   What are the two main concepts linked to repeat victimization?
8   What helps create opportunity for a residential area to be victimized?

Retrospective techniques

Analysts use their knowledge of place, opportunity, and the situational nature of crime when assessing criminogenic factors to guide the development of police responses. This chapter looks at retrospective techniques of mapping crime. They are retrospective because the data are from the past, and they only show where crime has occurred. These techniques will be distinguished from the prospective (predictive) techniques discussed in the next chapter. The most prevalent types of retrospective techniques are those related to mapping hot spots of crime. The history of hot spots, the base assumptions and analyses, and some more advanced methods will be discussed in this chapter.

HISTORY OF HOT SPOTS

As has been discussed in many places in this book, the foundation of exploring concentrations of crime began with the work of Guerry and Quetelet. It was greatly expanded in the work of the Chicago School in the 1920s and 1930s, particularly the work of Shaw and McKay. Interest in mapping crime and analyzing the geographic distribution of crime continued after the work of the Chicago School. But most of these maps and analyses were still conducted by hand.

As discussed in Chapter 12, the ability to digitize maps and to indicate crimes on those maps was developed from the 1980s, initially by academics. The problems both academics and police agencies had was the ability to get data sufficient to conduct analyses and the capability for GIS analysis. At that time, almost no police agencies had any access to GIS software that could even map the distribution of crime; so, any geographic representations were completed by hand, often with a large map on the wall with pins in it. What resources might be available at the city level were typically in the planning office and either unavailable to the police or the coordination was so complex it was almost not worth the effort. The introduction of GIS software on personal computers would change all of that (see, for example, Joelson and Fishbine, 1980).

By 1986, the Illinois Criminal Justice Information Authority (ILCJIA) had developed the Spatial and Temporal Analysis of Crime (STAC) program for finding and describing hot spots. This program identified high concentrations within a geographic area and bounded it with an ellipse. The way it did this was to count the number of points in a grid (raster) overlay of the area to find those that had a high concentration of points. The circle was then displayed on a map with the center over the mean location of the points. When the program was introduced to the ILCJIA board, the term used for these concentrations was called a "hot spot."

The work that made the term "hot spots of crime" popular was a project in Minneapolis, sponsored by the National Institute of Justice. This study found that relatively few areas had a concentration of crime (Sherman, Gartin, and Buerger, 1989). For example, 50 percent of the calls for police occurred in only 3 percent of the places in the city. One problem of this study was that it only coded a single address as a hot spot, regardless of the "size" of that location. For example, a very large apartment complex with hundreds of residents was coded as a single address for hot spot analyses. It also did not take into account that some places had a higher probability of a call for police. For example, a very large department store that hired extra security officers and had an aggressive shoplifting prevention plan would have a higher number of calls than a smaller department store that did not have such "guardianship" measures in place.

The popularity of hot spots research quickly spawned a number of analysis methods and geographic-based software to analyze the hot spots. Roncek (see, for example, Roncek, 1981; Roncek and Francik, 1981) and others were using GIS analyses by the late 1980s. There were people who were also working on better ways to analyze crime and place data – and were specifically working to overcome some of the problems of the Sherman et al. study.

TYPES OF HOT SPOT ANALYSES

Pin maps

Historically, the most common method of identifying hot spots was using point mapping (see Figure 13.1). This kind of analysis was shown as far back as Shaw and McKay (1942) and was routinely

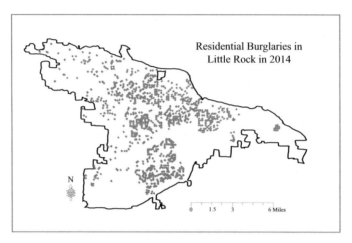

Figure 13.1 Pin Map of Burglaries in Little Rock

Figure 13.2 Ellipse Map of Hot Spots
Source: Eck et al. (2005).

used by police agencies when trying to analyze crime in their city. The reasons these kinds of maps were used were twofold. First, as discussed below, crimes occur at places. Therefore, using dot maps indicating specific locations makes sense. Further, it is much easier to place pins on a map and to update them than it is to use other methods.

A major problem of pin maps is that there is no real way to indicate the intensity of the occurrence at that location. Multiple data points at the same place look like one point. For example, a bar that had one incident and a bar that had 300 incidents look the same on a pin map. There are more recent mapping methods that partially overcome this issue while continuing to use a pin map; but, often, analysts and researchers use a different kind of map to display intensity.

An extension of pin maps specifically to display hot spots is using spatial ellipses to show the locations of hot spots (see Figure 13.2). This does not necessarily affect the analysis, but it does make it easier to distinguish hot spots from other locations, and it can assist with the analysis when hot spots have been identified using statistical analyses, which are then displayed on a map.

Choropleth maps

To overcome some of the issues of point mapping, choropleth, or thematic, maps are used (see Figure 13.3). These maps shade the areas with different markings to represent different degrees of the variable. Typical choropleth maps are where a boundary such as a police district or Census tract is shaded in to represent the concentration in the area. They have the advantage of clearly showing different levels of crime or other variables. Their only disadvantage is that the areas are larger, so they may overrepresent the variation that likely occurs within the area.

A growing number of spatial analysis programs are using raster or grid data as a part of their analyses. These typically produce grid-system maps, as shown in Figure 13.4. These analyses overlay a grid over the area to be examined and then compare data between the cells of the grid. A common method associated with grid-system maps is Local Indicators of Spatial Association (LISA). LISA statistics examine the spatial association between data by comparing local averages to global averages. For this reason, they are useful in adding definition to crime hot spots and placing a spatial limit on those areas of highest crime event concentration. One of the more applied LISA statistics on crime point events is the Gi* statistic (see Ratcliffe and McCullagh, 1999, for more details). The Gi* statistic is applied to a grid cell output, such as a quartic kernel density estimation map, from which local associations are compared against the global average.

Van Patten, McKeldin-Coner, and Cox (2009) used a LISA analysis to examine the robbery distribution in Roanoke, Virginia. For this LISA analysis, they generated a map with thousand-foot grid cells and then shaded them to represent the LISA output of concentrations of robbery. Their goal was to create a map where a high concentration of robberies were first-order neighbors to other cells with a high concentration. If the spatial autocorrelation between the cells was significant ($p < 0.05$) then the cell was categorized as a High-High cell. Similarly, cells were classified as Low-Low (low concentration neighboring a low concentration), Low-High, and High-Low cells. As shown in Figure 13.4, they were able to display in a grid-map where the concentrations of robbery lay in the city.

Smoothing maps

As already mentioned, one problem of pin map representation is that it becomes less effective when the pins stack on top of each other. For example, if there are 57 calls to a single address, the intensity of that address becomes lost because the pins just look like one call. A way around this is using a concentration procedure. Also, a common criticism of many maps, both point and choropleth, is that

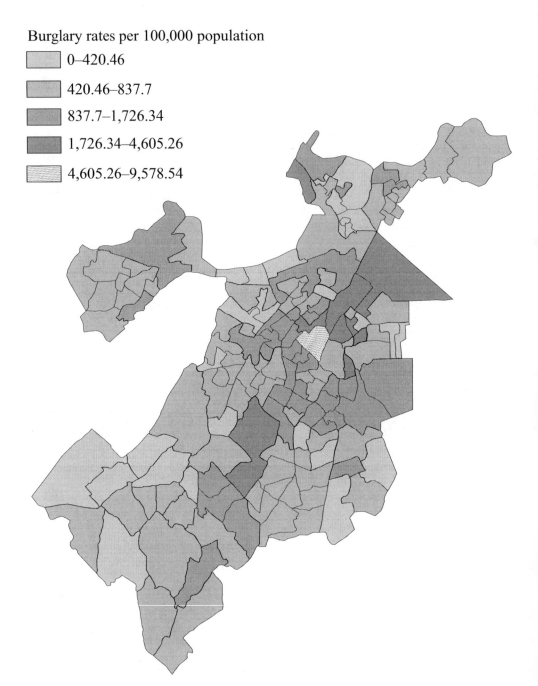

Burglary rates per 100,000 population

0–420.46

420.46–837.7

837.7–1,726.34

1,726.34–4,605.26

4,605.26–9,578.54

Figure 13.3 Thematic/Choropleth Map
Source: Eck et al. (2005).

they rely on government-created boundaries (mostly Census tracts or police boundaries, but they could be neighborhood boundaries as defined by the city or other types). Surface smoothing methods were designed to overcome this limitation. These types of maps (typically kernel density estimation

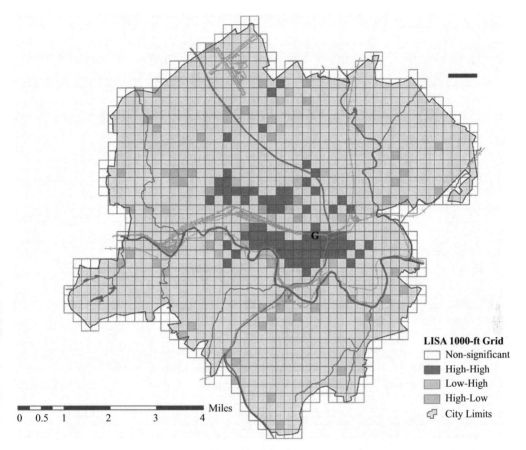

LISA 1000-ft Grid
☐ Non-significant
■ High-High
▨ Low-High
▨ High-Low
⌘ City Limits

Miles
0   0.5   1   2   3   4

Figure 13.4 Grid-System Map
Source: Van Patten et al. (2009).

and isopleth maps) ignore boundaries, and instead show the concentrations of crime in the form of intensity bands.

Kernel density estimation (KDE) maps, sometimes called heat maps, typically show a center hot spot and then gradients of reductions in crimes surrounding it. A KDE map of aggravated assault is shown in Figure 13.5. This type of map does not use an artificial boundary. A problem with these kinds of maps is that the size of the areas can distort the interpretation of the distribution. Large dark areas may look like major problems, whereas smaller dark areas may have a higher frequency of crime but concentrated in a smaller area, so it does not look like as big a problem.

There are other methods of examining microplaces of crime that are more mathematical than visual. These may be displayed on a map in some ways (such as the LISA analysis described above or the microplace analysis of Weisburd, Bushway, Lum, and Yang (2004), who used KDE maps to examine block segments in Seattle). Some of these methods are discussed in the next section.

HOT SPOT ANALYSES

As shown in the discussion above, there are several ways hot spots can be identified. Most police analyses prefer to use hot addresses because they are called to addresses for crimes. Sometimes the

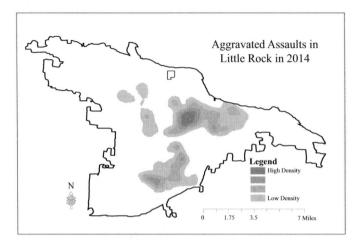

Figure 13.5 Kernel Density Map of Aggravated Assaults

police, and also researchers, examine hot blocks or clusters of blocks (microplaces). Researchers also examine larger areas for hot spots (Census block groups or tracts, etc.) because it is easier to blend social and economic data at this level.

A National Institute of Justice report (Eck, Chainey, Cameron, Leitner, and Wilson, 2005) on crime mapping argued that there are at least two critical factors in using hot spot analysis in policing. First, it proposed that hot spot analysis can be most effective for police agencies when it is guided by theories of crime related to the crime environment (such as those discussed in Chapter 3). It also argued that hot spot analysis requires multiple techniques to properly analyze the data.

The desire to increase the understanding of crime in microplaces resulted in the National Institute of Justice awarding a large, multi-year grant to study crime in Seattle. Perhaps the culmination of the analysis of this research is Weisburd, Groff, and Yang (2012). They examined crime at the street segment (generally conceptualized as a block on a single street). One of the improvements of this work over previous research was their analysis of street segments using trajectory analysis. Their findings were that a few street segments in both low and high disadvantaged neighborhoods consistently accounted for most of the crime in those areas. They proposed that these microplaces had characteristics that were different from other places, even within the same general area.

One problem of using hot spots to analyze crime data is that they are not truly static, which makes it difficult to be effectively analyzed over time. Traditional options to address fluctuations over time were to use an area that may be larger than needed to include minor fluctuations in the hot spot, or to ignore "wobble" in crimes that occur just outside the hot spot.

Short, Brantingham, Bertozzi, and Tita (2010) attempted to overcome this problem by creating an analysis procedure for examining the dynamics of hot spots. They essentially took the principles of routine activities theory and near-repeat offenses and applied mathematical formulas to them such that the level of risk of victims in a particular area produced hot spots. They could then examine the stability, decrease, or spatial diffusion of the risk to determine how spatially and temporally stable the hot spot was. They found that certain locations have an elevated risk of victimization. When a crime occurs, the area surrounding the victimization will also have an elevated risk for additional crimes. If this area does not come into contact with the area surrounding other crimes in the region, the result will be individual crimes. If the areas surrounding the crimes are so big that essentially a large region is completely covered by risk, then additional crimes may occur, but they will not represent hot spots. If the areas surrounding the crimes are small but do come into contact with other crimes in the immediate region, it has a mathematical increase in the likelihood of additional crimes occurring there, resulting in a hot spot of crime.

Similarly, Gorr and Lee (2014) found that hot spots tend to have small footprints; and that distance decay is strong. They used kernel density smoothing patterns to examine the concentration of violent crimes. They found that the primary ring of their identified hot spots had an average of 738 Part I violent crimes, while a second ring had only 372 crimes and the next ring had 214 crimes. They divided hot spots into those that were chronic (those lasting years or decades) and temporary (usually lasting less than a year, more often months). Think of chronic hot spots as neighborhoods that have been high in crime for a very long time and temporary hot spots as drug markets that may stay on a street corner for a while but then move. They found that chronic hot spots were more likely to be in commercial areas of disadvantaged neighborhoods. Temporary hot spots were more likely to be spread across a city and not necessarily concentrated in areas of disadvantage. Gorr and Lee (2014) argued that early detection of temporary hot spots can be key to shortening their existence. They also argued that early detection of these hot spots for more minor crimes could foretell an increase in more serious crimes in the same area. In a similar study, Cohen, Gorr, and Olligschlaeger (2007) found that understanding increases in less serious crimes enabled prediction of approximately 25 percent of increases in more serious and violent crimes a month in advance. A limitation of these kinds of analyses at present is that they require larger units of analysis (Census tracts) than is efficient for crime analyses.

One commonality about hot spots is that we tend to think of them as fairly defined areas with often sharp breaks outside of them. Think of an ellipse on a map. Whether it is real on the ground or not, the boundary of a microplace has an area inside the ellipse and one outside the ellipse. An example of this can be found in the Cohen et al. (2007) study. In this study, crime fell off dramatically when moving away from the hottest hot spots. While other cities show similar drop-offs, they are not always as sharp. The work by Frank, Park, Brantingham, Clare, Wuschke, and Vajihollahi (2010) found that, in some cases, this is an accurate portrayal of the microplace, where there are sharp boundaries in at least part of the microplace. In others, or in other parts of a microplace, there are often very gradual changes from higher to lower crime levels. Frank et al. (2010) also argued that not all microplaces of crime are perfect circles, or even oblong, or oval, circles. That is why it is important for crime analysts to know their city, the law enforcement agency, and the crime data so they can have the best possible analyses of the crime in that particular city. Crime analysts should know enough about the shape of their city to know when to stretch a microplace along a strip shopping development or to place it within a more circular ellipse around a shopping mall.

As discussed in Chapter 11, crime can also cluster in time and can cluster in space/time. For example, Braga and Clarke (2014) proposed that the flow of the population into, out of, and within a hot spot area makes a difference over the course of a day, and should be examined. There are methods of examining the spatio-temporal aspect of crime, as previously discussed. Again, these are more statistical analyses than geographic, although GIS systems are beginning to have temporal analysis modules in them.

WHAT TO DO ABOUT HOT SPOTS

The obvious reason we pay so much attention to hot spots of crime is to be able to reduce crime there. Over the years, many strategies have been put in place to address crime hot spots. Reports on many of these efforts can be found at the Center for Problem-Oriented Policing (www.popcenter.org). One would think addressing crime in chronic hot spots (those that have been high in crime for many years) would be simple – just put prevention measures in place and sustain them there. But it is more complicated than that. Some hot spots have social issues that are beyond the control of the criminal justice system.

Gorr and Lee (2014) proposed a strategy for detecting and dealing with temporary hot spots. Their strategy was to use crime data to identify temporary hot spots, work to deploy the right resources to address the problem, and to determine when the resources can be reduced or eliminated for that hot spot. The prevention methods they suggested were to identify the highest density chronic hot spots for sustained deployment of resources. They then proposed it was more effective to deploy resources to temporary hot spots rather than using them in larger areas of chronic hot spots.

CONCLUSION

As we continue to learn more about hot spot analyses from environmental criminology and crime analysis, we will be able to use more sophisticated analyses to refine our detection and forecasting of microplace crime. For example, Bosse and Gerritsen (2010) introduced an agent-based model of hot spots using agents in routine activities theory. An interesting finding of this research was that the guardians (police) almost always reacted to hot spots after they formed rather than anticipating them, even though the agents were not programed to be reactionary. This shows that police behavior of adapting to the movement of crime rather than anticipating it may be a normal occurrence; so crime analysts need to work to improve our ability to forecast where microplace crime will occur. This is the topic of the next chapter.

REFERENCES

Bosse, T. and C. Gerritsen. 2010. Social simulation and analysis of the dynamics of criminal hot spots. *Journal of Artificial Societies and Social Simulation*, 13(2): 5–28.
Braga, A.A. and R.V. Clarke. 2014. Explaining high-risk concentrations of crime in the city: Social disorganization, crime opportunities, and important next steps. *Journal of Research in Crime and Delinquency*, 51(4): 480–498.
Cohen J., W.L. Gorr, and A.M. Olligschlaeger. 2007. Leading indicators and spatial interactions: A crime-forecasting model for proactive police deployment. *Geography Analysis*, 39: 105–127.
Eck, J.E., S. Chainey, J.G. Cameron, M. Leitner, and R.E. Wilson. 2005. *Mapping Crime: Understanding Hot Spots*. Washington, DC: National Institute of Justice.
Frank, R., A.J. Park, P. Brantingham, J. Clare, K. Wuschke, and M. Vajihollahi. 2010. Identifying high risk crime areas using topology. Paper presented at the IEEE Intelligence and Security Informatics – Public Safety and Security Conference. Vancouver, Canada.
Gorr, W.L. and Y. Lee. 2014. Early warning system for temporary crime hot spots. *Journal of Quantitative Criminology*, 31(1): 25–47.
Joelson, M.R. and G.M. Fishbine. 1980. The display of geographic information in crime analysis. In D.E. Georges-Abeyie and K.D. Harries, (Eds.), *Crime: A Spatial Perspective* (pp. 247–263). New York, NY: Columbia University Press.
Ratcliffe, J.H. and M.J. McCullagh. 1999. Hotbeds of crime and the search for spatial accuracy. *Journal of Geographical Analysis*. 1: 385–398.
Roncek, D.W. 1981. Dangerous places. *Social Forces*, 60: 74–96.
Roncek, D.W. and J.M.A. Francik. 1981. Housing projects and crime. *Social Problems*, 29: 151–166.
Shaw, C.R. and H.D. McKay. 1942. *Juvenile Delinquency and Urban Areas*. Chicago, IL: University of Chicago Press.
Sherman, L.W., P.R. Gartin, and M.E. Buerger. 1989. Hot spots of predatory crime routine activities and the criminology of place. *Criminology*, 27: 27–56.
Short, M.B., P.J. Brantingham, A.L. Bertozzi, and G.E. Tita. 2010. Dissipation and displacement of hotspots in reaction–diffusion models of crime. *Proceedings of the National Academy of Sciences of the United States of America*, 107(9): 3961–3965.

Van Patten, I.T., J. McKeldin-Coner, and D. Cox. 2009. A microspatial analysis of robbery: Prospective hot spotting in a small city. *Crime Mapping: A Journal of Research and Practice,* 1(1): 7–32.

Weisburd, D., S. Bushway, C. Lum, and S. Yang. 2004. Trajectories of crime at places: A longitudinal study of street segments in the city of Seattle. *Criminology,* 42: 283–321.

Weisburd D.L., E.R. Groff, and S.M. Yang. 2012. *The Criminology of Place: Street Segments and Our Understanding of the Crime Problem.* New York, NY: Oxford University Press.

QUESTIONS AND EXERCISES

1   What are some reasons why a hot spot ellipse would need to be a shape other than round? Discuss these reasons in terms of the social and physical (buildings, businesses) aspects of an area.

2   What are some reasons why you would want to use pin maps over choropleth or smoothing maps when making a presentation of crime to the command staff of a police agency?

3   Other than the ways discussed in the chapter, how might you be able to display how a hot spot changes over time?

4   Find an article that uses hot spot analyses to examine crime in the area. What were their methods? What did their results show? Explain their results in terms of the social, economic, and physical environment (you should be able to go beyond what is provided in the article and offer additional explanations based on what you have learned so far in the class).

Chapter 14

Predictive techniques, analytics, and applications

Vijay F. Chillar

MOVING BEYOND HOT SPOTS

Many years of research has demonstrated crime incidents do not distribute uniformly or randomly across geographic places. Instead, they cluster, often referred to as hot spots (discussed in Chapter 13). Additionally, we know that crime is dynamic in nature and changes over time (Brantingham and Brantingham, 1995; Ratcliffe, 2010).

Hot spot analysis as a tool, as discussed in Chapter 13, has an inherent nature of being retroactive in that it is dependent on past crime occurring. This makes sense and provides a knowledge base of where crime occurred and where it significantly clustered; however, that is all the technique provides agencies. If we only use hot spot analysis, we are left with an inconclusive understanding of why the crimes occurred in the first place and where they are most likely to move (displacement) or to emerge next should they disappear from the original location. This limits what police can do with that knowledge in an attempt to lower and prevent crime at places. Additionally, this generally results in police chasing crime rather than understanding the underlying mechanisms influencing where, when, and why crime occurs throughout a jurisdiction. In crime analysis, it is imperative to note the importance of past crime incidents (retrospective techniques) in providing a foundational knowledge of spatial patterns. But there is more that can be accomplished with crime analysis than only looking at the past.

BUILDING TOWARD A BETTER UNDERSTANDING
OF CRIME AND PREVENTING CRIME AT PLACES

The spatial technique of identifying crime hot spots through GIS mapping has been successful (Braga, 2005). Utilizing a targeted approach, such as focused deterrence strategies by police within hot spots, has been supported by research and continues to be used by police agencies across the nation. Based on the research of crime and place, you might expect interventions to be associated with targeted policing initiatives that focus on the built environment of the identified place; however, police responses have typically taken an offender-focused approach. For example, the Operation Ceasefire initiative that took place in Boston (Braga et al., 2001) was based on enforcement actions aimed at reducing youth violence by disrupting street-level drug markets, serving warrants, and mounting federal prosecutions. The problem associated with focused aggressive police enforcement strategies is twofold: entire neighborhoods run the risk of acquiring a more negative self-image associated with the stigma of being labeled as a hot spot of crime, and the residents that comprise those neighborhoods could view the police as abusers of power who profile them as the "best fit" candidate (individual) for crime based on select demographical characteristics (Kennedy, Caplan, and Piza, 2011).

The core of hot spots is that there are clusters of crime, which may have been identified through the mapping techniques based on crime locations from a defined time period (week, month, quarter, year). This identification process and output would then be used as a means of where crime is expected to occur in the future (Harries, 1999). Knowing this, it would logically appear that police would target these areas to solve the problem at hand (i.e. place-based); however, the "stationary fallacy" posed by Brantingham and Brantingham (1981) emphasized that hot spots are combinations of unrelated incidents that occurred over time and are plotted in hot spots as though they are somehow connected beyond sharing a common geography. Instead of addressing the common thread of the incidents, interventions born out of hot spots policing typically involve the incapacitation of the offending individuals (agencies trying to arrest their way out of a problem), which may fail to cool off these areas as the location remains suitable for other offenders to commit crime (forming stable hot spot or chronic places of crime). This is captured by Caplan and Kennedy (2016), who describe police sentiment as that resembling a game of "whack-a-mole" with crime, in that a focus on hot spot areas causes crime to displace elsewhere (not always in the immediate surrounding area as researchers often measure) and then return to the original location once the focus shifts. With police and other law enforcement agencies being strained by tight fiscal budgets, it is not financially, nor practically, suitable to participate in a prolonged game of "whack-a-mole" because it can deplete valuable resources without producing noteworthy results – specifically, the reduction of crime.

Building on our understanding about the nature of crime, it is appropriate to surmise that crime prevention resources should be concentrated on targeted places rather than dispersed across a larger study area (Braga, 2001). This is well established within the hot spots policing literature in which police departments have funneled their resources into areas of high crime as a result of this geographical focus; typically, with measured effectiveness (Weisburd, 2008). A systematic review conducted by Braga (2001) identified nine studies examining police interventions at crime hot spots; seven of which reported statistically significant reductions in crime. Again, it should be noted that utilizing hot spots as a technique for mapping clusters of high crime areas is an empirically proven practice that has led to more geographically focused police practices with a strategic allocation of resources, resulting in noteworthy crime reductions.

Hot spot analysis has brought us to a point where we are able to identify the areas where crime clusters and utilize targeted practices to reduce their stability; but the approach leaves researchers and practitioners wanting more. Predictive techniques seek to extend this by providing an understanding of the relationship between crime and the built environment. Ideally, this will assist police in what to do with high-risk places for crime, and shift the focus from people to the environment as a means to reduce the spatial vulnerability of its features.

There are several predictive techniques and software programs utilized by police. Some of these only tell the police where they should be to prevent crime without providing any of the "why" or understanding. Others do more to include both the social and built environment in the analysis, and give police more information about the environment where the crime is occurring. In this chapter, we will focus on one predictive technique: Risk Terrain Modeling.

RISK TERRAIN MODELING (RTM)

Risk Terrain Modeling (RTM) is a spatial diagnostic tool that identifies significant place features from the environment (i.e. types of businesses, parks, etc.) and models how the features co-locate in space to create behavior settings for crime (see: www.riskterrainmodeling.com). For example, imagine you are walking through a town; instinctively there are features that you would avoid (tall bushes, alleyways, vacant properties, etc.) and others that you would seek to increase your perceptions of safety (street lighting, residential buildings, schools, etc.). The way those place features co-locate help you to determine the level of risk that is posed – a sidewalk that is adjacent to tall bushes and is absent of street lighting has a higher perceived risk level than a sidewalk that is well lit and is adjacent to residential buildings. We can see that each feature has its own risk; and, when we begin to add different features together, the risk varies with each combination. While the outcome may classically be a typology of crime, RTM has been applied to various topics such as injury prevention, public health, child maltreatment, traffic accidents, and pollution studies to name a few.

By examining places rather than people, RTM shifts the focus away from individual characteristics to the way people interact and use their environments (Caplan and Kennedy, 2016). RTM is composed of three concepts, defined as:

1   *Risk:* the probability of an occurrence of an unwanted outcome (i.e. crime) determined by the increased spatial vulnerabilities at places.
2   *Terrain:* cells whose attributes quantify vulnerabilities at each place.
3   *Modeling:* attributing the presence, absence, influence, or intensity of qualities of the real world to places within a terrain to study their simultaneous effect on the risk for undesired outcomes.

Through three key processes, RTM first seeks to cartographically operationalize qualities of a landscape to a geographic map whose layers represent spatial influences of environmental features – often crime generators and attractors. Here, spatial influence is defined as the "measurable link between features of a landscape and their impacts on people and the ways in which they use space" and is operationalized as proximity, density, or both (Caplan and Kennedy, 2016: 21). For example, we may want to know what the relative risk, or the likelihood of occurrence based on the risk factors, is for a motor vehicle theft if we are within a certain proximity or within a cluster of a certain environmental feature. Proximity, as the term suggests, means that being at a place close to a potential risk factor (a bar, bodega, strip-club, etc.) has a greater likelihood for crime than places not in close proximity to those factors. Density refers to when multiple facilities of the same type cluster in space and create a riskier place for crime. Using hotels as an example, places where hotels cluster are at greater risk for motor vehicle theft than places where hotels do not cluster. By operationalizing the spatial influences of features within a landscape, we are able to measure the theoretical and behavioral links between people and their geographies.

It is important to note that no two study areas are alike; and, thus, the risk factors selected must be chosen in a way that incorporates the knowledge of the defined area to ensure they are practically meaningful. For example, if we know that the presence of bars correlates with an increased risk for robbery but the study area does not contain any bars, it would not be relevant to include them within the risk terrain model. By combining both the theoretical and the empirical risk factors, we apply informed risk factors to ensure that the model of "best fit" will be able to properly diagnose risky places within the environment that are at a statistically higher likelihood of experiencing crime.

To quantify risk across a study area and assist in the RTM steps, the Risk Terrain Modeling Diagnostics (RTMDx) Utility was developed (Caplan and Kennedy, 2013). RTMDx is a means of automating the RTM process to produce an output list of environmental risk factors and their spatial influence on the outcome event (see Caplan, Kennedy, and Piza, 2013). The output from RTMDx indicates specific vulnerabilities at places by computing a relative risk value (RRV), according to their relative spatial influences on crime events – this allows for the prioritization of risk factors during intervention planning as a way to maximize allocated resources. The parameters of RTMDx are briefly listed below, followed by an example of how RTM can be used to better understand crime in a jurisdiction. This can show the applicability of predictive modeling programs such as RTM for police agencies.

1   *Study Area Boundary:* Shapefile of area being studied (i.e. city or police district).
2   *Block Length:* Should be set to the mean length of a block face in the study area.
3   *Raster Cell Size:* Should be set to half the block length.
4   *Model Type:* Aggregative (negative effects) or Protective (detractors of crime).
5   *Outcome Event Data:* Outcome of interest (i.e. shootings, robberies, auto theft, etc.).
6   *Risk Factor Data:*
    i   Operationalization: Proximity, Density, or Both
    ii   Max Spatial Influence: 1 Block – 4 Blocks
    iii   Analysis Increments: Half Block, Whole Block.

These are used to display spatial vulnerabilities in the results of a RTM analysis (see below). The results are displayed using tabular (Figure 14.3) and cartographic (Figure 14.4) outputs in which the spatial influences of the identified factors are combined to display areas of high risk for the outcome event. The results of the analyses are to communicate meaningful information to produce actionable intelligence.

Example of RTM analyses

In this section, we work through an example of RTM analysis to show the steps of RTM and how to use the RTMDx Utility. Figure 14.1 displays the interface of RTMDx Utility and the way in which information will be entered to construct the model.

First, you begin by selecting an outcome event of interest, which in this case is automobile theft. Second, choose the study area; we chose Little Rock, Arkansas, as our study area (during this step, you will need to find boundary files for your selected study area). Third, determine the time period for the study (here calendar year 2013). Fourth, identify risk factors that may be applicable to automobile theft (www.rutgerscps.org/publications.html contains literature reviews for possible associated risk factors for various outcome events). In this case, we chose banks, big box retail stores, bus stops, check cashing facilities, grocery/supermarkets, liquor stores, public high schools, pawn shops, fast food chains, and convenience stores. In each of these cases, you must obtain the spatial data for the locations of the risk factors as well as for the outcome event.

At this point, we have the necessary data to begin utilizing the RTMDx Utility. Keep in mind, that when utilizing the RTMDx Utility you will also need to provide the associated parameters of the model: the block length of the study area (432 feet), the cell size (216 feet), and the type of model you want to run (aggravating). The next step is to make a decision as to the operationalization of the spatial influence for each factor. If you select both proximity and density, the software will determine which operationalization is optimal for the model. A conscious decision should be made at this step because it will be important to interpreting the results and turning them into actionable intelligence. Included within this step is selecting the spatial influence of the factor, which can range from one to four blocks. For this example, we selected a spatial influence of three blocks with half block analysis increments. Figure 14.2 displays the risk factors that were empirically selected and input into the RTMDx, inclusive of their spatial influence parameters.

Once the factors are selected and the parameters are set, the software will select the statistically significant factors and weight them. To determine the influence of each factor, we consult the relative risk value (RRV) in the table (see Figure 14.3). Those with larger relative risk values have a larger influence on the outcome event of the study, which in this case is automobile theft in Little Rock, AR, during 2013. The software will produce an output page of the findings of the model of best fit. The tabular results are displayed in Figure 14.3.

In this model, there were six risk factors identified in the final RTM. The largest relative risk value were banks, convenience stores, big box retail, bus stops, fast food, and liquor stores. As illustrated, a place located within a proximity of 216 feet (approximately half a block) of a bank has a relative risk value of 12.01. Another way to think of the RRV is, being at a place within a half-block of a bank is 12 times as risky for an automobile theft than places beyond a half-block. It is also possible to calculate differences between risk locations. For example, when comparing a place influenced by convenience stores to a place influenced by a bus stop, we find that the expected risk of automobile theft is approximately three times higher (11.9/4.2 = 2.83). Knowing this information, police can prioritize which risk factor to target based on their relative risk value. In this case, we may choose to address banks to reduce the relative risk they pose to those within their proximity of experiencing potential automobile theft.

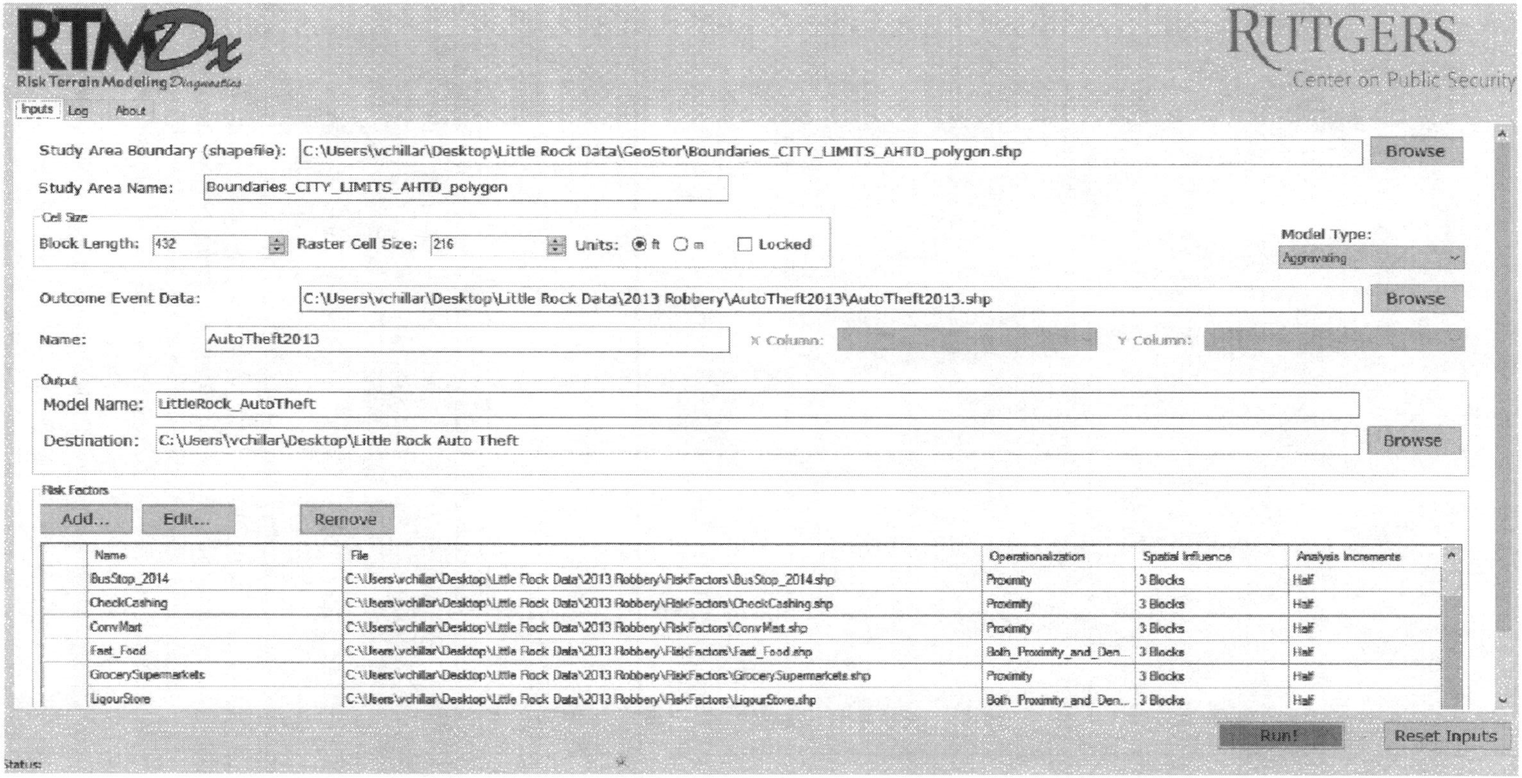

RTMDx
Risk Terrain Modeling Diagnostics

Inputs Log About

RUTGERS
Center on Public Security

Study Area Boundary (shapefile): C:\Users\vchillar\Desktop\Little Rock Data\GeoStor\Boundaries_CITY_LIMITS_AHTD_polygon.shp   Browse

Study Area Name: Boundaries_CITY_LIMITS_AHTD_polygon

Cell Size
Block Length: 432   Raster Cell Size: 216   Units: ⦿ ft ◯ m   ☐ Locked

Model Type: Aggravating

Outcome Event Data: C:\Users\vchillar\Desktop\Little Rock Data\2013 Robbery\AutoTheft2013\AutoTheft2013.shp   Browse

Name: AutoTheft2013

X Column: Y Column:

Output
Model Name: LittleRock_AutoTheft
Destination: C:\Users\vchillar\Desktop\Little Rock Auto Theft   Browse

Risk Factors
Add...   Edit...   Remove

Name	File	Operationalization	Spatial Influence	Analysis Increments
BusStop_2014	C:\Users\vchillar\Desktop\Little Rock Data\2013 Robbery\Risk Factors\Bus Stop_2014.shp	Proximity	3 Blocks	Half
CheckCashing	C:\Users\vchillar\Desktop\Little Rock Data\2013 Robbery\Risk Factors\CheckCashing.shp	Proximity	3 Blocks	Half
ConvMart	C:\Users\vchillar\Desktop\Little Rock Data\2013 Robbery\Risk Factors\ConvMart.shp	Proximity	3 Blocks	Half
Fast_Food	C:\Users\vchillar\Desktop\Little Rock Data\2013 Robbery\Risk Factors\Fast_Food.shp	Both_Proximity_and_Den...	3 Blocks	Half
GrocerySupermarkets	C:\Users\vchillar\Desktop\Little Rock Data\2013 Robbery\Risk Factors\Grocery Supermarkets.shp	Proximity	3 Blocks	Half
LiquorStore	C:\Users\vchillar\Desktop\Little Rock Data\2013 Robbery\Risk Factors\LiquorStore.shp	Both_Proximity_and_Den...	3 Blocks	Half

Run!   Reset Inputs

Status:

Figure 14.1 RMTDx Utility Parameters for Automobile Theft in Little Rock (2013)

Analysis Parameters

The Utility was provided with the following risk factors and parameters:

Name	Feature Count	Operationalization	Spatial Influence	Analysis Increment
Banks	23	Both_Proximity_and_Density	3 Blocks	Half
Big_Box_Retail_Stores	51	Proximity	3 Blocks	Half
BusStop_2014	1155	Proximity	3 Blocks	Half
CheckCashing	6	Proximity	3 Blocks	Half
ConvMart	88	Proximity	3 Blocks	Half
Fast_Food	90	Both_Proximity_and_Density	3 Blocks	Half
GrocerySupermarkets	61	Proximity	3 Blocks	Half
LiqourStore	51	Both_Proximity_and_Density	3 Blocks	Half
PublicHighSchools	5	Proximity	3 Blocks	Half
Pawn	16	Proximity	3 Blocks	Half

Figure 14.2 Empirically Selected Risk Factors for Automobile Theft in Little Rock (2013)

Type	Name	Operationalization	Spatial Influence	Coefficient	Relative Risk Value
Rate	Banks	Proximity	216	2.4859	12.0119
Rate	ConvMart	Proximity	216	2.4767	11.9019
Rate	Big Box Retail Stores	Proximity	216	2.0371	7.6683
Rate	BusStop 2014	Proximity	1080	1.4350	4.1996
Rate	Fast Food	Proximity	432	0.9130	2.4918
Rate	LiqourStore	Density	1296	0.5428	1.7208
Rate	Intercept	--	–	-5.1524	–
Overdispersion	Intercept	–	–	-0.2922	–

Figure 14.3 RTM Output (Tabular) for Automobile Theft in Little Rock (2013)

Now that we know the influence of each individual factor, we can combine them via a quantitative process and represent the findings cartographically. There are many ways to visually represent the spatial vulnerabilities of a study area identified through RTM. A typical way in RTMDx is to use its .tif file output function (that users can convert in a mapping/GIS-friendly layer to symbolize in a more visually and statistically appealing way). This output is shown in Figure 14.4.

Traditionally, the map should be symbolized by utilizing the data classification method of standard deviation breaks of the mean: mean to 1 standard deviation, 1 standard deviation to 2 standard deviations, and above 2 standard deviations. The places with risk scores above 2 standard deviations from the mean are considered the highest risk places. In addition to the RTM map shown in Figure 14.4, you can also create pin maps (Figure 14.5), kernel density maps (hot spots), and Getis-Gi* maps to convey the data in a meaningful way to whomever the audience is you are trying to engage. All of the maps can be made within ArcGIS with the assistance of the *IPIR ArcGIS 10.1 Toolset and Tutorial* (from NIJ Project; it can be found at www.rutgerscps.org/software.html).

There were 74,173 raster grid cells used in this analysis, of which 688 contained automobile theft incidents for calendar year 2013. The relative risk scores ranged from 1 (for the lowest risk place) to 1,643 (for the highest risk place) – thus, the places of highest risk are 1,643 times more likely to experience automobile theft in comparison to places with a risk score of 1. Locations in

Little Rock

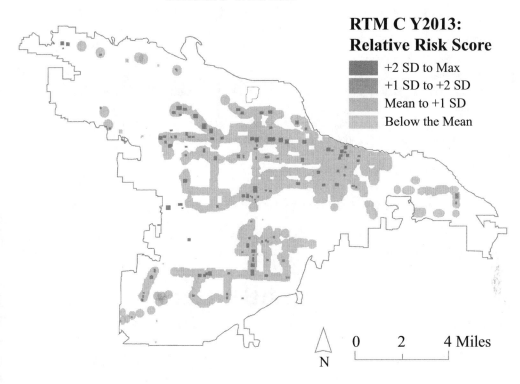

RTM C Y2013:
Relative Risk Score

■ +2 SD to Max
■ +1 SD to +2 SD
■ Mean to +1 SD
□ Below the Mean

N   0   2   4 Miles

Figure 14.4 RTM (Cartographic) for Automobile Theft in Little Rock (2013)

Figure 14.4 with the dark blue shading represent the locations that are 2 standard deviations above the mean relative risk value, and are considered to be the highest risk locations for automobile theft.

By way of review, the steps to Risk Terrain Modeling are as follows – each step is covered via one of the three processes:

1   Choose an outcome event (i.e. automobile theft).
2   Choose a study area (i.e. Little Rock, AR).
   i   RTM can be applied to any geographic level; however, you should select a study area for which the information provided by the RTM and related cartographic visualizations will be meaningful and actionable.
3   Choose a time period (i.e. 2013).
   i   Just as vulnerability to crime varies geographically, so too does it vary temporally in terms of dependent risk levels.
   ii   The time period should be meaningful for the data used such that the information to be communicated by the RTM will allow for sound decision making.
4   Identify the best available (possible) risk factors (i.e. hotels/motels, big box retail, fast food, convenience stores, and banks).

5   Obtain spatial data.
   i   Internal sources such as city agencies/departments can have better, more updated data.
   ii   Jurisdictions that have open data portals such as the Open Data Philly, or the Chicago Data Portal can be used to obtain spatial data easily for free.
   iii   The U.S. Geological survey and the Census Bureau are also good sources of base maps such as roads and study area outlines.
6   Map spatial influence of factors.
   i   Data with a "fleeting" nature (calls-for-service, shots fired, etc.) should be operationalized as density.
   ii   When operationalizing a risk factor as "both," the RTMDx Utility will make an empirical decision with regard to the spatial influence of that feature on the locations of outcome events.
7   Select model factors.
8   Weight model factors.
9   Quantitatively combine model factors.
10   Communicate meaningful information (tabular and cartographic representations of results).

While RTM identifies the environmental features that pose a significant risk of experiencing the outcome event, it is conceivable that some interaction effects between risk factors will be more influential

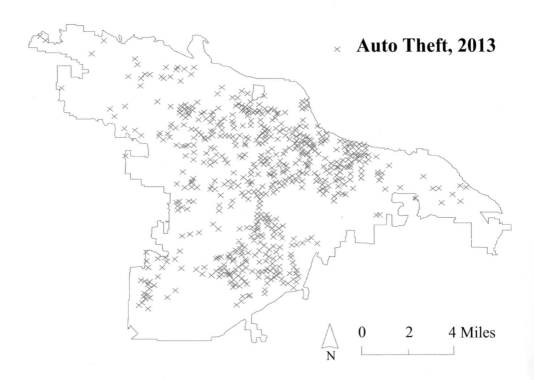

Figure 14.5 Pin Map for Automobile Theft in Little Rock (2013)

than others. RTM identifies significant risk factors and the respective risk values, but does not provide the interactions between those measures. The Relative Risk Score in the output provides an overall risk score for risk factors co-locating, but RTM does not indicate what those are at each place. For example, while one risk factor (such as a high school) is risky, a place where high schools and vacant properties co-locate (overlapping spatial influence) could be at even greater risk for crime. Furthermore, there could be certain interactions that could be stronger than other combinations of risk factors, leading to a greater relative frequency of crime. Because RTM does not address these issues, other analyses should be conducted that can assist in these. One way to examine the interactions of risk factors is with Conjunctive Analysis.

CONJUNCTIVE ANALYSIS OF RISK FACTOR CONFIGURATIONS (CARFC)

Conjunctive analysis is an analytic tool that can be used to supplement the findings of RTM. Conjunctive analysis can be performed in many software packages, such as SPSS, STATA, and SAS. Conjunctive analysis is a multipurpose tool in that the technique is not solely a spatial addition but can examine case (risk factor) configurations to detect underlying interactions (see Hart and Miethe, 2011; Hart and Zandbergen, 2012; Miethe, Hart, and Regoeczi, 2008). In spatial analyses, the technique allows you to explore spatial interactions between environmental risk factors. The number of possible combinations is a function of the number of possible risk factors and the categories within them, which is a dummy code indicating the presence (1) or absence (0) of influence. For example, within the analysis of automobile thefts above, there were six risk factors, which means that there are 64 possible combinations (e.g. $2^6 = 64$) or potential "behavior settings" (see Miethe et al. 2008). Typically, you will want to focus on dominant behavior settings – those that appear in the study at a frequency of ten times or more – and exclude those that fail to reach this distinction (unless potential value is identified in the excluded configurations).

The data matrix displayed in Table 14.1 is the final step of the conjunctive analysis. It identifies six dominant behavior settings, and is an example of the way in which the results should be communicated. As we can see, a problematic interaction occurs between banks and bus stops. This behavior setting has the largest Relative Frequency of Crime (RFC) (20.00) and appears ten times within the study settings. Additionally, it contains two crimes, which amounts to 0.2 percent of all crimes in the study setting during the study period. This might seem like a small percentage, but keep in mind Little Rock was comprised of over 74,000 cells. The data matrix also indicates that bus stops appear frequently within the most problematic behavior settings, which suggests that these factors consistently aggravate the risk posed by other factors within the risk terrain model.

It is important to note that decisions regarding the overall number of behavior settings to display, and the thresholds used to make those determinations, are solely based on the preference of the individuals performing the analysis (Barnum, 2016). Overall, while the RTM analysis in this case suggested that the co-location of weighted risk factors at particular locations created an increased likelihood of experiencing an outcome event, conjunctive analysis suggested that the spatial interaction of risk factors created risky locations for crime. In terms of policing intelligence and operations, RTM informs officers with the spatial knowledge as to which environmental factors are related to the risk of crime. Conjunctive analysis adds to this understanding of the space in which officers operate by informing them of the most influential combinations of environmental risk factors on the outcome crime(s) of interest. Crime analysts can utilize this knowledge to inform the agency as to which environmental factors they should focus on within areas identified as high risk, and to assist in the way resources are

Table 14.1 Conjunctive Analysis Data Matrix of Behavior Settings for Incidents of Auto Theft in Little Rock (2013)

Behavior Setting	Banks	Convenience Mart	Big Box Retail	Liquor Store	Fast Food	Bus Stop	Crimes	Cell Count	Percent Crime	Relative Frequency of Crime Rate
1	1	0	0	0	0	1	2	10	0.20	20.00
2	0	0	0	1	1	1	29	203	2.91	14.29
3	0	1	0	1	0	1	2	18	0.20	11.11
4	0	0	0	0	1	1	31	301	3.11	10.30
5	0	0	0	0	1	0	7	69	0.70	10.14
6	0	1	0	0	0	1	3	31	0.30	9.68

allocated to reduce the risk of the crime in question. By doing so, they are making connections about the way in which risk factors correlate with the outcome crime – individually and combined (behavior settings) – and are beginning the process otherwise known as ACTION. ACTION is where the results of predictive analytic techniques can be turned into operational activity of the police. This is described in the next section.

ACTION (ASSESSMENT, CONNECTIONS, INTERVENTIONS, OUTCOMES, AND NOTIFICATIONS)

Once a predictive analysis is completed (and any other analytical techniques such as conjunctive analysis), the focus should turn to the stakeholders (police departments, store owners, residents, city agencies/departments, etc.) within the jurisdiction to develop an understanding of how they view the problem (crime). How law enforcement views a crime problem can be different from a community perspective. This allows for the intervention to not only be grounded in the empirical findings of the analyses, but also to be informed by the social, cultural, economic, and political atmospheres in which the outcome event is occurring (Caplan and Kennedy, 2016). Predictive analyses provide the necessary information; but the stakeholders provide context (and potential solutions) to the problem. For example, an analysis could indicate that pawn stores and parking lots are significant risk factors for robbery; but the understanding of the police as to why can be left incomplete. Yes, we could make assumptions, but the police may not have all the information about the environment of the area that lets them understand all that could be coming together to produce the crime. Meetings with stakeholders enables the police to gain a better understanding by connecting potential risk factors and their spatial influences to outcome events. From these meetings, they may come to understand that the robbery may occur within parking lots, and the pawn store is where the criminals go to exchange the stolen property for quick cash and to rid themselves of the evidence of the robbery. Additionally, by meeting with various stakeholders, a form of distributed leadership can be followed, where each agency/stakeholder could be assigned a task pertaining to the overall goal of the intervention, otherwise known as the Intervention Planning Intel Report (IPIR), discussed below.

After the planning and implementation phases are complete, the attention is turned to understanding if what was completed, intervention wise, had the desired effect; essentially, evaluating what was done. It is important at this step to take note of the downfalls and successes to be able to build from the experience moving forward. Once the intervention strategies are evaluated, notifying the stakeholders and greater public audience helps continue the sense of a partnership in solving the problem. Involving outside stakeholders assists law enforcement in addressing problems affecting the greater community.

This process, beginning with the assessment of the way in which the risk factors relate to the outcome event and ending with the notification of others, has been coined ACTION (Assessment,

Table 14.2 ACTION Plan Outline

Step	Description	Occurrence	Questions to consider
Assessment of the Risk Narrative	Spoken or written account of connected events and the way in which they relate to other phenomena in the environment	At the start	What is the problem to be addressed? How are the events related? What is the history of the problem?
Connections	Identify factors that might spatially correlate with the priority crime	During risk narrative; before and after predictive analyses	What attracts the problematic behavior? Why do events cluster at certain places over time?
Task Management	Decide upon the feasibility and responsibilities for performing tasks to collect data, perform analyses, and respond to information and spatial intelligence	Prior to intervention planning; ongoing	Who can collect and manage data? Who can perform analyses?
Intervention Planning Intel Report – IPIR	Outline the way in which the problem in question occurs in the study area, and the factors that are important in elevating risks of it continuing	After a risk assessment is completed and a risk narrative is clearly articulated	What information is needed in the IPIR? Who should be at the table to operationalize the IPIR?
Outcome Evaluation	In addition to measuring changes in crime count, also measure changes in the spatial patterns of crime occurrence; consider diffusion of benefits and assess whether crime displacement occurred	After intervention is implemented	How will you define success? How will you collect data on intervention activities and outcome measures?
Notifying Others	Share key information about risk management efforts with the stakeholders involved as well as the general population	During and after intervention implementation	Who will you "keep in the loop", and how will you do it?

Connections, Interventions, Outcomes, and Notifications). Overall, it is a guide for applied problem solving in which the steps need not be linear but can occur concurrently with others. Table 14.2 is a brief description of each step, when it should occur, and questions to consider.

It is important to note that because the ACTION framework is inclusive of community stakeholders, they are made aware of the intervention that is to be implemented and become invested in the activities and outcomes. This enables community partnerships to be constructed with police departments via the sharing of insights and data that can help to further understand the problem in question. The ACTION framework is not meant to be a one-time event but a reiterative process, each time learning from the past. This will help tailor prevention strategies and overcome obstacles encountered in prior iterations. Overall, ACTION allows law enforcement agencies to take what is found via predictive analyses, along with other analytical methods, and supplement the findings with stakeholder input to develop a holistic approach toward reducing the crime problem in question.

INTERVENTION PLANNING INTEL REPORT (IPIR)

Within the ACTION framework is an IPIR or Intervention Planning Intel Report. Predictive analyses fit into this step as it is a fundamental part of the IPIR and the resulting evidence-based intervention strategies. The IPIR allows for law enforcement agencies (and stakeholders) to determine where place-based interventions are needed, and allows for the prioritization of risk factors to be addressed based upon their impact on the problem (usually derived from the analyses). This ensures that resources can be properly allocated in a way to maximize potential results, and provides information of what may be influencing crime in particular places. This is important due to limited resources that many police agencies have available and allows for the game of "whack-a-mole" to be avoided. Furthermore, it provides guidance on what the analytical information means, and offers suggestions for steps that can be taken to translate the data analysis into actionable intelligence and defined tactics for intervention. By this we mean that you can utilize what you have learned to make decisions about which factors within the environment you want to address and at which selected target areas to do so. It does not make sense from a financial and resource allocation standpoint to address a selected environmental risk factor that has a low relative risk value (i.e. liquor stores from the previous example of automobile theft); however, this does not mean that strategies should be avoided for these places (more general crime prevention through environmental design (CPTED) approaches could be discussed). Additionally, it would not be wise to address every select environmental risk factor (i.e. every hotel/motel from the automobile theft analysis) within the extent of the study area. Instead, you should set up "target sites" and focus on the significant environmental risk factors that contribute to the level of risk within those defined areas.

Typically, an IPIR is inclusive of pin maps, hot spot maps (kernel density maps), near-repeat analysis, and predictive analysis, each technique building from the prior. This does not mean that additional spatial analytic techniques cannot be incorporated as well. Pin maps allow for a visual inspection of the clustering of crimes, while a Nearest Neighbor (NN) analysis statistically examines whether the distribution of crimes is significantly clustered. Kernel density maps add to the intuition provided by pin maps and NN analysis by indicating areas of high concentration of crime incidents throughout the study area. Depending on the law enforcement agency, hot spot maps are the norm, so leaving them out will prompt questions. It might ease the transition in the discussion of predictive analysis by including hot spot analyses at the start. As this chapter has discussed, however, hot spot analyses often do not address what is contributing to crime in the area that has allowed it to remain hot, and why crime has been occurring in the same areas for a duration of time despite police efforts. If the intervention strategies that are being employed by police are not causing the hot spots to cool, this gives rise for the need to change the environment itself in relation to the behaviors accepted at those places. Predictive analyses help to diagnose the underlying characteristics influencing the presence of crime and forecast where crime is likely to occur in the future.

As stated above, when the IPIR is completed, continued conversations with police agencies and other stakeholders should take place to continue to examine risk, to select or adjust target areas, to schedule intervention start and end dates, and to formalize the management of tasks. Once these steps are completed, police and other stakeholders can address proposed actions that can be taken to mitigate the spatial influence of each risk factor. Ultimately, these actions will become part of the intervention in which multiple activities can be performed to address a single risk factor. For example, if your IPIR found that the presence of vacant buildings increased the risk of experiencing a robbery, you could propose that the police conduct directed patrols in the target areas or that a city agency tear down the buildings.

There are seven principles outlined by Caplan and Kennedy (2014) that should be considered when utilizing the IPIR to develop a risk-based intervention:

1   Have clearly defined target areas that are distinctly identified as high risk.
2   Risk actors in the target areas should be clearly identified so the intervention can focus on these risks; let the IPIR inform police what to do when they get to the target areas.
3   Develop strategies for both action and analysis. With an understanding of the mechanisms for how risk factors affect nearby crime incidents, develop actions to mitigate them.
4   The collection of data needs to be both valid and reliable. The actions that are done in an area should clearly relate to the intervention strategy directed at specific risks. Collect accurate geo-located measures of these actions to be able to identify where and when the intervention took place relative to the risk.
5   Expect that risk factors may become less risky over time. Routinely reassess the meaningfulness of target areas, risk factors, and intervention strategies as they may change with the dynamic nature of illegal behavior and crime patterns.
6   Allow the analysis to inform the intervention and the results to inform subsequent analyses to better later intervention strategies.
7   Consider the expected daily crime count and plan intervention lengths accordingly so you can measure outcomes reliably and with sufficient power – you must have sufficient cases in the target areas for a statistically valid evaluation to be performed.

In general, risk-based interventions should include at least three simultaneous activities relating to each of the following categories: reducing the spatial influence of one or more of the risk factors, developing evidence-based practices (i.e. target hardening, situational prevention, community awareness, etc.), and using policing activities to deter known offenders.

RISK-BASED POLICING

To this point, the chapter has focused on how to utilize predictive analytic techniques to reduce the risk of crime by examining the environment and the way in which certain features influence behavior. When police agencies adopt the mindset and operational practice of reducing and managing crime risk, they are utilizing place-based policing (Weisburd, 2008) or risk-based policing. Risk-based policing focuses on five elements: problem solving, evidence-based decision making, sustainability, better utilization of resources, and increased transparency. By utilizing risk-based policing, the benefits are distributed across various stakeholders, inclusive of police officers (better measurement of performance and productivity), crime analysts (more informative and actionable analytical products), community members (more effective, responsive, and transparent police agencies), elected officials (strengthen police–community relations), and command staff/directors (evidence-based support for decisions help to justify need for financial or personnel resources to manage risk) to name a few.

Risk-based policing has the focus of actions that can be used to decrease crime based on spatial analyses. There are three steps in employing risk-based policing. The first is the most crime analysis heavy approach. Here, crime analysis is used to determine attractors of crime through risk analysis, producing better and more informative intelligence products, forecasting crimes, and targeting high-risk areas. Predictive analyses are often at the core of this approach. The second step is to employ interventions and risk reduction strategies to lower crime, make evidence-based decisions, improve officer safety and wellness, mitigate risky places, and identify priorities for crime prevention. At this level, crime analysis is used to reduce crime by managing risks. The last step is having new goals for the agency and using crime analysis to find better ways to make intelligence actionable for policy and planning, achieve multi-stakeholder responsibility for public safety, strengthen community relations, make efficient allocations of resources, use better performance measures, make better use of technology, forecast crime, and save money. At this level, crime analysis and risk reduction strategies are used to achieve agency and leadership objectives. Overall, all these steps go together to achieve the agency and leadership objectives of risk-based policing.

A study that demonstrates predictive analysis within the ACTION plan, and provides evidence of significant crime reductions through risk-based policing, is the National Institute of Justice study conducted by Caplan, Kennedy, and Piza (2015). The study began with conducting a RTM analysis in each city (Chicago, IL; Colorado Springs, CO; Glendale, AZ; Kansas City, MO; and Newark, NJ). Next, each police agency developed an intervention strategy that targeted the spatial influences of select significant risk factors. The police agencies also collaborated with the research team in the selection of target areas for the intervention. To evaluate the intervention, statistical comparisons were made to equivalent control areas, which were selected through propensity score matching. The findings of the study showed significant reductions in targeted crimes in the five cities and also showed the ability of predictive analyses to identify risky areas. For example, in Colorado Springs, the highest risk identified covered about 4 percent of the study area while accounting for approximately 43 percent of all crime incidents. Risk-based policing strategies produced a 33 percent crime reduction in the target areas compared to the control areas.

As this study showed, the use of risk-based policing has the ability to influence specific crimes by altering the environment and addressing the spatial influence of the factors that increase risk within select target areas. This brings together the use of predictive analyses and police action to reduce crime.

CONCLUSION

Analyzing the way in which spatial dynamics influence crime is essential to address the crime issues that arise within communities. Predictive spatial analysis techniques such as Risk Terrain Modeling and conjunctive analysis have advanced the field of spatial analytics by building on the successes of hot spot mapping and by providing context for the underlying influences of crime at particular places. These analyses provide police knowledge and a working strategy to follow. Crime analysts will continue to have to expand their technical capabilities and will be asked to perform more analyses as more agencies begin to rely on evidence-based policing practices. The information that is produced by these analyses becomes pivotal for targeted, place-based and risk-based interventions. Overall, it is important to remember that, when conducting predictive analyses, the results are only as good as the data you are able to obtain; thus, utilizing as many empirically supported risk factors that model the built environment is advised. Crime analysts will be tasked with greater data responsibilities, but the potential benefits become valuable insights for not only police departments but for the greater community.

REFERENCES

Barnum, J.D. 2016. *Tutorial for Conjunctive Analysis of Risk Factors Configurations (CARFC)*. Newark, NJ: Rutgers Center on Public Security.

Braga, A.A. 2001. The effects of hot spots policing on crime. *Annals of the American Academy of Political and Social Science*, 578(1), 104–125.

Braga, A.A. 2005. Hot spots policing and crime prevention: A systematic review of randomized controlled trials. *Journal of Experimental Criminology*, 1(3): 317–342.

Braga, A.A., D.M. Kennedy, E.J. Waring, and A.M. Piehl. 2001. Problem-oriented policing, deterrence, and youth violence: An evaluation of Boston's Operation Ceasefire. *Journal of Research in Crime and Delinquency*, 38(3): 195–225.

Brantingham, P.J. and P.L. Brantingham. 1981. *Environmental Criminology*. Beverly Hills, CA: Sage Publications.

Brantingham, P.J. and P.L. Brantingham. 1995. Criminality of place: Crime generators and crime attractors. *European Journal on Criminal Policy and Research*, 3: 1–26.

Caplan, J.M. and L.W. Kennedy. 2013. *Risk Terrain Modeling Diagnostics Utility* (version 1.0). Newark, NJ: Rutgers Center on Public Security.

Caplan, J.M. and L.W. Kennedy. 2014. 7 Principles for Implementing Risk-Based Interventions. www.riskterrain modeling.com/uploads/2/6/2/0/26205659/risk-basedtxprinciples.pdf

Caplan, J.M. and L.W. Kennedy. 2016. *Risk Terrain Modeling: Crime Prediction and Risk Reduction*. Berkeley: University of California Press.

Caplan, J.M., L.W. Kennedy, and E. Piza. 2013. Joint utility of event-dependent and environmental crime analysis techniques for violent crime forecasting. *Crime and Delinquency*, 59(2): 243–270.

Harries, K. 1999. *Mapping Crime: Principles and Practice*. Washington, DC: National Institute of Justice.

Hart, T.C. and T.D. Miethe. 2011. Violence against college students and its situational contexts: Prevalence, patterns, and policy implications. *Victims and Offenders*, 6(2): 157–180.

Hart, T.C. and P.A. Zandbergen. 2012. *Effects of Data Quality on Predictive Hotspot Mapping*. Washington, DC: National Institute of Justice.

Kennedy, L.W., J.M. Caplan, and E. Piza. 2011. Risk clusters, hotspots, and spatial intelligence: Risk terrain modeling as an algorithm for police resource allocation strategies. *Journal of Quantitative Criminology*, 27(3): 339–362.

Kennedy, L.W., J.M. Caplan, and E. Piza. 2015. *A Multi-jurisdictional Test of Risk Terrain Modeling and a Place-based Evaluation of Environmental Risk-Based Patrol Deployment Strategies*. Washington, DC: National Institute of Justice. www.rutgerscps.org/uploads/2/7/3/7/27370595/nij6city_results_inbrief_final.pdf

Miethe, T.D., T.C. Hart, and W.C. Regoeczi. 2008. The conjunctive analysis of case configurations: An exploratory method for discrete multivariate analyses of crime data. *Journal of Quantitative Criminology*, 24(2): 227–241.

Ratcliffe, J. 2010. The spatial dependency of crime increase dispersion. *Security Journal*, 23(1): 18–36.

Weisburd, D. 2008. *Place-based Policing. Ideas in Policing Series*. Washington, DC: Police Foundation.

QUESTIONS AND EXERCISES

1   When analyzing the output of the RTMDx, how should the results be interpreted to turn them into actionable intelligence for researchers and practitioners? Specifically, what value is most important in determining the riskiest criminogenic factor?

2   With regard to generalizability, what are some limitations that must be considered when utilizing an RTM approach?

3   If you were meeting with a police chief, how would you explain risk-based policing to him/her to encourage its use within the department?

4   When selecting risk factors to use within your model, what are some important aspects to consider to safeguard against the notion of garbage in garbage out?

5   After running a model, you find that bars and hotels are significant risk factors for experiencing an aggravated assault. Bars are operationalized as proximity with a spatial influence of 640 feet (2-blocks) and relative risk value of 15. Hotels are operationalized as density with a spatial influence of 160 feet (1/2 block) and relative risk value of 45. Describe each risk factor's effect on aggravated assault, and compare both risk factors to one another in terms of riskiness.

Future directions

In the bigger picture, crime analysis is still relatively new in that not all police agencies even have the analytical capabilities within their agencies. Even larger cities, where you think it would be common, sometimes do not have crime analysts. There is a larger movement in law enforcement to become more transparent, which may require agencies to be able to assess their operations more clearly. The public will start to expect a greater understanding of steps taken by law enforcement agencies to reduce crime and how they interact with the public. This is where crime analysis gains importance and value. There are other places crime analysis is likely to grow, and to provide more employment opportunities for crime analysts. These are discussed here.

ENVIRONMENTAL CORRECTIONS

The need for crime analysts within law enforcement agencies will continue to increase, and also with growth in probation and parole. A majority of the book up to this point has focused on examples related to police, but policing is only one aspect of the criminal justice system. Specifically, corrections (including community corrections) could greatly benefit from adopting a similar position as a crime analyst. Cullen, Eck, and Lowenkamp (2002) discuss how tenets of environmental criminology lend support to an environmental corrections paradigm.

We know probationers and parolees are going to re-enter the community, and the likelihood of recidivism is high within three years post-release (Durose, Cooper, and Snyder, 2014). Recidivism research all too often focuses on individual characteristics, such as race, gender, age, and criminal history, with limited acknowledgment to neighborhood influences (see Kubrin and Stewart, 2006). This is a bit concerning given the amount of research that focuses on neighborhoods and crime and crime and place. The neighborhood environment where ex-offenders return to should be taken into account when determining service expectation and potential risk of recidivism. For example, the risk of crime throughout a neighborhood could be examined and weighted against the availability of social services in close proximity to the neighborhood to determine neighborhood risk separate from individual risk level.

This is a fruitful future direction for both practitioners and researchers to approach. Bridging the two, often siloed, fields of policing and corrections is a promising direction for crime analysis. With such a high percentage of past offenders returning to the criminal justice system, at some point the two fields need to move in conjunction with one another to better understand the problem versus continuing to react after crimes occur. That is, both corrections and policing often deal with the same people; and because of this, it would be of interest to proactively develop working relationships to reduce recidivism from both a policing and corrections standpoint.

PREDICTIVE ANALYTICS

Predicting crime would seem to be a great goal for crime analysis. If you can predict crime, then you should be able to reduce crime. If only it was that simple. At this point, we know crime patterns in time and space, allowing for a degree of predictability. Now it comes to how accurate we can be with our crime predictions. It is an attention grabber if you can say "I predict 65 percent of crime will occur in 8 percent of the land area in city." Law enforcement agencies could focus on that 8 percent of land area hoping to get the most "bang for the buck" when directing resources. But these tactics have shown to have serious negative consequences with only small reductions in crime.

To see how much predictive crime analytics have become a big deal in law enforcement, do an Internet search on "predictive crime analytics". Most likely, there are a number of vendors on the first page offering analytical services/products. Some of these services are incredibly expensive and have potentially promising results at crime reductions for a jurisdiction. Predictive approaches will continue to be utilized by law enforcement agencies with the expectation of crime reductions, often through the use of a sophisticated algorithm. But how much these predictive techniques will actually make a difference in crime is still subject to debate.

RAND (www.rand.org) released a report (Perry, McInnis, Price, Smith, and Hollywood, 2013) on predictive policing, and highlighted some common myths concerning predictive policing (pp. xix–xx). These are:

Myth 1: The computer actually knows the future.
Myth 2: The computer will do everything for you.
Myth 3: You need a high-powered (and expensive) model.
Myth 4: Accurate predictions automatically lead to major crime reductions.

These four myths show some of the problems that are being faced by crime analysts. Computer models are not the be-all and end-all in crime forecasting and reduction. The output from the predictive analytics only gives a law enforcement agency so much information. If the agency does not understand the data being input into the models, the output is not valuable. The computer cannot simply tell you where to go to stop crime. Computer models are only as good as the data being put into them and the interpretation of that data; hence, crime analysts become crucial to understanding the problem.

The progression of technology has the potential to impact numerous types of jobs, even crime analysts. Police departments will continue to be approached by outside companies trying to sell new programs capable of analyzing crime and directing police where to go. These programs could be beneficial; however, someone within the agency has to have the understanding of what the program is doing and what the output means. A bunch of numbers from a computer program does little to inform the agency of what the root issue contributing to crime is and how to approach the problem. This is often overlooked in hopes to lower crime by numbers alone. If chasing numbers is what an agency wants to do, these types of programs could be useful; but for agencies truly wanting to understand their crime problems, crime analysts provide a level of human capital vital to dissecting issues that arise in a jurisdiction. A crime analyst can be the person to understand the data, modeling, and output for predictive analytics. If the crime analyst is removed from the equation, when questions arise from officers and police administration about the modeling, it is hard to imagine analytic vendors being able to respond in a timely manner to each question.

All of these software programs are, and will be, extremely benefical for law enforcement agencies. Agencies will lean on crime analysts to guide them through this process and determine what works best for them. Oftentimes, crime analysts will be asked to review multiple software programs and recommend what has the greatest potential to assist the department.

DATA AT YOUR FINGERTIPS

Access to information and data has continued to expand, even during the time of writing this textbook. The use and popularity of social media has required law enforcement agencies to become more transparent in their efforts; and law enforcement are also using social media in crime investigations. Numerous law enforcement agencies have Facebook and Twitter pages so residents can be made aware of events and issues at a local level. These notifications can include a variety of topics, from community-oriented policing efforts and fundraisers to active homicide crime scenes, including the address of where the incident occurred. Additionally, through Facebook Live, police agencies can stream press conferences.

Typically, through data portals, law enforcement agencies provide daily, weekly, or monthly crime information rather than in real time. This introduces a lag-time from when crimes occurr to the public having access to the data. While daily, or real-time, is ideal for data transparency, there is a need to validate the data before releasing them to the public. Crime analysts could find their roles continuing to expand into data validation for real-time availability through different portals, websites, or media accounts.

The ability to relay pertinent information quickly will continue to grow as technology continues to advance. Additionally, depending on where you reside and the type of phone you have, emergency alerts are also sent out for missing/kidnapped children or even when crimes occur in your area. For these types of notifications, crime analysts could take on the role of resident notification. This could provide police departments with assistance solving crimes while notifying residents of potentially dangerous situations.

Just as police departments can notify residents, the growth of technology at our fingertips allows residents to notify/report issues to police. Smartphones have a multitude of features that make reporting easier. The ability to take photos and attach a GPS location becomes valuable data for police departments. There are numerous apps developed to connect residents and law enforcement agencies together. Through these apps, residents can report crime to law enforcement agencies beyond the traditional call-in method. This can provide a real-time opportunity for crime analysts to respond to active situations. This will be an area of growth as law enforcement agencies turn to residents to assist them in public safety endeavors since police cannot be everywhere at all times. Crime analysts will then be responsible for taking the collected data and turning them into valuable insights and intelligence the department can use to develop strategies to prevent/reduce crime.

CONCLUSION

The focus of this book has been to provide a background in theory, statistics, and applications often used in crime analysis. The foundational knowledge this book covers will make the transition into more advanced classes pertaining to crime analysis easier. All too often, students jump into a GIS/crime mapping course without knowing the background. This creates problems since students are not familiar with the theory. Having only a GIS course is understandable because being proficient in GIS is a great skill to have when looking for a job. But only knowing how to map does not mean you have the skills needed for quality crime analyses.

There has been a growing interest in academic departments in providing classes geared toward crime analysis. A degree or a certificate in crime analysis identifies that you have a toolset and knowledge base that separates you from more traditional criminal justice degrees. This is valuable when on the job market and trying to get your first job in crime analysis. Even if there are not crime mapping type courses offered in your department, geography or other departments may have a GIS course. You would just take that knowledge and apply it to a criminal justice paradigm.

Similar to any career, it is important to continue learning and being aware of new/upcoming approaches to understanding crime. Consider the analogy of adding a new tool to your toolbox. You might not always need it or it may not work as well as other tools, but you can say you tried the tool. By doing so, you start to learn new applications and the limitations of certain methodologies. Do not be afraid of change, even if the larger agency as a whole does not want to change. As an analyst, your tools need to remain sharpened and up to date.

There are numerous ways to keep up with current techniques/approaches and upcoming training opportunities. An easy way to be alerted about new research is creating a Google Scholar Alert for keywords such as: GIS and crime, crime analysis, environmental criminology, crime and place, among numerous others that might interest you. The Google Scholar Alert will email you a list of new publications that contain your keywords. Of course, not all of the articles are going to directly pertain to your interests, but you can quickly read the abstract to determine if the study is connected to your needs in crime analysis. These emails can save quite a bit of time and act as a reminder when it could escape your mind to look up new research.

The International Association of Crime Analysts (IACA) has an email list-serve that provides many benefits. You can pose questions to fellow analysts throughout the world while also being made aware of upcoming training/conference opportunities. Training through IACA webinars or at conferences is a great benefit to take advantage of when trying to stay up to date and learn new techniques. Some of the webinars are low cost or affordable if an agency is willing to cover the cost of additional training (see http://www.iaca.net/training.asp). The IACA conference also has in-person training opportunities that allow you to learn from fellow analysts/researchers/law enforcement personnel as well as attending the conference.

ESRI, the developer of ArcGIS, is a valuable resource when learning how to map. ESRI has a Crime Analyst extension you can download to make features available to you. ESRI also has numerous webinars geared toward crime analysis that are often free for users. Along with webinars, ESRI offers a number of Massive Open Online Courses (MOOCs) that are designed for you to take at your own pace. There are usually assignments along the way; and, once completed, certification is often available. The MOOCs might not directly relate to criminal justice, but much of what is covered is applicable to criminal justice. It is up to you as crime analysts to get creative and take what you have learned and apply it to your work.

Depending on where you live, there are a number of regional crime analysis groups that offer similar training opportunities. These are just a few ways of keeping up with what is going on in the larger crime analysis field. Continual training provides you with ability to not only extend your knowledge base but make new contacts and strengthen your network.

Crime analysts can provide numerous benefits to law enforcement agencies. There will be a learning curve for agencies adding a crime analyst unit. Obviously, the agency realizes the potential value of having an analyst; but there may be push-back because, as an analyst, you will now be examining the data. You were hired because of your skills. Show them your value and how the data relate to what is known (i.e. ease the transition). Go be a crime analyst.

REFERENCES

Cullen, F.T., J.E. Eck, and C.T. Lowenkamp. 2002. Environmental corrections: A new paradigm for effective probation and parole supervision. *Federal Probation: A Journal of Correctional Philosophy and Practice*, 66: 28–37.

Durose, M.R., A.D. Cooper, and H.N. Snyder. 2014. *Recidivism of Prisoners Released in 30 States in 2005: Patterns from 2005 to 2010*. Washington, DC: Bureau of Justice Statistics.

Kubrin, C.E. and E. Stewart. 2006. Predicting who reoffends: The neglected role of neighborhood context in recidivism studies. *Criminology*, 44(1): 165–197.

Perry, W.L., B. McInnis, C.C. Price, S.C. Smith, and J.S. Hollywood. 2013. *Predictive Policing: The Role of Crime Forecasting in Law Enforcement Operations*. Santa Barbara, CA: Rand Corporation.

QUESTIONS AND EXERCISES

1   List three MOOCs currently offered related to crime analysis.
2   What are examples of smartphone apps that connect police departments with their constituents?
3   Does your city have a data portal? If so, what data are available? If not, does the county or state provide data for your city?
4   What social media presence do law enforcement agencies have in your area?
5   Does your university have a text alert system for crime on/near campus? Is there a delay in notification from crime occurrence?
6   What are three examples of predictive policing tools? What makes these tools so valuable? What data do these tools utilize for prediction?
7   Have there been recent developments in environmental corrections? In other words, do community correction agencies employ similar positions as crime analysts (i.e. data analysts)?

Crime analyst questionnaire responses

QUESTIONNAIRE #1

Name: Diane Weber

Department/Agency: Los Angeles Police Department, Operations-Valley Bureau (OVB)

Serving Population Size: 3,792,621 Citywide; 1,426,071 in OVB, 37.6% of the total City population

Title: Crime & Intelligence Analyst II

Years as Analyst: 13

Crime Analysis Experience: Management Assistant in lieu of Analyst I at Devonshire, Analyst II at Mission (both Area assignments), Analyst II at COMPSTAT (main analysis section downtown), Analyst II at Valley Bureau (one of four Bureaus, handles seven geographic Areas of the 21 Citywide)

Other Related Work Experience: Management Analyst in Dept. of Sanitation, needed to take the position to get into the job class.

Education: BA in History (required for Management Analyst), California DOJ Certificate in Crime & Intelligence Analysis.

Starting Salary Range: CIAN1: $54.8K–$80.1K; CIAN2: $64.6K–$94.5K; SrCIAN: $76.3K–$111.6K

How Did You Get into Crime Analysis: Accidentally. I was working for another City Department, and on the promotional list for Management Assistant (entry level management position). I was selected for LAPD, not expecting to find a career, and finally found my niche. It is about solving puzzles, which is how my mind works, and very satisfying work.

Main Duties: Area analysts read and code reports, prepare crime alerts, map everything that moves, and analyze their crime patterns, providing various documents to their detectives and command staff. Bureau analysts report to the Deputy Chief, and handle a great deal of admin analysis, perform audits of the Areas' analysis units, and prepare various documents for the Bureau command. Up until recently, we had two squads of officers that could be assigned anywhere in the Bureau based on analysis of current crime problems. It was the duty of me and my staff (of one) to determine where the squads needed to deploy, and provide them with information regarding the specific problem they were deployed to handle and any patterns, suspects or activity in that area.

Highlights of Job: Seeing results based on my analysis – reading the sergeants' logs every morning to see how they did and what arrests were made.

Favorite Task/Analysis/Approach: Looking at the patterns of crime type, time of day, day of week and seeing what resources we have to address the specific problems.

Words of Wisdom/Thoughts for Up-and-Comers: NEVER ASSUME! We experienced a series of car break-ins at fire stations. Firefighters leave all kinds of stuff in their cars, and the cars unlocked, feeling safe within the confines of their own parking lots. All the stations were adjacent to two freeways, and I assumed that the suspect was driving up and across the two freeways to get to the various stations. I projected three likely locations for future hits, based on distance from these freeways. One was correct, four others were not. Most of the property taken was fire department radios, iPads, iPods, cell phones, etc. However, we got lucky, and the suspect used one of the victim's credit cards to buy a sandwich at Subway, which gave us excellent photos of the suspect. He also used the card to fill up a Metro TAP (Transit Access Pass) card. We got information from Metro regarding the locations the card was used. They only provided lat/long information, but by plugging that into Google, we were able to determine what station the suspect was using most frequently, and what time the card was scanned. There is a subway and busway line that parallel the two freeways, and are also close, and in most cases closer, to the fire stations that were targeted. Two metro stations were targeted in the wee hours of the morning, and the suspect walked up to the metro station and into custody. Suspect was homeless, and rode the subway and bus line up from downtown and out into the Valley to caper. He just liked fire stations, and waited till they were out on a call to break into the cars. Los Angeles is a commuter city, and I assumed that the suspect would be driving. Not a mistake I will make again.

QUESTIONNAIRE #2

Department/Agency: Virginia State Police

Serving Population Size: 8,279,884 (whole state of VA)

Title: Insurance Fraud Analyst

Years as Analyst: 14+ years

Crime Analysis Experience: 14+ years

Other Related Work Experience: Accounting background

Education: Dual MBA (Forensic Accounting/Financial Analysis)

Starting Salary Range: $48,000 year

How Did You Get into Crime Analysis: Job opening

Main Duties: Inquire databases to analyze criminal activity of insurance fraud (e.g. stage accidents, slip and fall claims, homeowner, repeated offenders, commercial slip and falls, workers' compensation).

Highlights of Job: Catching criminals who display a pattern of criminal behavior.

Favorite Task/Analysis/Approach: Networking with others who share information on solved cases.

Words of Wisdom/Thoughts for Up-and-Comers: Many ways to catch a criminal but the best way is critical analyzing – details, details, details, provides a pattern.

QUESTIONNAIRE #3

Name: Neha Gupta

Department/Agency: United States Marine Corps, Provost Marshall's Office (PMO)

Serving Population Size: 3500

Title: Crime and Intelligence Analyst

Years as Analyst: 3

Crime Analysis Experience: The majority of my experience has been as an intern with the Los Angeles Police Department Devonshire Division Crime and Intelligence Analyst, I was in this position for the purpose of completing the required 400 hour internship for certification, which I started in July 2011. I continued to work to gain experience and knowledge until July 2014.

Other Related Work Experience: I have some experience working with the Gwinnett County Police Department, Lawrenceville, Georgia. Other work experiences with law enforcement include the position of Police Service Representative – Dispatcher with the Los Angeles Police Department Communications Division.

Education: Associates of Arts in Criminal Justice, Crime and Intelligence Analyst Certification, and Bachelor's of Science in Criminal Justice Administration with a concentration in Cybercrimes.

How Did You Get into Crime Analysis: I was first introduced to crime analysis in one of my criminal justice classes while I was pursuing my Associates degree, from that brief introduction to some further research on my own into the field I decided to pursue the certification that was offered. I am glad I did, this has proven to me to be a great start into my career in law enforcement.

Main Duties: Prepare comprehensive written reports, presentations, maps, and charts based on research, collection, and analysis of intelligence data. Assist and facilitate the work of staff in the review and analysis of crime reports and related criminal data to identify and evaluate crime series, trends, and patterns. Manage and update the division daily role call PowerPoint presentation for officers and present this in a slideshow format using Smart Board technology. Read crime reports and aid in drafting a weekly intelligence report using Microsoft Office Word. Prepare Crime Alerts, Crime Bulletins, and Community Alert Flyers by instruction and requests of detectives. Manage and update case status of individual crime reports. Collaborate with representatives from other government and intelligence organizations to share information or coordinate intelligence activities. Assist and train staff and other officers in the proper use of crime analysis computer applications, various spreadsheets, and databases. Perform related duties and responsibilities as required.

Highlights of Job: Everyday there is something new to do, something new to learn. Working directly with law enforcement officers and knowing that at any given moment your input and suggestions based on analysis of patterns or trends can in fact mean a great deal. Patrol suggestions and meeting with command staff disseminating information for officer safety. Creating documents and presentations for public awareness, it all comes together and falls into place as a busy and fulfilling day.

Favorite Task/Analysis/Approach: My most favorite task has been mapping crime incidents and looking for any hotspots that may exist. The patterns or trends that may be emerging in an area that needs to be addressed. Creating crime alerts and bulletins for officer safety and public awareness.

QUESTIONNAIRE #4

Name: Paul Byers

Department/Agency: Cincinnati Police

Serving Population Size: 300,000

Title: Police Officer

Years as Analyst: 15

Other Related Work Experience: Police officer and prosecuting attorney

Education: J.D.

Starting Salary Range: $62,000.00

How Did You Get into Crime Analysis: Sworn position became available

Main Duties: Provide technical and data resource for District Analysts, RTCC [Real-Time Crime Center] Analysts, and others

Highlights of Job: Analyze Data for Problem Solving Projects

Favorite Task/Analysis/Approach: Conduct Background Work-Ups on criminal suspects

Words of Wisdom/Thoughts for Up-and-Comers: Volunteering to work in a crime analysis unit gives the student real-life analyst experience and a recommendation for employment.

QUESTIONNAIRE #5

Serving Population Size: we have [federal] jurisdiction (with a population of 8+ million) and conduct investigations under the lead of the Office of the Attorney General on organized crime, money laundering, counterterrorism, state protection, etc.

Title: Operational Crime Analyst

Years as Analyst: 13

Crime Analysis Experience:

2001, internship with a State Police and basic training;

2003–2008, Operational Crime Analyst and Instructor, on and off-the-job training (Analysis, IT);

2009–Present, Deputy Head of Section, on and off-the-job training (Analysis, IT, OSINT, leadership)

Education:

1999, MAS in Political Sciences;

2003, DESS in Criminology

How Did You Get into Crime Analysis: 2001, I discovered the Crime Analysis Unit during my internship with a State Police. I was so enthusiastic that I extended the internship from 3 weeks to 10 months (all spent then in the CAU).

Main Duties:

- Law Enforcement: we support investigations and preliminary investigations (case-oriented);
- Intelligence-Led Policing: we (should) participate in specific intelligence projects;
- Instruction: Operational Crime Analysis; Analysis Software and Databases; Case Management;
- IT Support;
- Networking: National and International.

Highlights of Job:

- To serve and help when needed, thanks to the specific skills that you learn;
- Independency and responsibility;
- Teaching;
- Networking.

Favorite Task/Analysis/Approach:

- Social Network Analysis;
- Criminal Geographic Profiling;
- OSINT.

Words of Wisdom/Thoughts for Up-and-Comers:

"[. . .] *no longer will we have to fight 21st-century crimes with 19th-century tools*" [Janet Reno, US Attorney General, 12/10/1997]

QUESTIONNAIRE #6

Name: Rhea-Lyn Gerstenkorn

Department/Agency: Delray Beach Police Department

Serving Population Size: Census data: around 60,000. During season or our regular highly attended events our service population can more than double.

Title: Crime Analyst

Years as Analyst: 10

Other Related Work Experience: UCR and Florida Public Records

Education: Bachelor's degree, I'm also certified through the Florida Department of Law Enforcement, and recently earned my certification in geographic profiling analysis through CGPATC (Committee for Geographic Profiling Analyst Training and Certification).

Starting Salary Range: 44,000–60,000

How Did You Get into Crime Analysis: By chance. At a previous department we were changing to a new RMS system that was going to alleviate most of the data entry. They came up with some options for us, Crime Analysis was one of them, and I was the only one who showed interest. The rest is history for me.

Main Duties: Reading reports and determining patterns and trends, social media analysis – identifying and connecting people, preparing and presenting our weekly tactical intel meeting, creating bulletins and fliers, forwarding information from outside agencies, tying people to crimes or crime locations, identifying our "prolific offenders" (those who are actively committing crimes, even if we don't have PC [probable cause], and they aren't in custody) and our known offenders (people who have a criminal history, on probation/parole, part of or associated with a gang. These people may not be actively committing crimes, and could be incarcerated somewhere), documenting associations between people in RMS [records management system], run pictures through a shared facial recognition software, network with our local agencies to facilitate sharing information on related crimes.

Highlights of Job: Finding that little nugget that blows an investigation wide open, finding and identifying a suspect or person that we didn't have before, the feeling that on some days I've made a difference in the world, even if just a minuscule level.

Favorite Task/Analysis/Approach: Social media analysis. I love connecting people and finding those ties, and following whatever path we go. Sometimes it becomes a rabbit hole, and I don't know how I got there. But when you find what you're looking for, it becomes very rewarding. I'm very curious by nature and I like to just dig and dig into people until I can't go any further.

Words of Wisdom/Thoughts for Up-and-Comers: Be confident in yourself and your opinions. You will come across individuals who don't believe in what we're doing – most still don't understand what we're supposed to do. As an analyst your job is to have an opinion, if you've done your due diligence then have the confidence to stand by your analysis and don't let naysayers push you down. This is a rewarding career, we may not be out there putting handcuffs on people, but that doesn't mean we didn't play a part in their arrest. Don't get complacent. Always strive to learn new skills, be open to different thought processes in crime analysis, challenge yourself, be passionate about your career. You will find that people will strongly disagree on different methods and theories. Use what works for you, and build on your successes. Push yourself out of your comfort zone from time to time, but never lose your integrity.

QUESTIONNAIRE #7

Name: Shannon Lawson

Department/Agency: City of Santa Clara

Serving Population Size: approx. 116,000

Title: Management Analyst

Years as Analyst: 13

Crime Analysis Experience: 9

Other Related Work Experience: Dispatching police and fire/9–1–1 operator/paralegal/retail security

Education: B.S. in Criminal Justice, M.S. in Emergency Services, Certified DOJ/Cal State Crime Analyst, Paralegal certification

Starting Salary Range: $85,000 (this is a bit misleading though as our city has a total compensation approach to benefits so we pay some into our retirement and medical/dental benefits and our agency still pays social security when many agencies do not)

How Did You Get into Crime Analysis: I was working in the city in the Communications Department (9–1–1 center) and our Department was melded into the Police Department in 2005. At that time, an interim Communications Department head who was a retired Assistant Police Chief asked if I was interested in Crime Analysis as the Police Department had not had one for a few years. I was interested, the department sent me to the certification course and arranged other training and since then, I have worked a dual role as crime analyst/communications analyst. I am just now being able to get away from the communications work.

Main Duties: Assist with some technical aspects of our CAD (computer aided dispatch system), manage the Emergency Medical Dispatching program (am hoping to soon be rid of these two duties but . . .) – for Crime Analysis, I support all divisions of the police department with statistics that include crime statistics, officer activity statistics, nuisance suppression, neighborhood watch related statistics, Clery requests, grant requests, etc. Compile monthly statistics regarding Part I crimes. Update sex registrant and parole data monthly. Create presentations for all the above as needed. Am familiar with multiple software programs to include Microsoft Office Suite, ArcGIS for mapping, i2 Analysts notebook, Crystal Reports for data mining, etc.

Highlights of Job: I enjoy the job most when I find that something I have done helps someone else do their job easier or helps them solve a crime – I have found that sometimes when I think something is insignificant or of less importance, it is of the utmost importance to the person I've helped. I do not enjoy attention or accolades for my work but when someone just says "thanks" or "your help really made a difference" that will set me up on Cloud 9 for days and days!

Favorite Task/Analysis/Approach: I enjoy working with numbers and mapping to tell a story. Communicate – while it sounds easy, it isn't always. My approach is to be sure that whoever you are doing the work for has a say in the finished project – I always approach it with "Here's a first draft . . . does it work for what you need? If not, how do you want it to work for you . . . or do you have any suggestions on finishing it?" Don't hesitate to approach your co-workers and ask if there is anything you can do to help them. You might get a lot of 'no, thanks' but every now and then someone will take you up on the offer. I always ask "When do you need this by?" and if I can't accommodate that, I'm very clear up front or, (as I usually do because I have a hard time saying no) be flexible – reassess your work load and see if something can be moved around on the priorities list.

Words of Wisdom/Thoughts for Up-and-Comers: There is a lot to learn and you can easily get overwhelmed. Don't hesitate to ask for help from other analysts. Join professional organizations and forums such as the IACA. Go to conferences and trainings and network. Get names and contact information. Never hesitate to ask a question as there is almost always someone with an answer! Overall – for a support position in law enforcement – the Analyst job is one of the best!

QUESTIONNAIRE #8

Name: Tommy L. Smith

Department/Agency: Tallahassee Police Department, Florida

Serving Population Size: Approximately 190,000; with student and transient population, it could easily be between 300,000 and 350,000 (inclusive of FSU, FAMU, and TCC students).

Title: Crime Analyst

Years as Analyst: 2.5 years

Other Related Work Experience: Five (5) years with a local sheriff's office in the following positions: Emergency Telecommunications Specialist and Training Coordinator with certifications as a CJIS Local Agency Instructor (LAI) and Terminal Agency Coordinator (TAC).

Education: Master's Degree in Homeland Security with Concentration in Criminal Justice, (*expected graduated 2016*), American Military University; Bachelor's Degree in Criminal Justice with Concentration in Forensic Science (*with honors*), 2010–2014, American Military University

Starting Salary Range: $32,000–39,000; I personally was hired at the maximum rate and have since gotten several salary increases.

How Did You Get into Crime Analysis: I always knew I wanted to be something "more" in the criminal justice and law enforcement communities, and on the back of my mind, I'd always wanted to be famous in show business of some sort. I did not, however, know what crime analysis was, or that it even existed. By fate I suppose, I was browsing job postings for the northern Florida panhandle area and found one that said "Crime Analyst" for the City of Tallahassee Police Department. Immediately after reading the job description, I submitted my résumé and application. The minimum requirements listed a bachelor's degree or equivalent work experience in some sort of analytical or criminal justice capacity. I did not know for sure if I would even be considered, since I really was not an analyst and I had not yet completed my degree – but I did have several years of criminal justice experience. To my surprise, I heard back from the unit supervisor within a couple of weeks. I came in, interviewed with a panel of four (4) agency representatives, which included supervisors, future colleagues, and sworn section commanders. After the interview, I took an extensive one (1) hour written and computer test, which included topics such as bulletin writing, statistics, Excel "fluency," crime analysis concepts, formulas, etc. and ended up scoring the highest of all applicants. The next step was an interview with the Captain whom I would be working under, and the next thing I knew, I was sitting in my new office.

Main Duties: In this position, I am responsible for reviewing police reports, especially those of burglary, robbery, sexual battery, homicide, auto theft, and firearm incidents in order to timely disseminate pertinent information to agency personnel. In this assignment, I am responsible for the entire Northern Sector of the City of Tallahassee, which includes two major college campuses – Florida State University (FSU) and Tallahassee Community College (TCC). I generate weekly "tracked crime" reports for patrol operations and deployment, as well as regular crime bulletins which identify trends, patterns, series, sprees, etc. In a nutshell, I perform two major functions: analysis of geographical crime patterns; and similar offense pattern analysis. Another aspect of the job includes creating complex link analysis charts to assist criminal investigators in linking suspects to cases.

Highlights of Job: Highlights of my job include being able to help citizens who need to be reassured that we are constantly looking at crime in their neighborhoods to try and make it a safer place to live, as well as providing actionable information to patrol officers to be in the right place at the right time.

Favorite Task/Analysis/Approach: I would have to say that my absolute favorite tasks in my current assignment are creating Pivot Tables in Excel, bulletin writing, and forming a great and comprehensive analysis report. My favorite analysis approach goes a little something like this: look at geographical patterns first before jumping to conclusions about an M.O. in one incident matching that of another. If a residential burglary occurs five (5) miles from another one and the only thing the analyst has to go on is a kicked-in rear door, it's not enough to warrant an alert or bulletin.

Words of Wisdom/Thoughts for Up-and-Comers: Don't get caught up in numbers – numbers mean absolutely nothing on their own for a crime analyst. You have to look at the "meat" in the data.

QUESTIONNAIRE #9

Name: Tracey Lowey

Department/Agency: Calgary Police Service

Serving Population Size: 1.2 million

Title: Crime and Intelligence Analyst – Major Crimes Section – Homicide Unit

Years as Analyst: 18

Crime Analysis Experience: 3 years in the District, 12 years in Organized Crime and 3 Years in Homicide.

Other Related Work Experience: I'm an Instructor at Mount Royal University and I am currently Acting Coordinator in Criminal Justice for Athabasca University. I teach Crime and Intelligence Analysis (in class and online) at both MRU and AU. I have taught Crime Scene Investigations, Forensic History, Risk Population and Issues, Aberrant Behavior, Introduction to Criminal Justice, Introduction to Criminology, Introduction to Human Relations, Diversity, Young Offenders and the Law, Victims of Crime and Psychological Explanation of Criminal Behavior.

Education: Master of Science Degree in Criminal Justice

Starting Salary Range: $90,000.00

How Did You Get into Crime Analysis: I completed a Master's Degree in Criminal Justice, volunteered for Calgary Police Service and then analyst positions were created.

Main Duties: Analysis of cell phone data, crime mapping and creating charts in i2 Analyst Notebook.

Highlights of Job: Main focus is on cell phone data analysis and testifying in court.

Favorite Task/Analysis/Approach: Working in i2, cell tower mapping, creating profiles, presenting the life history and story of the target.

Words of Wisdom/Thoughts for Up-and-Comers: To be a successful analyst you must be a life-long learner. There is always new technology available that allows us to complete our analytical tasks more efficiently and effectively. Embrace the change. And, ask for specific training on software including i2 Analyst Notebook, ArcGIS and Excel.

QUESTIONNAIRE #10

Name: Victoria

Department/Agency: Sarasota Police Department

Serving Population Size: about 52,000

Title: Crime Analyst

Years as Analyst: 4

Crime Analysis Experience: I have been a crime analyst at Orange County Sheriff's Office in Orlando, FL, Manatee County Sheriff's Office in Bradenton, Florida and now at Sarasota Police Department in Sarasota, FL.

Education: Bachelor's Degree in Criminal Justice and certificate in Crime Analysis & Mapping from the University of Central Florida, Orlando.

How Did You Get into Crime Analysis: I learned about the certificate in college, decided to take a few courses and then was lucky enough to get the Crime Analysis internship at the Orange County Sheriff's Office. I decided it was a great option for me because I wanted to be in law enforcement, but wasn't sure I wanted to be an officer.

Main Duties: In a small agency I have a myriad of duties like identifying patterns and trends and communicating them to patrol, creating and disseminating bulletins, identifying suspects and obtaining relevant information and assisting anyone who calls and requests statistics.

Highlights of Job: When you identify a pattern, give an analysis and watch everything unfold and an arrest be made because of what you did. Another highlight is helping detectives with their cases and making their job easier.

Favorite Task/Analysis/Approach: My favorite task is compiling recent crimes and identifying commonalities in day, time, location and modus operandi to identify the trends.

Words of Wisdom/Thoughts for Up-and-Comers: Don't give up on what you want to do and where you want to go. You'll make it there one day.

National Incident-Based Reporting System (NIBRS) group offenses

GROUP A OFFENSES

1 Arson
2 Assault Offenses
    2.1   Aggravated Assault
    2.2   Simple Assault
    2.3   Intimidation
3 Bribery
4 Burglary/Breaking and Entering
5 Counterfeiting/Forgery
6 Destruction/Damage/Vandalism of Property
7 Drug/Narcotic Offenses
    7.1   Drug/Narcotic Violations
    7.2   Drug Equipment Violations
8 Embezzlement
9 Extortion/Blackmail
10 Fraud Offenses
    10.1   False Pretenses/Swindle/Confidence Game
    10.2   Credit Card/Automatic Teller Machine Fraud
    10.3   Impersonation
    10.4   Welfare Fraud
    10.5   Wire Fraud
11 Gambling Offenses
    11.1   Betting/Wagering
    11.2   Operating/Promoting/Assisting Gambling
    11.3   Gambling Equipment Violations
    11.4   Sports Tampering
12 Homicide Offenses
    12.1   Murder and Nonnegligent Manslaughter
    12.2   Negligent Manslaughter
    12.3   Justifiable Homicide
13 Kidnapping/Abduction
14 Larceny/Theft Offenses
    14.1   Pocket-Picking
    14.2   Purse-Snatching
    14.3   Shoplifting

GROUP B OFFENSES

Data analysis add-in for Microsoft Excel

Step 1: Click on the File tab in the top left corner
Step 2: Click on Options at the bottom of the list

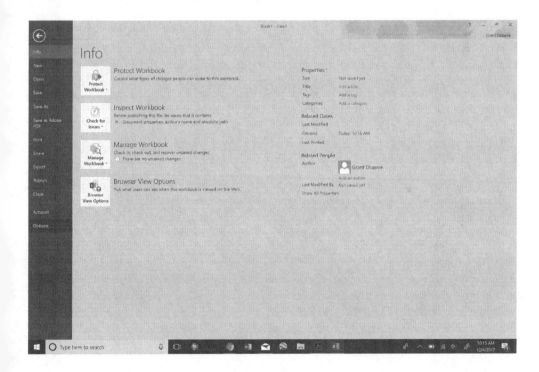

Step 3: Click on the Add-ins tool on the left
Step 4: Select Analysis ToolPak from the list generated then click Go . . .

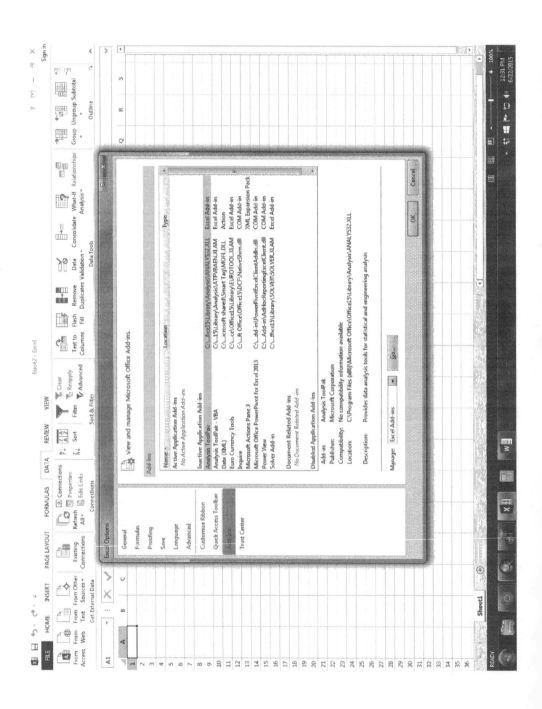

Step 5: Check the box for Analysis ToolPak then click OK

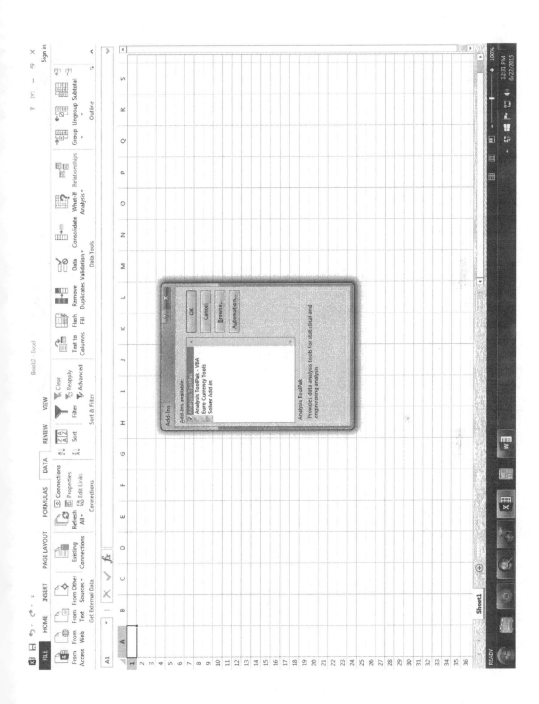

Step 6: Now if you look in the top right corner, you will see Data Analysis, click Data Analysis

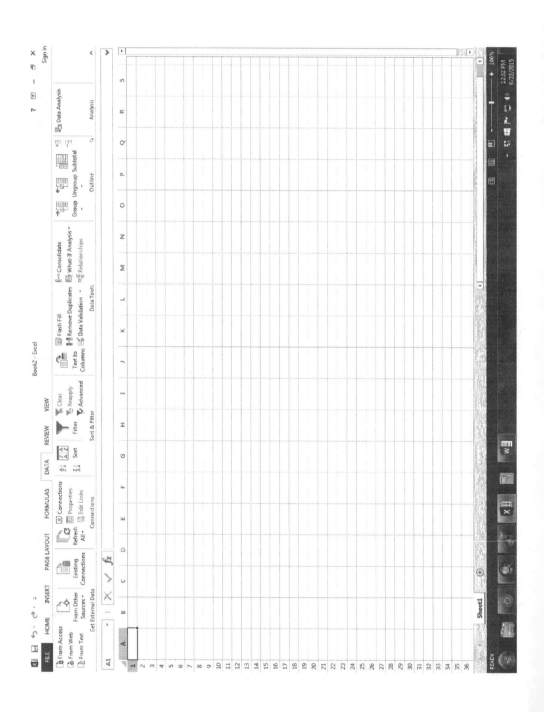

Step 7: Scroll through the different analytical functions within the ToolPak

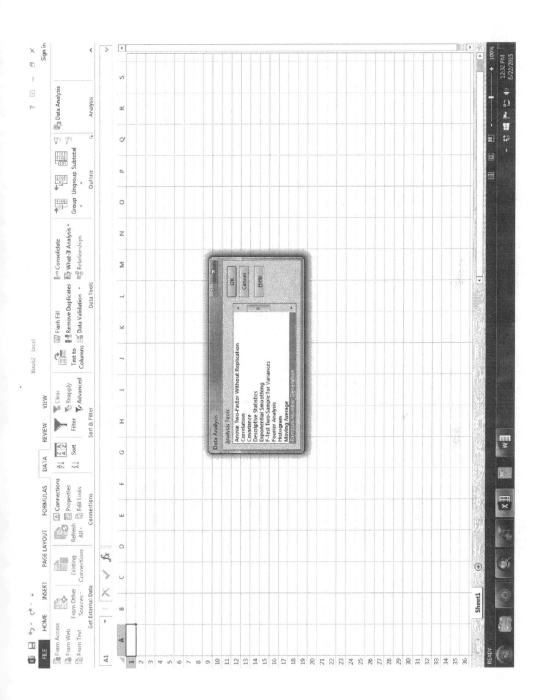

INDEX